Pocket Rough Guide

PARIS

written and researched by

RUTH BLACKMORE AND
JAMES McCONNACHIE

with additional contributions by

CLAIRE WILLIAMS

Contents

<< CAFÉ DE LA MAIRIE, ST-GERMAIN
< THE LOUVRE AND PYRAMIDS

INTRODUCTION TO

PARIS

A trip to Paris, famous as the most romantic of destinations, is one of those lifetime musts. Long the beating heart of European civilization, it remains one of the world's most refined yet passionate cities. The very fabric of the place is exquisite, with its magnificent avenues and atmospheric little back streets, its grand formal gardens and intimate neighbourhood squares. And for all the famed pride and hauteur of its citizens, Paris has a warmth about it these days: its cafés, restaurants and nightlife venues hum with cosmopolitan chatter, while new schemes to reclaim the city for bikes and pedestrians have brought the streets to life.

BRASSERIE DE L'ILE ST-LOUIS

Best places for a Parisian picnic

Picnicking on the grass is rarely allowed in central Paris – except on the elegant place des Vosges. But public benches make civilized alternatives: try the pedestrian bridge, the Pont des Arts; the lime-tree-shaded Square Jean XXIII, behind Notre-Dame; the intimate Jardin du Palais Royal; or the splendid Jardin du Luxembourg. Further out, the parks of Buttes Chaumont, Monceau, Montsouris and André-Citroën offer idyllic spots for lounging on the grass.

The city is divided into twenty arrondissements in a spiral, centred on the Louvre. The inner hub comprises arrondissements 1er to 6e, and it's here that most of the major sights and museums are to be found. Through the heart of the city flows the Seine, skirting the pair of islands where Paris was founded. The historic pillars of the city, the church of Notre-Dame and the royal palace of the Louvre, stand on the riverbank, along with one of the world's most distinctive landmarks – the Eiffel Tower. At times, the fabric of the city can feel inhuman, the magnificence of its monuments encompassing the bombastic grandeur of the Panthéon, the industrial chic of the Eiffel Tower and the almost spiritual glasswork of the Louvre pyramid. The city's art galleries can be equally intimidating: the enormous collections at the Louvre, Musée d'Orsay and Pompidou Centre are unrivalled.

Yet there is a host of smaller museums, many devoted to just one artist, and alongside the great civic monuments lie distinct *quartiers* that make Paris feel more a collection of sophisticated villages than a modern-day metropolis. Traditional communities still revolve around long-established and well-loved cafés and restaurants, and the student, gay and immigrant quarters are, by and large, lively and well-defined. So too are the wealthier districts, with their exclusive boutiques and restaurants. Neighbourhoods such as the elegant Marais, chichi St-Germain and romantic Montmartre are ideal for shopping, sitting in cafés and aimless wandering, while throughout the city you can find peaceful green spaces, ranging from formal gardens and avant-garde municipal parks to ancient cemeteries.

Above all, Paris is a city defined by its food. Few cities can compete with the thousand-and-one cafés, brasseries, *bistrots*, restaurants, bakeries, food shops and markets that line the boulevards and back alleys alike. You'll find anything from ultra-modern fashion temples to traditional mirrored palaces, and from tiny neighbourhood *bistrots* to crowded Vietnamese diners. Parisian nightlife is scarcely less renowned: its theatres and concert halls pull in artists of the highest calibre, while the tiny venues hosting jazz gigs, art events and Parisian *chanson* nights offer a taste of a more local, avant-garde scene. The café-bars and clubs of the Champs-Elysées, Bastille and the Left Bank fill with the young and style-conscious from all over.

When to visit

Spring is the classic time to visit Paris; the weather is mild (average daily 6–20°C), and plentiful bright sunny days are balanced by occasional freshening rain showers. Autumn, similarly mild, and winter (1–7°C) can be very rewarding, but on overcast days the city can feel melancholic, and cold winds can really cut down the boulevards; winter sun, however, is the city's most flattering light, and hotels and restaurants are relatively uncrowded in this season. Paris in high summer (15–25°C) is not the best time to go: large numbers of Parisians desert the capital between July 15 and the end of August for the beach or mountains, and many restaurants and shops close down for much of this period.

VIEW OVER PARIS AT DUSK

PARIS AT A GLANCE

>>EATING

There's a real buzz about the current Paris dining scene, as talented young chefs open up new *bistrots* – the **Marais and eastern districts** are good areas to try. For more traditional French cuisine, you don't have to look far: every *quartier* has its own local *bistrot*, serving staples such as *steak au poivre*. For a really authentic experience, go for a classic brasserie such as *Gallopin* (see p.75) off the **Grands Boulevards**, where you can dine amid splendid original decor. You can almost always eat more cheaply at lunchtime, when most places offer set menus from around €15. Even some of the haute cuisine restaurants become just about affordable at lunch.

>>DRINKING

It's easy to go drinking in Paris: most cafés stay open late and serve alcoholic drinks as well as coffee, and old-fashioned wine bars and English-style "pubs" can be found everywhere. That said, certain areas specialize in late-night drinking. The **Marais** offers trendy but relaxed café-bars; further east, the **Bastille and Oberkampf** areas have lots of youthful venues, many doubling as clubs. On the Left Bank, the **Quartier Latin** has lots of postage-stamp-sized studenty dives, while **St-Germain** is the place for cheery posh partying.

>>SHOPPING

One of the most appealing shopping areas is **St-Germain**, with its wide variety of clothes shops and gourmet food stores. Designer wear and haute couture are concentrated around the Champs-Elysées and on **rue du Faubourg-St-Honoré**, while more alternative fashion boutiques can be found in the Marais, especially around **rue Charlot**, and in Montmartre, in particular on **rue des Martyrs**. If you're short on time, make for one of the department stores, such as Printemps or Galeries Lafayette on the Right Bank, or Bon Marché on the Left Bank. For quirky one-off buys and curios, head for the atmospheric *passages* (nineteenth-century shopping arcades), just off the **Grands Boulevards**.

>>NIGHTLIFE

The best clubs in Paris double up as live venues, but dancefloors rarely warm up before 1am. Good eclectic venues include the boats moored beside the **Bibliothèque Nationale**, and **Oberkampf** classics such as *L'Alimentation Générale* and *Le Nouveau Casino*. Serious clubbers should chase down the latest soirée, though the clubs *Rex*, *Showcase* and *Social Club* are generally good bets. **Rue des Lombards** has some classic venues, notably the jazz club *Le Sunside*.

OUR RECOMMENDATIONS FOR WHERE TO EAT, DRINK AND SHOP ARE LISTED AT THE END OF EACH PLACES CHAPTER

Day One in Paris

1 Ile de la Cité > p.36. Paris was founded on this tiny island, which rises out of the River Seine.

2 Notre-Dame > p.38. The magnificent Gothic cathedral of Notre-Dame is the uplifting, historic heart of the city.

3 Sainte-Chapelle > p.37. This chapel is an exquisite jewel box, walled in medieval stained glass.

4 Pont Neuf > p.36. The riverbank quays lead west to the Pont Neuf, the oldest bridge in the city, and beyond to the Square du Vert Galant, where you can sit and watch the Seine flow by.

Lunch > p.120. Step south into the Latin Quarter for lunch at a classic brasserie, such as *Brasserie Balzar*.

5 Jardin du Luxembourg > p.127. These gardens are filled with people playing tennis or chess and couples strolling round the elegant lawns.

6 Pont des Arts > p.122. This handsome pedestrian bridge runs from St-Germain to the Louvre; you can pick up the Batobus beside it and head downriver.

7 Musée d'Orsay > p.123. This grand old railway station houses some of the most beguiling Impressionist works ever painted.

8 Eiffel Tower > p.54. Continue on the Batobus to this ever-thrilling structure, at its best at night or around sunset.

Dinner > p.130. Head back to St-Germain to an elegant *bistrot*, such as *Au 35*.

Day Two in Paris

1 Pompidou centre > p.78. Begin the day with a crash course in modern art – the Musée National d'Art Moderne has an unbeatable collection of Matisses, Picassos, and more.

2 Rue Montorgueil > p.81. Stroll down this picturesque market street, where grocers, horse butchers and fishmongers ply their trade alongside traditional restaurants and trendy cafés.

Lunch > p.74. Stop off at *Bistrot des Victoires*, an old-fashioned *bistrot* serving *confit de canard* and other staples.

3 Galerie Vivienne > p.70. One of a number of nineteenth-century shopping arcades dotted around the area, this is probably the finest, with its lofty glass ceiling, floor mosaics and Grecian motifs.

4 Palais Royal > p.69. The handsome arcaded buildings of the Palais Royal enclose peaceful gardens and shelter quirky antique shops selling pipes, Légion d'Honneur medals and lead soldiers.

5 Jardin des Tuileries > p.50. Saunter along the chestnut-tree-lined alleys of the Jardin des Tuileries, admiring the grand vistas, formal flower beds and fountains.

6 Place de la Concorde > p.50. An impressive piece of town planning, with a gold-tipped obelisk at its centre, broad avenues radiating off it, and grand monuments, such as the Arc de Triomphe, in every direction.

Dinner > p.52. Treat yourself to a gourmet meal at *La Table du Lancaster*, perfect for an intimate dinner.

Art lover's Paris

Paris was long the undisputed international capital of art. The cafés of Montmartre and Montparnasse may now be haunted only by the ghosts of the great Impressionists and Modernists, but in the city's galleries you can come face to face with their living works.

1 Musée de l'Art Moderne de la Ville de Paris > p.58. The museum celebrates Paris's modernists, and has a stunning mural by Matisse and a great view across the Seine.

2 Site de Création Contemporaine > p.58. The gallery's distressed-chic interior is home to cutting-edge contemporary art.

3 Musée Rodin > p.62. Rodin's stirring sculptures are housed in the most refined and elegant of Parisian mansions.

🍴 **Lunch** > p.64. Stop for a hearty lunch at the relaxed *La Fontaine de Mars*.

4 Musée Jacquemart-André > p.48. An exceptional Italian Renaissance collection set in a lavish nineteenth-century mansion.

5 Louvre > p.42. If you're going to tackle the mighty Louvre, take on a less well-known wing, such as French sculpture or Objets d'Art.

🍴 **Dinner** > p.82. Head a few steps east to the Beaubourg *quartier* for dinner at a brasserie, such as the centuries-old *Au Chien Qui Fume*.

Budget Paris

Despite Paris's reputation as an expensive city, there are many treats to be enjoyed for free, plus plenty of good-value deals to be had at restaurants.

1 Hotel Bonséjour Montmartre > p.173. Set on a quiet street, this hotel is a steal at €56 for a simple double with sink, or €68 for one with a shower.

2 Buses > p.182. Touring by bus is enjoyable and inexpensive; try the #29 from Gare St-Lazare, which goes past the Opera Garnier, through the Marais, and on to Bastille.

3 Sacré-Coeur > p.146. There's no charge to visit this Parisian landmark, but the real draw is the view from the terrace.

4 Musée Carnavalet > p.88. One of the city's best free museums is the Musée Carnavalet, devoted to the history of Paris.

Lunch > p.96. For a cheap and filling lunch, get a takeaway from *L'As du Fallafel* in the Marais' Jewish Quarter.

5 Place des Vosges > p.89. Lounge on the grass beneath the elegant facades of the place des Vosges, and enjoy the entertainment from buskers playing in the arcades.

6 Maison de Victor Hugo > p.90. It's free to visit the stately place des Vosges mansion that Victor Hugo lived in.

7 Petit Palais > p.48. The Petit Palais hosts free lunchtime classical concerts on Thursdays, and there's no charge to visit the museum's fine collection of art.

Dinner > p.109. The French cuisine at charming restaurant *L'Encrier* is excellent value, with set menus from €19.30.

Big sights

1 Eiffel Tower It may seem familiar from afar, but close up the Eiffel Tower is still an excitingly improbable structure. **> p.54**

2 Pont Neuf The "new bridge" is actually the oldest in the city, and, with its stone arches, arguably the loveliest. **> p.36**

4 Notre-Dame Islanded in the Seine stands one of the world's greatest Gothic cathedrals, Notre-Dame. **> p.38**

3 Sacré-Coeur steps From the steps of Sacré-Coeur, atop Montmartre's hill, the silvery roofs of Paris spread to the horizon. **> p.146**

5 The Panthéon The domed Panthéon shelters the remains of the French Republic's heroes – and offers a superb view. **> p.116**

Cultural Paris

1 Musée Moreau Gustave Moreau's eccentric canvases cover every inch of his studio's walls; below is the apartment he shared with his parents. > **p.148**

3 Musée Guimet Visiting the Buddhist statues and sculptures at the beautifully designed Musée Guimet is a distinctly spiritual experience. > **p.57**

2 Musée Jacquemart-André The Jacquemart-André couple's sumptuous Second Empire residence displays their choice collection of Italian, Dutch and French masters. > **p.48**

4 Musée Carnavalet This fascinating museum brings the history of Paris to life through an extraordinary collection of paintings, artefacts and restored interiors. > **p.88**

5 Musée National du Moyen Age Set in a fine Renaissance mansion, Paris's Museum of the Middle Ages houses all manner of exquisite objets d'art. > **p.113**

Dining

1 **Le Train Bleu** The glamour of the *belle époque* lives on in the Gare de Lyon's restaurant, with its gilt decor and crystal chandeliers. **> p.109**

2 L'Os à Moëlle Even Right-Bankers are making the trip out to this chef-run *bistrot* at the edge of the city. > **p.140**

3 Gallopin It's hard to go wrong with this handsome brasserie, with its charming service and well-executed classic cuisine > **p.75**

4 Le Gaigne This pocket-sized contemporary *bistrot* serves excellent, cutting-edge cuisine. > **p.95**

5 L'Arpège Alain Passard's unique menu includes exquisitely inventive morsels of rare vegetables in elegant sauces. > **p.64**

Romantic Paris

1 Lapérouse The private dining rooms at gourmet restaurant, *Lapérouse*, are full of faded elegance; close the door and summon your waiter with a buzzer.
> **p.130**

2 Lady with the Unicorn Tapestry, Musée du Moyen Age These five medieval tapestries, depicting the senses, comprise perhaps the most sensual work of art ever made. **> p.113**

3 Mixed steam session, Les Bains du Marais At weekends, the fashionable steam rooms of Les Bains du Marais are opened to male-female couples. **> p.89**

4 Time out in the Tuileries Taking time out in one of Paris's elegant gardens can be the most romantic thing of all. **> p.50**

5 Seine-watching From various points around the city, you can sit and watch the Seine slide by.

21

Paris shopping

1 Anne Willi Willi designs simple, flattering clothes in luxurious fabrics, as well as cute children's outfits. **> p.107**

2 Galeries Lafayette The queen of Paris's department stores, with floor upon floor of clothes and cosmetics. > **p.72**

3 Abbesses boutiques Shoppers with a quirky eye should make for the independent designers and boutiques around place des Abbesses. > **p.149**

4 Haut Marais boutiques Currently the city's hottest fashion spot, the Haut Marais is full of stylish independent boutiques. > **p.92**

5 Isabel Marant Isabel Marant is renowned for her exciting, ready-to-wear collections, at prices that won't make your eyes water. > **p.107**

Bars and nightlife

1 La Fourmi Cool young bohemians gather at this café-bar; perfect for pre-club drinks and finding out where to go next. **> p.151**

2 Au Limonaire At this tiny backstreet venue, you can dine while listening to young *chanson* singers, poets and vaudevillean acts. **> p.77**

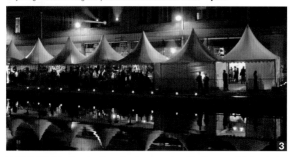

3 Point Ephémère An alternative-leaning arts collective uses this buzzingly boho ex-canal boathouse for exhibitions and gigs. **> p.111**

5 Le Nouveau Casino Smallish but superb venue with esoteric live acts and varied DJ soirées later on. **> p.111**

4 Batofar There's not much space for a club on an old lightship, but Batofar is a classic, friendly venue. **> p.141**

Paris calendar

1 Paris in spring The Seine-side beach of summer, the café terraces of winter and the autumn leaves all have their appeal, but spring remains the loveliest time to visit Paris.

2 Nuit Blanche During Nuit Blanche (the Sleepless Night) hundreds of galleries, cafés and public buildings stage events all night. > **p.188**

3 Paris Plage For four weeks in summer, tonnes of sand are laid out as a beach along a stretch of the Seine. > **p.188**

4 Patinoire de l'Hôtel de Ville From early December to the end of February there is an ice-skating rink in front of the town hall. > **p.91**

5 Bastille Day July 14 is the country's most important national holiday, celebrated with dancing, fireworks and a military parade down the Champs-Elysées. > **p.188**

Paris for kids

1 Disneyland Disney's vast theme park may not be very French, but the children will love it. **> p.162**

2 Jardin du Luxembourg boats
One of the timeless pleasures of the Luxembourg gardens is hiring a toy boat and sailing it across the circular pond. > **p.127**

3 Parc de la Villette The Géode Omnimax cinema is just one of the many attractions for kids in this futuristic park. > **p.102**

4 Jardin d'Acclimatation No child could fail to be enchanted by this wonderland of mini-canal and train rides, adventure parks and farm animals. > **p.153**

5 Jardin des Plantes These delightful gardens have plenty of plants, but also a small zoo and the Grande Galerie de l'Évolution. > **p.117**

29

Green Paris

1 Jardin des Tuileries The French formal garden par excellence: sweeping vistas, symmetrical flower beds and straight avenues. **> p.50**

3 Jardin du Palais Royal

Enclosed by a collection of arcaded shops, the Jardin du Palais Royal makes a wonderful retreat from the city bustle. > **p.69**

2 Jardin du Luxembourg For
all its splendid Classical design, the Luxembourg is still the most relaxed and friendly of Paris's parks. > **p.127**

4 Place des Vosges The place des Vosges's ensemble of pink-brick buildings
form an elegant backdrop to the attractive garden at its centre. > **p.89**

5 Promenade Plantée This disused railway line, now an elevated walkway,
is a great way to see a little-known part of the city. > **p.98**

Parisian's Paris

1 The Café de la Mosquée The Paris mosque serves North African snacks and mint tea at its café, and has a hammam (steam bath) next door. **> p.117**

2 Cinema The city's historic cinemas, such as The Rex, are the ideal venues for a French classic. **> p.184**

3 Raspail organic market On Sunday mornings, Paris's fashionable foodies flock to the exquisite Marché Bio, or organic market, which runs down boulevard Raspail. **> p.128**

4 Vélib' Launched in 2007, the city's wonderful pick-up and drop-off bike scheme has been hugely successful. **> p.182**

5 Les Trois Baudets The best place to catch up-and-coming stars of French *chanson* – the classic, Parisian singer-songwriter tradition. **> p.151**

PLACES

The Islands

There's no better place to start a tour of Paris than its two river islands, Ile de la Cité, the city's ancient core, and charming, village-like Ile St-Louis. The Ile de la Cité is where Paris began. It was settled in around 300 BC by a Celtic tribe, the Parisii, and in 52 BC was overrun by the Romans who built a palace-fortress at the western end of the island. In the tenth century the Frankish kings transformed this fortress into a splendid palace, of which the Sainte-Chapelle and the Conciergerie prison survive today. At the other end of the island they erected the great cathedral of Notre-Dame. The maze of medieval streets that grew up around these monuments was largely erased in the nineteenth century by Baron Haussmann, Napoleon III's Préfet de la Seine (a post equivalent to mayor of Paris), and much of the island is now occupied by imposing Neoclassical edifices, including the Palais de Justice, or law courts.

PONT NEUF

Ⓜ Pont Neuf. MAP P.38–39, POCKET MAP C16

Despite its name, the Pont Neuf is Paris's oldest surviving bridge, built in 1607 by Henri IV, one of the city's first great town planners. A handsome stone construction with twelve arches, the bridge links the western tip of the Ile de la Cité with both banks of the river. It was the first in Paris to be made of stone rather than wood, hence the name. Henri is commemorated with a stately equestrian statue.

PONT NEUF

SQUARE DU VERT-GALANT

Ⓜ Pont Neuf. MAP P.38–39, POCKET MAP C16

Enclosed within the triangular "stern" of the island, the square du Vert-Galant is a tranquil, tree-lined garden and a popular lovers' haunt. The square takes its name (a "Vert-Galant" is a "green" or "lusty" gentleman) from the nickname given to Henri IV, whose amorous exploits were legendary.

PLACE DAUPHINE

Ⓜ Cité. MAP P.38–39, POCKET MAP C16

Red-brick seventeenth-century houses flank the entrance to place Dauphine, one of the city's most secluded and attractive squares, lined with venerable townhouses. The noise of traffic recedes here, likely to be replaced by nothing more intrusive than the gentle tap of boules being played in the shade of the chestnuts.

THE SAINTE-CHAPELLE

4 bd du Palais Ⓜ Cité. Daily: March–Oct 9.30am–6pm; Nov–Feb 9am–5pm. €8.50, combined ticket with the Conciergerie €12.50. MAP P.38–39, POCKET MAP D16

The slender spire of the Sainte-Chapelle soars high above the Palais de Justice buildings. Though damaged in the Revolution, it was sensitively restored in the mid-nineteenth century and remains one of the finest achievements of French High Gothic, renowned for its exquisite stained-glass windows.

The building was constructed by Louis IX between 1242 and 1248 to house a collection of holy relics, including Christ's crown of thorns and a fragment of the True Cross, bought from the bankrupt empire of Byzantium. First you enter the lower chapel, where servants would have

INSIDE THE SAINTE-CHAPELLE

worshipped; very simply decorated, it gives no clue as to the splendour that lies ahead in the upper chapel. Here you're greeted by a truly dazzling sight – a vast, almost uninterrupted expanse of magnificent stained glass, supported by deceptively fragile-looking stone columns. When the sun streams through, the glowing blues and reds of the stained glass dapple the interior and it feels as if you're surrounded by myriad brilliant butterflies. The windows, two-thirds of which are original (the others are from the nineteenth-century restoration), tell virtually the entire story of the Bible, beginning on the north side with Genesis and various other books of the Old Testament, continuing with the Passion of Christ (east end) and ending with the Apocalypse in the rose window.

THE CONCIERGERIE

2 bd du Palais ⓜ Cité. Daily 9.30am–6pm.
€8.50, combined ticket with Sainte-Chapelle
€12.50. MAP P.38–39, POCKET MAP D16

Located within the Palais de Justice complex, the Conciergerie is Paris's oldest prison, where Marie-Antoinette and, in their turn, the leading figures of the Revolution were incarcerated before execution. It was turned into a prison – and put in the charge of a "concierge", or steward – after Etienne Marcel's uprising in 1358 led Charles V to decamp to the greater security of the Louvre. One of its towers, on the corner of the quai de l'Horloge, bears Paris's first public clock, built in 1370 and now fully restored.

Inside the Conciergerie are several splendidly vaulted Gothic halls, among the few surviving vestiges of the original Capetian palace. Elsewhere a number of rooms and prisoners' cells, including Marie-Antoinette's cell, have been reconstructed to show what they might have been like at the time of the French Revolution.

CATHÉDRALE DE NOTRE-DAME

ⓜ Cité & ⓜ/RER St-Michel. Cathedral daily 8am–6.45pm; free. Towers daily: April–Sept 10am–6.30pm, till 11pm Sat & Sun July–Aug; Oct–March 10am–5.30pm; €8, under-18s free. Guided tours in English Wed & Thurs 2pm, Sat 2.30pm; 1hr–1hr 30min; free; meet at welcome desk.
MAP P.38–39, POCKET MAP E17

One of the masterpieces of the Gothic age, the Cathédrale de Notre-Dame rears up from the Ile de la Cité like a ship moored by huge flying buttresses. It was among the first of the great Gothic cathedrals built in northern France and one of the most ambitious, its nave reaching an unprecedented 33m. It was begun in 1160 and completed around 1345. In the seventeenth and eighteenth centuries it fell into decline, suffering its worst depredations during the Revolution. It was only in the 1820s that the cathedral was at last given a

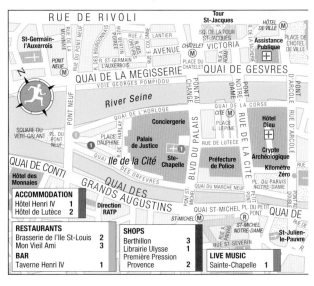

much-needed restoration, a task entrusted to the great architect-restorer Viollet-le-Duc, who carried out a thorough – some would say too thorough – renovation, remaking much of the statuary on the facade (the originals can be seen in the Musée National du Moyen Age) and adding the steeple and baleful-looking gargoyles, which you can see close up if you climb the towers (entrance outside).

NOTRE-DAME

The cathedral's facade is one of its most impressive exterior features; the Romanesque influence is still visible, not least in its solid H-shape, but the overriding impression is one of lightness and grace, created in part by the delicate filigree work of the central rose window and the gallery above.

Inside, you're struck by the dramatic contrast between the darkness of the nave and the light falling on the first great clustered pillars of the choir. It is the end walls of the transepts

which admit all this light, being nearly two-thirds glass, including two magnificent rose windows coloured in imperial purple. These, the vaulting and the soaring shafts reaching to the springs of the vaults, are all definite Gothic elements, while there remains a strong sense of Romanesque in the stout round pillars of the nave and the general sense of four-squareness.

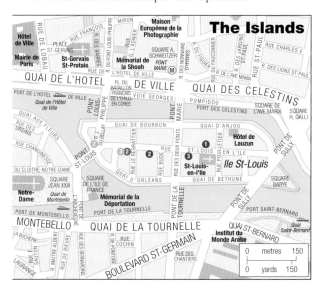

KILOMÈTRE ZÉRO

Ⓜ Cité. MAP P.38–39, POCKET MAP D17

On the pavement by the west door of Notre-Dame is a spot, marked by a bronze star, known as Kilomètre Zéro, from which all main-road distances in France are calculated.

THE CRYPTE ARCHÉOLOGIQUE

Place du Parvis-Notre-Dame Ⓜ Cité & Ⓜ/RER St-Michel. Tues–Sun 10am–6pm. €4. MAP P.38–39, POCKET MAP D17

The atmospherically lit Crypte Archéologique is a large excavated area under the place du Parvis revealing the remains of the original cathedral, as well as vestiges of the streets and houses that once clustered around Notre-Dame: most are medieval, but some date as far back as Gallo-Roman times.

LE MÉMORIAL DE LA DÉPORTATION

Ⓜ Cité. Daily 10am–noon & 2–7pm, closes 5pm in winter. Free. MAP P.38–39, POCKET MAP E17

Scarcely visible above ground, the stark and moving Mémorial de la Déportation is the symbolic tomb of the 200,000 French who died in Nazi concentration camps during World War II – among them Jews, Resistance fighters and forced labourers. Stairs barely shoulder-wide descend into a space like a prison yard and then into a crypt, off which is a long, narrow, stifling corridor, its walls covered in thousands of points of light representing the dead. Above the exit are the words "Pardonne, n'oublie pas" ("Forgive; do not forget").

ILE ST-LOUIS

Ⓜ Pont-Marie. MAP P.38–39, POCKET MAP E17–F18

The smaller of the two islands, Ile St-Louis, is prime strolling territory. Unlike its larger neighbour, it has no heavy-weight sights; rather, the island's allure lies in its handsome ensemble of austerely beautiful seventeenth-century houses, tree-lined quais and narrow streets, crammed with restaurants, art galleries and gift shops. For centuries the Ile St-Louis was nothing but swampy pastureland, a haunt of lovers, duellists and miscreants on the run, until in the seventeenth-century the real-estate developer, Christophe Marie, filled it with elegant mansions.

Shops

BERTHILLON

31 rue St-Louis-en-l'Île ⓜ Pont-Marie.
Wed–Sun 10am–8pm. MAP P.38–39, POCKET MAP F17

Long queues form for
Berthillon's exquisite ice creams
and sorbets that come in all
sorts of unusual flavours, such
as rhubarb and Earl Grey tea.

LIBRAIRIE ULYSSE

26 rue St-Louis-en-l'Île ⓜ Pont-Marie.
Tues–Fri 2–8pm. MAP P.38–39, POCKET MAP F17

A tiny bookshop, piled from
floor to ceiling with new and
secondhand travel books.

PREMIÈRE PRESSION PROVENCE

51 rue St-Louis-en-l'Île ⓜ Pont-Marie. Daily
11am–7pm. MAP P.38–39, POCKET MAP F17.

This shop is devoted to
top-quality olive oil from
Provence; choose from among
36 varieties, many on tap.
Pesto, tapenades, truffles and
chutneys are also available.

Restaurants

BRASSERIE DE L'ILE ST-LOUIS

55 quai de Bourbon ⓜ Pont-Marie
☎ 01.43.54.02.59. Daily except Wed noon–
midnight; closed Aug. MAP P.38–39, POCKET MAP E17

A bustling place with a rustic,
dark-wood interior and flirty
waiters dishing out dollops of
sauerkraut with ham and
sausage and other brasserie
staples (mains around €20).

MON VIEIL AMI

69 rue St-Louis-en-l'Île ⓜ Pont-Marie
☎ 01.40.46.01.35. Wed–Sun 11.30–2.30pm &
7–10.30pm; closed 3 weeks in Jan & Aug.
MAP P.38–39, POCKET MAP E17

Overseen by Michelin-starred
Alsatian chef Antoine
Westermann, this charming
bistrot offers bold, zesty
cuisine made with seasonal

ingredients, and a wine list
including a selection of
Alsatian vintages. Three course
menu €43.

Bar

TAVERNE HENRI IV

13 place du Pont-Neuf ⓜ Pont-Neuf.
Mon–Fri 11.30am–9.30pm, Sat noon–5pm;
closed Aug. MAP P.38–39, POCKET MAP C16

An old-style wine bar, buzziest
at lunchtime when lawyers
from the Palais de Justice drop
in for generous meat and
cheese platters (around €12)
and toasted sandwiches.

Live music

SAINTE-CHAPELLE

4 bd du Palais ⓜ Cité ☎ 01.42.77.65.65;
bookings also at any FNAC (see p.107) or
Virgin Megastore, 60 av des Champs-Elysées.
MAP P.38–39, POCKET MAP D16

Classical music concerts are
held in the splendid surround-
ings of the chapel more or less
daily. Tickets €29–44.

BRASSERIE DE L'ILE ST-LOUIS

41

The Louvre

The Louvre is one of the world's truly great museums. Opened in 1793, during the Revolution, it soon acquired the largest art collection on earth, thanks to Napoleon's conquests. Today, it houses paintings, sculpture and precious art objects, from Ancient Egyptian jewellery to the beginnings of Impressionism. Separate from the Louvre proper, but within the palace, are three design museums under the aegis of Les Arts Décoratifs, dedicated to fashion and textiles, decorative arts and advertising.

THE PALACE

MAP P.44, POCKET MAP B15–C15

For centuries the site of the French court, the palace was originally little more than a feudal fortress, begun by Philippe-Auguste in 1200. It wasn't until the reign of François I that the foundations of the present-day building were laid, and from then on almost every sovereign added to the Louvre, leaving the palace a surprisingly harmonious building. Even with the addition in 1989 of the initially controversial glass **Pyramide** in the cour Napoléon – an extraordinary leap of imagination conceived by architect I. M. Pei – the overall effect of the Louvre is of a quintessentially French grandeur and symmetry.

PAINTING

The largest of the museum's collections is its paintings. The early **Italians** are perhaps the most interesting, among them Leonardo da Vinci's *Mona Lisa*. If you want to get near her, go during one of the evening openings, or first thing in the day. Other highlights of the Italian collection include two Botticelli frescoes and Fra Angelico's *Coronation of the Virgin*. Fifteenth- to seventeenth-century Italian paintings line the Grande Galerie, including Leonardo's *Virgin and Child with St Anne* and *Virgin of the Rocks*. Epic-scale nineteenth-century French works are displayed in the parallel suite of rooms, among them the *Coronation of Napoleon I*, by David, Ingres' languorous nude, *La Grande Odalisque*, and Géricault's harrowing *Raft of the Medusa*.

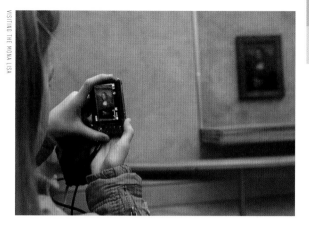

A good point to start a circuit of **French paintings** is with the master of French Classicism, Poussin; his profound themes, taken from antiquity, the Bible and mythology, were to influence generations of artists. You'll need a healthy appetite for Classicism in the next suite of rooms, but there are some arresting portraits. When you move into the less severe eighteenth century, the more intimate paintings of Watteau come as a relief, as do Chardin's intense still lifes. In the later part of the collection, the chilly wind of Neoclassicism blows through the paintings of Gros, Gérard, Prud'hon, David and Ingres, contrasting with the more sentimental style that begins with Greuze and continues into the Romanticism of Géricault and Delacroix. The final rooms take in Corot and the Barbizon school, the precursors of Impressionism. The Louvre's collection of French painting stops at 1848, a date picked up by the Musée d'Orsay (see p.123).

Visiting the Louvre

Ⓜ Louvre Rivoli/Palais Royal-Musée du Louvre ☎ 08.92.68.36.22, Ⓦ www.louvre.fr. Mon, Thurs, Sat & Sun 9am–6pm, Wed & Fri 9am–10pm. €10; free to under-18s & under-26s from (or studying in) EU countries, and everyone on the first Sunday of each month. Same-day readmission allowed.

You can buy tickets in advance by phone, online or from branches of FNAC and Virgin Megastore. The main entrance is via the Pyramide, but you can also try the entrance directly under the Arc du Carrousel, accessible from 99 rue de Rivoli and from the Palais Royal-Musée du Louvre métro stop. Pre-booked ticket-holders can enter from the Passage Richelieu.

Owing to the sheer volume of exhibits, you won't have time to see everything. The Denon wing, with the Mona Lisa, is a popular place to start; relatively peaceful alternatives are the grand chronologies of French painting and sculpture, the sensual collection of Objets d'Art, or the dramatic Medieval Louvre section. Pick up a free floor plan at the start.

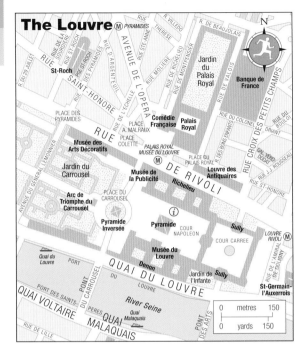

The Louvre Ⓜ PYRAMIDES

THE GALERIE D'APOLLON

ANTIQUITIES

The **Oriental Antiquities** and **Arts of Islam** categories cover the Mesopotamian, Sumerian, Babylonian, Assyrian and Phoenician civilizations, and the art of ancient Persia, India and Spain. One of the collection's most important exhibits is the Code of Hammurabi, a basalt stele from around 1800 BC covered in Akkadian script setting down King Hammurabi's rules of conduct for his subjects.

The **Egyptian Antiquities** collection starts with the atmospheric crypt of the Sphinx. Everyday life is illustrated through cooking utensils, jewellery, the principles of hieroglyphics, sarcophagi and a host of mummified cats. The collection continues with the development of Egyptian art.

The biggest crowd-pullers after the *Mona Lisa* are found in the **Greek and Roman Antiquities** section: the *Winged Victory of Samothrace*, and the late-second-century BC *Venus de Milo*, striking a classic model's pose.

OBJETS D'ART

The vast Objets d'Art section presents the finest tapestries, ceramics, jewellery and furniture commissioned by France's wealthiest patrons. It begins with the rather pious Middle Ages section and continues through 81 relentlessly superb rooms to a salon decorated in the style of Louis-Philippe, the last king of France. Walking through the complete chronology gives a powerful sense of the evolution of aesthetic taste at its most refined and opulent. The circuit also passes through the breathtaking apartments of Napoleon III's minister of state.

SCULPTURE

The sculpture section covers the development of the art in France from the Romanesque to Rodin in the Richelieu wing, and Italian and northern European sculpture in the Denon wing, including Michelangelo's *Slaves*, designed for the tomb of Pope Julius II. The huge glass-covered courtyards of the Richelieu wing – the cour Marly with the Marly Horses, which once graced place de la Concorde, and the cour Puget with Puget's *Milon de Crotone* as the centrepiece – are very impressive.

LES ARTS DÉCORATIFS

107 rue de Rivoli ⓦ www.lesartsdecoratifs .fr. Tues–Sun 11am–6pm, Thurs till 9pm. €9.50.

Separate from the rest of the Louvre, Les Arts Décoratifs comprises three museums devoted to design and the applied arts.

The core of the collection is found in the **Musée des Arts Décoratifs**, displaying superbly crafted furniture and objets. The medieval and Renaissance rooms show off curiously shaped and beautifully carved pieces, religious paintings and Venetian glass. The Art Nouveau and Art Deco rooms include a 1903 bedroom by Hector Guimard – the Art Nouveau designer behind the original Paris métro stations. Individual designers of the 1980s and 90s, such as **Philippe Starck,** are also represented.

The **Musée de la Mode et du Textile** holds high-quality temporary exhibitions demonstrating cutting-edge Paris fashions from all eras, such as Jackie Kennedy's famous dresses of the 1960s.

On the top floor, the **Musée de la Publicité** shows off its collection of advertising posters through cleverly themed, temporary exhibitions.

Cafés

CAFÉ MOLLIEN

First floor, Denon wing. Daily except Tues 10.15am–5pm, until 7pm Wed & Fri.

The busiest of the Louvre's cafés has a prime position near the Grande Galerie, with huge windows giving onto a terrace (open in summer only).

CAFÉ RICHELIEU

First floor, Richelieu wing. Same hours as *Café Mollien.*

The most prim and elegant of the Louvre's cafés, *Café Richelieu* serves a range of full meals, as well as drinks and snacks. The spectacular outdoor terrace is open for business in the summer months.

The Champs-Elysées and Tuileries

The breathtakingly ambitious Champs-Elysées is part of a grand, nine-kilometre axis, often referred to as the "Voie Triomphale", or Triumphal Way, that extends from the Louvre at the heart of the city to the Défense business district in the west. Combining imperial pomp and supreme elegance, it offers impressive vistas along its entire length and incorporates some of the city's most famous landmarks – the place de la Concorde, Tuileries gardens and the Arc de Triomphe. The whole ensemble is so regular and geometrical it looks as though it might have been laid out by a single town planner rather than successive kings, emperors and presidents, all keen to add their stamp and promote French power and prestige.

THE CHAMPS-ELYSÉES

MAP P.48–49, POCKET MAP B5–E6

The celebrated avenue des Champs-Elysées, a popular rallying point at times of national crisis and the scene of big military parades on Bastille Day, sweeps down from the Arc de Triomphe towards the place de la Concorde. Its heyday was during the Second Empire when members of the haute bourgeoisie built themselves splendid mansions along its length and fashionable society frequented the avenue's cafés and theatres. Nowadays, this broad, tree-lined avenue is still an impressive sight, especially when viewed from the place de la Concorde, and although fast-food outlets and chain stores tend to predominate, it has been steadily regaining some of its former cachet as a chic address: the Louis Vuitton flagship store (see p.51) has undergone a glitzy revamp, while once-dowdy shops such as the Renault show room at no. 53 and the Publicis advertising agency, near the Arc de Triomphe, have had stylish makeovers. New, fashionable restaurants and bars are constantly popping up in the streets that spar off the avenue.

THE ARC DE TRIOMPHE

THE ARC DE TRIOMPHE

Ⓜ Charles-de-Gaulle. Daily: April–Sept 10am–11pm; Oct–March 10am–10.30pm. €9.50. MAP P.48–49, POCKET MAP B5

Crowning the Champs-Elysées, the Arc de Triomphe sits imposingly in the middle of place Charles de Gaulle, also known as l'Etoile ("star") on account of the twelve avenues radiating from it. Modelled on the ancient Roman triumphal arches, this imperial behemoth was built by Napoleon as a homage to the armies of France and is engraved with the names of 660 generals and numerous French battles. The best of the exterior reliefs is François Rude's *Marseillaise*, in which an Amazon-type figure personifying the Revolution charges forward with a sword, her face contorted in a fierce rallying cry. A quiet reminder of the less glorious side of war is the tomb of the unknown soldier placed beneath the arch and marked by an eternal flame that is stoked up every evening by war veterans. The climb up to the top is well worth it for the panoramic views.

THE GRAND PALAIS

Ⓜ Champs-Elysées-Clemenceau Ⓦ www .grandpalais.fr. Galeries nationales du Grand Palais: daily except Tues times vary. €12. MAP P.48–49, POCKET MAP D6

At the lower end of the Champs-Elysées is the Grand Palais, a grandiose Neoclassical building with a fine glass and ironwork cupola, created for the 1900 Exposition Univer-selle. The cupola forms the centrepiece of the *nef* (nave), a huge, impressive exhibition space, used for large-scale installations, fashion shows and trade fairs. In the north wing of the building is the Galeries nationales, Paris's prime venue for major art retrospectives.

The Grand Palais' western wing houses the Palais de la Découverte (Ⓦ palais -decouverte.com; Tues–Sat 9.30am–6pm, Sun 10am–7pm; €8), Paris's original science museum dating from the late 1930s, with interactive exhibits, an excellent planetarium and engaging exhibitions, such as recent ones on dinosaurs and the history of clay.

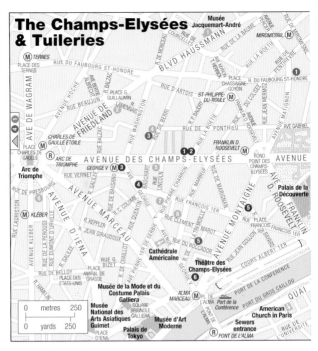

THE PETIT PALAIS

Av Winston Churchill Ⓜ Champs-Elysées-
Clemenceau ☎ 01.53.43.40.00, Ⓦ www
.petit-palais.paris.fr. Tues–Sun 10am–6pm.
Free. MAP P.48–49, POCKET MAP D6-7

The Petit Palais houses the
Musée des Beaux Arts. Built
at the same time as its larger
neighbour the Grand Palais,
the building is hardly "petit"
but certainly palatial, with
beautiful spiral wrought-iron
staircases and a grand gallery
on the lines of Versailles' Hall
of Mirrors. The museum has
an extensive collection of
paintings, sculpture and decorative artworks, ranging from
the ancient Greek and Roman
period up to the early twentieth
century. At first sight it looks
like it's mopped up the leftovers
after the city's other galleries
have taken their pick, but there
are some real gems here, such
as Monet's *Sunset at Lavacourt*

and Courbet's provocative
*Young Ladies on the Bank of
the Seine*. There's also fantasy
jewellery of the Art Nouveau
period, a fine collection of
seventeenth-century Dutch
landscape painting, Russian
icons and effete eighteenth-
century furniture and porcelain.
A stylish café overlooks the
interior garden, and popular
free lunchtime concerts are
held most Thursdays at 12.30
by Radio France (turn up about
an hour in advance to collect
a ticket).

MUSÉE JACQUEMART-ANDRÉ

158 bd Haussmann Ⓜ Miromesnil/
St-Philippe-du-Roule ☎ 01.45.62.11.59,
Ⓦ www.musee-jacquemart-andre.com. Daily
10am–6pm. €11. MAP P.48–49, POCKET MAP D5

The Musée Jacquemart-André
is set in a magnificent
nineteenth-century *hôtel
particulier* (mansion), hung

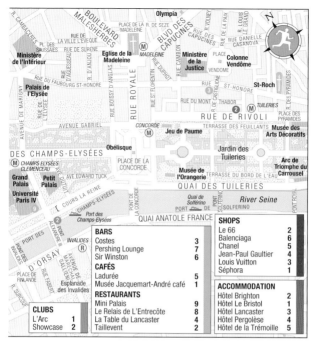

BARS	
Costes	3
Pershing Lounge	7
Sir Winston	6
CAFÉS	
Ladurée	5
Musée Jacquemart-André café	1
RESTAURANTS	
Mini Palais	9
Le Relais de L'Entrecôte	8
La Table du Lancaster	4
Taillevent	2

SHOPS	
Le 66	2
Balenciaga	6
Chanel	5
Jean-Paul Gaultier	4
Louis Vuitton	3
Séphora	1

ACCOMMODATION	
Hôtel Brighton	2
Hôtel Le Bristol	1
Hôtel Lancaster	3
Hôtel Pergolèse	4
Hôtel de la Trémoille	5

CLUBS	
L'Arc	1
Showcase	2

with the superb artworks accumulated on the travels of banker Edouard André and his wife, former society portraitist Nélie Jacquemart. A stunning distillation of fifteenth- and sixteenth-century Italian genius, including works by Tiepolo, Botticelli, Donatello, Mantegna and Uccello, forms the core of the collection. Almost as compelling as the splendid interior and collection of paintings is the insight gleaned into a grand nineteenth-century lifestyle.

PLACE DE LA CONCORDE

Concorde. MAP P.48-49, POCKET MAP E6-7

The vast place de la Concorde has a much less peaceful history than its name suggests. Between 1793 and 1795, some 1300 people died here beneath the Revolutionary guillotine, Louis XVI, Marie-Antoinette and Robespierre among them. Today, constantly circum-navigated by traffic, the centrepiece of the place is a gold-tipped obelisk from the temple of Ramses at Luxor, offered as a favour-currying gesture by the viceroy of Egypt in 1829.

JARDIN DES TUILERIES

Concorde/Tuileries. Daily: April–June & Sept 7.30am–9pm; July & Aug 7.30am–11.45pm; Oct–March 7.30am–7.30pm. MAP P.48-49, POCKET MAP E7-F7

The Jardin des Tuileries, the formal French garden par excel-lence, dates back to the 1570s, when Catherine de Médicis cleared the site of the medieval warren of tilemakers (*tuileries*) to make way for a palace and grounds. One hundred years later, Louis XIV commissioned André Le Nôtre to redesign them, and the results are largely what you see today: straight avenues, formal flower beds and splendid vistas. The central alley is lined with clipped chestnuts and manicured lawns, and framed at each end by ornamental pools, surrounded by an impressive gallery of copies of statues by the likes of Rodin.

ORANGERIE

Jardin des Tuileries Concorde
☎ 01.44.77.80.07, www.musee-orangerie.fr. Daily except Tues 9am–6pm. €7.50.
MAP P.48-49, POCKET MAP E7

The Jardin des Tuileries' Orangerie, an elegant Neoclassical-style building designed to protect the garden's orange trees, now houses a private collection of late nineteenth-century art, including eight of Monet's giant water-lily paintings. Highlights from the rest of the collection include sensuous nudes by Renoir and a number of Cézanne still lifes.

JEU DE PAUME

Jardin des Tuileries Concorde
☎ 01.47.03.12.50, www.jeudepaume.org. Tues noon–9pm, Wed–Fri noon–7pm, Sat & Sun 10am–7pm. €8.50. MAP P.48-49, POCKET MAP E6-7

The Neoclassical Jeu de Paume is a major exhibition space dedicated to photography and video art. It's not as well lit as you might expect from the soaring, light-filled foyer, but it's one of the top venues for catching major retrospectives of photographers.

THE JARDIN DES TUILERIES

Shops

LE 66

66 av des Champs-Elysées Ⓜ George V.
Mon–Sat 11am–8pm, Sun 2–8pm. MAP P.48–49,
POCKET MAP C6

This stylishly designed glass-walled concept store stocks a great selection of high-end street-wear labels such as Evisu, Raf Simons, American Retro and Acne for both men and women, as well as accessories, international art books and magazines, all in a minimalist space. Jeans from €100, T-shirts from €50.

BALENCIAGA

10 av George V Ⓜ Alma Marceau/George V.
Mon–Sat 10am–7pm. MAP P.48–49, POCKET MAP C7

The Spanish fashion house (now owned by a French multinational and led by Nicolas Ghesquière), once famed for its bubble skirts, is currently producing some of the most exciting designs in Paris.

CHANEL

42 av Montaigne Ⓜ Franklin D. Roosevelt.
Mon–Sat 10am–7pm. MAP P.48–49, POCKET MAP C6

Born in 1883, Gabrielle "Coco" Chanel engendered a way of life that epitomized elegance, class and refined taste. Her most famous signatures are the legendary No. 5 perfume, the black evening dress and the once-omnipresent tweed suit.

JEAN-PAUL GAULTIER

44 av George V Ⓜ George V. Mon–Sat
10.30am–7pm. MAP P.48–49, POCKET MAP C6

The primordial young turk of Paris fashion, whose denim collection is within reach of those not being chased by paparazzi.

LOUIS VUITTON

101 av des Champs-Elysées Ⓜ George V.
Mon–Sat 10am–8pm, Sun 11am–7pm. MAP

LOUIS VUITTON SHOP FRONT

P.48–49, POCKET MAP C5

Louis Vuitton's stylish flagship store doesn't just sell luxury luggage and handbags, it also has a contemporary art space on its seventh floor, accessed from within the store or round the corner at 60 rue de Bassano. Artworks, such as a video wall by Olafur Eliasson (who did the sun-like installation *The Weather Project* at the Tate Modern in London), have also been incorporated into the shop.

SÉPHORA

70 av des Champs-Elysées Ⓜ Franklin-D.
Roosevelt. Mon–Sat 10am–midnight, Sun
11am–midnight. MAP P.48–49, POCKET MAP C6

A huge perfume and cosmetics emporium, stocking every conceivable brand, including Sephora's own line of fun, girly and reasonably priced cosmetics. There are lots of testers, and you can get free makeovers plus pampering and beauty consultations from the solicitous sales staff. It's also open till midnight, handy if you're out on the town without your lipstick.

THE LADURÉE TEA ROOMS

Cafés

LADURÉE

75 av des Champs-Elysées Ⓜ George V. Daily 7.30am–11.30pm. MAP P.48-49, POCKET MAP C6

This Champs-Elysées branch of the Ladurée tea rooms, with its luxurious gold and green decor, is perfect for a shopping break. It's justly famed for its melt-in-the-mouth macaroons with their gooey fillings (the chocolate and blackcurrant ones are hard to beat), and the light-as-air meringues and mille-feuilles are almost as good.

MUSÉE JACQUEMART-ANDRÉ

158 bd Haussmann Ⓜ Miromesnil/ St-Philippe-du-Roule. Daily 11.45am–5.30pm. MAP P.48-49, POCKET MAP D5

The city's most sumptuously appointed *salon de thé* set within the splendid Musée Jacquemart-André. The high ceilings are decorated with frescoes by Tiepolo and the walls hung with antique tapestries. In summer you can sit out on the lovely terrace, set in the mansion's interior courtyard. On the menu are delicious salads and quiches, and the exquisite cakes and pastries are not to be missed.

Restaurants

MINI PALAIS

Av Winston Churchill Ⓜ Champs-Elysées-Clemenceau ☎ 01.42.56.42.42.Daily 10am–2am. MAP P.48-49, POCKET MAP D6

A meal at the Grand Palais' lofty dining room or out on the colonnaded terrace is a real treat. The menu is a sophisticated mix of French classics and more international dishes. You can also come just for a snack, or a drink at the bar. Mains cost €15–35.

LE RELAIS DE L'ENTRECÔTE

15 rue Marbeuf Ⓜ Franklin D. Roosevelt. Daily noon–2.30pm & 7–11.30pm; closed Aug. MAP P.48-49, POCKET MAP C6

Don't worry if a menu isn't forthcoming here – there isn't one. The only dish is *steak frites*, widely considered the best in Paris and served with a delicious sauce, the ingredients of which are a closely kept secret. Count on around €25 including a salad starter. No reservations are taken so you may have to queue, or arrive early.

LA TABLE DU LANCASTER

7 rue de Berri Ⓜ George V ☎ 01.40.76.40.18. Noon–2.30pm & 7–10.30pm; closed Sat lunch. MAP P.48-49, POCKET MAP C5

An elegant haute cuisine restaurant within the five-star boutique *Hospes Lancaster*, perfect for an intimate dinner. The menu, overseen by chef Michel Troisgros, is arranged around different themes, with dishes characterized by exotic ingredients (such as cod with koshihikari rice). In summer, sit out in the Japanese-style garden. Lunch *menu* (Mon–Fri) €56; dinner *menu* from €115.

TAILLEVENT

15 rue Lamennais Ⓜ George V
☎ 01.44.95.15.01. Mon–Fri 12.15–2.30pm &
7.15–11.30pm; closed Aug. MAP P.48–49.
POCKET MAP C5

The Provençal-influenced cuisine of Alain Solivérés is outstanding, with the emphasis on the classic; dishes include spelt risotto with frogs' legs. The main dining room, with its light-wood panelling and grey-green colour scheme, creates a soothing ambience, and waiters treat you like royalty. There's a set menu for €82 at lunch, otherwise it's €125–200 a head, excluding wine.

Bars

COSTES

Hôtel Costes, 239 rue St-Honoré
Ⓜ Concorde/Tuileries. Daily until 2am.
MAP P.48–49, POCKET MAP A13

A favourite haunt of fashionistas and celebs, this is a fabulously glamorous place for an aperitif or late-night drinks amid a decadent nineteenth-century decor of red velvet, swags and columns. Cocktails around €20.

PERSHING LOUNGE

Pershing Hall, 49 rue Pierre Charron
Ⓜ George V. Daily 6pm–2am. MAP P.48–49,
POCKET MAP C6

The *Pershing Hall* hotel lounge bar is a delightful retreat from the bustle of the city, with its thirty-metre-high vertical garden. It's a bit of a jetsetters' hangout, with cocktails priced to match.

SIR WINSTON

5 rue du Presbourg Ⓜ Kléber/Charles-de-
Gaulle-Etoile. Daily 9am–2am (Thurs–Sat till
4am). MAP P.48–49, POCKET MAP B5

A British-Indian themed bar-restaurant, with comfy leather chesterfields and snug booths perfect for lingering over a martini cocktail (€10). Evenings see DJ sets with a world music slant.

Clubs

L'ARC

12 rue du Presbourg Ⓜ Charles-de-Gaulle-
Etoile Ⓦ larc-paris.com. Restaurant: Mon–Fri
noon–2pm, Sat 7–11pm; club: Thurs–Sat
11.30pm–5am .MAP P.48–49, POCKET MAP B5

A suitably triumphal entry on the Champs-Elysées scene, this sleek restaurant and club has quickly become a favourite with the city's glamorous crowd. After you've dined in the restaurant, you can party the night away downstairs in the Sixties-style neon-lit club.

SHOWCASE

Below Pont Alexandre III Ⓜ Champs-
Elysées-Clemenceau ☎ 01.45.61.25.43,
Ⓦ www.showcase.fr. Fri & Sat 10pm–dawn,
Sun 11am–3pm. MAP P.48–49, POCKET MAP D7

This superclub, facing onto the river, has a 1500 capacity, slick decor and a fun crowd. Electronica, particularly techno, is the order of the day, with Chloe from Paris regularly on the decks. Dress up to get in, or sign up online. Entry up to €20.

PERSHING LOUNGE

The Eiffel Tower area

The swathe of the 7^e arrondissement from the Eiffel Tower east to St-Germain has little in common with the rest of the Left Bank. Boutique bars and bohemians are few, while mansions and public monuments dominate. Dwarfed by the tower, which casts its timeless spell, the district is also defined by the great military edifices of the École Militaire and Hôtel des Invalides. On a more human scale are the exotic museum of non-Western art, the Musée du Quai Branly, and the intimate Musée Rodin. Across the river, the swish strip of the 16e arrondissement that runs alongside the Seine echoes the staid monumental tone, though a handful of museums – in particular the Site de Création Contemporaine, the Musée Guimet and the Cité de l'Architecture – offer some of the city's most exciting exhibitions.

THE EIFFEL TOWER

RER Champ de Mars–Tour Eiffel
ⓦ www.tour-eiffel.fr. Daily: mid-June to Aug 9am–12.45am; Sept to mid-June 9.30am–11.45pm; last entry 45min before closing time. Lift: top level €13.40; second level €8.20, or stairs to second level €4.70; stairs then lift to top level €9.90 (top level only accessible by lift; access closes 6pm Sept to mid-June).MAP P.56–57, POCKET MAP B8

It's hard to believe that the Eiffel Tower, the quintessential symbol both of Paris and the brilliance of industrial engineering, was designed to be a temporary structure for the 1889 Exposition Universelle. When completed, the 300m tower was the tallest building in the world. Outraged critics protested against this "grimy factory chimney", though Eiffel himself thought it was beautiful in its sheer structural efficiency: "To a certain extent," he wrote, "the tower was formed by the wind itself".

THE EIFFEL TOWER FROM BELOW

Unless you arrive before opening time, or in bad weather, you will queue at the bottom, for lifts at the changeovers, and when descending. It's absolutely worth it, however, not just for the view, but for the exhilaration of being inside the structure. The views are usually clearer from the second level, but there's something irresistible about taking the lift all the way up. Dusty brown by day, the tower is spectacular after dark, an urban lighthouse illuminated by a double searchlight. For the first ten minutes of every hour thousands of effervescent lights fizz about the structure, defining the famous silhouette in luminescent champagne.

PALAIS DE CHAILLOT

Ⓜ Trocadéro. MAP P.56–57, POCKET MAP A7

From behind its elaborate park and fountains, the sweeping arcs of the Palais de Chaillot seem designed to embrace the view of the Eiffel Tower, which stands on the far side of the river. The totalitarian Modernist-Classical architecture dates the palace to 1937, when it was built as the showpiece of the Exposition Universelle, one of Paris's regular trade and culture jamborees. The central terrace

between the palace's two wings provides a perfect platform for photo opportunities, curio-sellers and skateboarders.

CITÉ DE L'ARCHITECTURE ET DU PATRIMOINE

Palais de Chaillot, 1 place du Trocadéro
Ⓜ Trocadéro ☎ 01.58.51.52.00, Ⓦ www
.citechaillot.fr. Mon, Wed & Fri–Sun
11am–7pm, Thurs 11am–9pm; €8.
MAP P.56–57, POCKET MAP A7–B7

The Cité de l'Architecture et du Patrimoine, in the east wing of the Palais de Chaillot, is a fine museum of architecture. On the loftily vaulted ground floor, the Galerie des Moulages displays giant plaster casts taken from great French buildings at the end of the nineteenth century. You'd never guess these moulds weren't the real thing, and they vividly display the development of national (mainly church) architecture from the Middle Ages to the nineteenth century. The top floor offers a sleek rundown of the modern and contemporary, including a reconstruction of an apartment from Le Corbusier's Cité Radieuse, in Marseille. The Galerie des Peintures Murales, with its radiant, full-scale copies of great French frescoes occupies the top floors.

MUSÉE NATIONAL DE LA MARINE

Palais de Chaillot, place du Trocadéro Ⓜ Trocadéro ☎ 01.53.65.69.69, ⓦ www
.musee-marine.fr. Mon & Wed–Fri 11am–6pm,
Sat & Sun 11am–7pm. €7, €9 including
temporary exhibitions. MAP P.56–57.
POCKET MAP A7

While its super-scale models of
French ships, ranging from
ancient galleys through
Napoleon's imperial barges to
nuclear submarines, are
undeniably impressive, most of
the displays in this specialist
museum are (ironically) dry as
dust – it's best visited if you
have a particular interest in one
of the high-profile, lively
temporary exhibitions, all on
seafaring themes. It's also home
to the original Jules Verne
trophy, awarded for nonstop
round-the-world sailing – a
hull-shaped streak of glass
invisibly suspended by magnets
within its cabinet.

CINÉAQUA

Jardins du Trocadéro Ⓜ Trocadéro
☎ 01.40.69.23.01, ⓦ www.cineaqua.com.
Daily 10am–7pm. €19.90, children 3–12
€12.90, children 13–17 €15.50. MAP P.56–57.
POCKET MAP B7

A mysterious grotto-like
entrance hidden away in the
Jardins du Trocadéro leads
you down into this bizarre,
high-concept subterranean
space – an aquarium-cum-
multimedia complex. The
unlikely-sounding combina-
tion of animation workshops,
state-of-the-art tanks, film
museum and classic movie
screenings – with a Japanese
restaurant for good measure
– shouldn't work, but it does.
Admittedly, it's geared more
towards French-speakers, but
most cartoon-loving kids will
enjoy it.

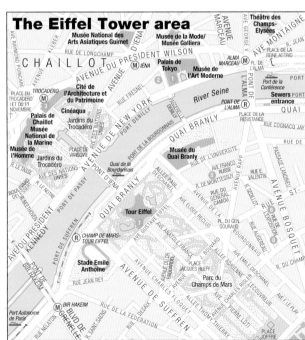

THE MUSÉE GUIMET

4

THE EIFFEL TOWER AREA

MUSÉE GUIMET

6 place d'Iéna Ⓜ Iéna ☎ 01.56.52.53.00, Ⓦ www.guimet.fr. Daily except Tues 10am–6pm; €7.50, €8 for temporary exhibitions. MAP P.56–57, POCKET MAP B7

The Musée National des Arts Asiatiques-Guimet boasts a stunning display of Asian, and especially Buddhist, art. Four floors groan under the weight of imaginatively displayed statues of Buddhas and gods, and a roofed-in courtyard provides an airy space in which to show off the museum's world-renowned collection of Khmer sculpture. The Buddhist statues of the Gandhara civilization, on the first floor, betray a fascinating debt to Greek sculpture, while the fierce demons from Nepal, the many-armed gold gods of South India and the pot-bellied Chinese Buddhas are stunningly exotic. One of the most moving exhibits is one of the simplest: a two-thousand-year-old blown-glass fish from Afghanistan.

The third-floor rotunda was used by founder Emile Guimet for the first Buddhist ceremony held in France. His original collection, brought back from Asia in 1876, is exhibited in the temple-like Galeries du Panthéon Bouddhique, at 19 avenue d'Iéna (same hours and ticket as museum).

ACCOMMODATION

Hôtel du Champs-de-Mars	3
Hôtel du Palais Bourbon	2
Hôtel Saint Dominique	1

CAFÉS

| Café Carlu | 3 |
| Café du Marché | 9 |

RESTAURANTS

L'Arpège	10
Au Bon Accueil	5
La Fontaine de Mars	6
Le Jules Verne	7
Aux Marchés du Palais	2
Au Petit Tonneau	4
Le P'tit Troquet	8
Tokyo Eat	1

| 0 | metres | 250 |
| 0 | yards | 250 |

MUSÉE DE LA MODE DE LA VILLE DE PARIS

Palais Galliera, 10 av Pierre 1ᵉʳ de Serbie
Ⓜ Iéna/Alma-Marceau ☎ 01.56.52.86.00,
Ⓦ www.galliera.paris.fr. Tues–Sun
10am–6pm. €7. Closed until spring 2013. MAP
P.56–57, POCKET MAP B7

Behind the Palais de Tokyo, the grandiose Palais Galliera – another Neoclassical hulk – is home to the Musée de la Mode, which rotates its magnificent collection of clothes and accessories from the eighteenth century to the present day in a few themed exhibitions a year. During changeovers the museum is closed, so check in advance.

MUSÉE D'ART MODERNE DE LA VILLE DE PARIS

Palais de Tokyo, 13 av du Président Wilson
Ⓜ Iéna/Alma-Marceau ☎ 01.53.67.40.00,
Ⓦ www.mam.paris.fr. Tues–Sun 10am–6pm;
during exhibitions also Thurs 10am–10pm.
Permanent collection free; temporary shows
€5–11. MAP P.56–57, POCKET MAP B7

While it's no competition for the Pompidou, the cool white Palais de Tokyo is a more contemplative space, offering a fitting Modernist setting for the city's own collection of modern art. Paris-based artists such as Braque, Chagall, Delaunay, Derain, Léger and Picasso are well represented in its strong early twentieth-century collection, and many works have Parisian themes. The enormous centrepieces are two versions of Matisse's *La Danse* and Dufy's giant mural, *La Fée Électricité*, commissioned by the electricity board, which fills an entire curved room with 250 lyrical panels recounting the story of electricity from Aristotle to the 1930s. Temporary exhibitions fill the ground-floor space.

SITE DE CRÉATION CONTEMPORAINE

Palais de Tokyo, 13 av du Président Wilson
Ⓜ Iéna/Alma-Marceau ☎ 01.47.23.54.01,
Ⓦ www.palaisdetokyo.com. Tues–Sun
noon–midnight €6. MAP P.56–57, POCKET MAP B7

The Palais de Tokyo's western wing hosts the Site de Création Contemporaine, a cutting-edge gallery whose brutalist space focuses exclusively on conceptual and avant-garde art. A changing flow of exhibitions and events – anything from a show by Paris-born Louise Bourgeois to a temporary "occupation" by squatter-artists – keeps the atmosphere lively, with an exciting, counter-cultural, buzz. Artists and art students pay just €1 to get in.

THE SITE DE CRÉATION CONTEMPORAINE

PLACE DE L'ALMA

Ⓜ Alma-Marceau. MAP P.56–57, POCKET MAP C7

From most angles, place de l'Alma looks like just another busy Parisian junction, with cars rattling over the cobbles and a métro entrance on the pavement. Over in one corner, however, stands a replica of the flame from the Statue of Liberty, which was given to France in 1987 as a symbol of Franco-American relations.

This golden torch has been adopted by mourners from all over the world as a memorial to Princess Diana, who was killed in the underpass beneath in 1997.

THE SEWERS

Place de la Résistance, RER Pont de l'Alma/ Ⓜ Place d'Iéna ☎ 01.53.68.27.81. Sat–Wed: May–Sept 11am–5pm; Oct–April 11am–4pm. €4.30. MAP P.56–57, POCKET MAP C7

Opposite the Pont de l'Alma on the northeast side of the busy junction of place de la Résistance, is the entrance to one of Paris's more unusual attractions – a small, visitable section of the sewers, or *les égouts*. Underground, it's dark, damp and noisy from the gushing water; the main exhibition runs along a gantry walk poised above a main sewer. The photographs, lamps, specialized sewermen's tools and other antique flotsam and jetsam render the history of the city's water supply and waste management surprisingly interesting. The air down here is as smelly and unappealing as you might expect, so those of a nervous disposition might want to give it a miss.

RUE CLER AND AROUND

Ⓜ La Tour-Maubourg. MAP P.56–57, POCKET MAP C8

A little further upstream, the **American Church** on quai

SEWERMEN'S LAMPS ON DISPLAY AT THE SEWERS

d'Orsay, together with the American College nearby at 31 av Bosquet, is a focal point in the well-organized life of Paris's large American community, its notice board usually plastered with job and accommodation offers and requests. Immediately to the south, and in stark contrast to the austerity of much of the rest of the quarter, lies a villagey wedge of early nineteenth-century streets between avenue Bosquet and the Invalides. Chief among them is **rue Cler**, whose food shops act as a kind of permanent market. The crossstreets, rue de Grenelle and rue St-Dominique, are full of neighbourhood shops, posh *bistrots* and little hotels.

PARC DU CHAMPS DE MARS

Ⓜ École Militaire. MAP P.56–57, POCKET MAP B8–C9

Parading back from the Eiffel Tower are the long, rectangular and tourist-thronged gardens of the **Champs de Mars**, leading to the eighteenth-century **École Militaire**, originally founded in 1751 by Louis XV for the training of aristocratic army officers, and attended by Napoleon, among other fledgling leaders.

MUSÉE DU QUAI BRANLY

37 Quai Branly ⓂIéna/RER Pont de l'Alma
☎01.56.61.71.72. ⓦwww.quaibranly.fr.
Tues, Wed & Sun 11am–7pm, Thurs–Sat
11am–9pm. €8.50, €10 including temporary
exhibits. MAP P.56–57, POCKET MAP B7–8

A short distance upstream of the Eiffel Tower, on quai Branly, stands the intriguing Musée du Quai Branly, designed by the French state's favourite architect, Jean Nouvel. The museum – which gathers together hundreds of thousands of non-European objects bought or purloined by France over the centuries – was the brainchild of President Chirac, whose passion for what he would no doubt call *arts primitifs* helped secure funding. Nouvel's elaborate design, which aims to blur the divide between structure and environment, unfurls in a long glazed curve, pocked with coloured boxes, through the middle of an enormous garden. Inside, areas devoted to Asia, Africa, the Americas and the Pacific ("Oceania") snake through dimly lit rooms lined by curving "mud" walls in brown leather. The 3500 folk artefacts on display at any one time – Hopi kachina dolls, ancient Hawaiian feather helmets – are as fascinating as they are beautiful; the tone of the place, however, is muddled. While the objects are predominantly displayed – and easily experienced – as works of art, there's an uneasy sense that they are being presented above all in terms of their exotic "otherness". This is not helped when the museum loses the courage of its convictions, shifting into outdated anthropological mode, using written (and often poorly translated) panels to give lofty cultural context.

HÔTEL DES INVALIDES

ⓂVarenne/La Tour-Maubourg Ⓦwww
.invalides.org. MAP P.56–57, POCKET MAP D8

There's no missing the overpowering facade of the Hôtel des Invalides, topped by its resplendent gilded dome. Despite its palatial, crushingly grand appearance, it was built as a home for wounded soldiers in the reign of Louis XIV – whose foreign wars gave the building a constant supply of residents, and whose equestrian statue lords it over a massive central arch. It today houses two churches – one for the soldiers, the other intended as a mausoleum for the king but now containing the mortal remains of Napoleon – and the

MUSÉE DU QUAI BRANLY

Musée de l'Armée, an enormous national war museum. The most interesting sections of the museum are detailed below, but the remainder, dedicated to the history of the French army from Louis XIV up to the 1870s, is really for fanatics only.

MUSÉE DE L'ARMÉE

Hôtel des Invalides ⓂLa Tour-Maubourg/ Varenne ☎01.44.42.38.77, ⓌWww.invalides .org. Daily: April–Sept 10am–6pm, Oct–March 10am–5pm; Oct–June closed first Mon of every month. €9 ticket also valid for Napoleon's tomb. MAP P.56–57, POCKET MAP D8

By far the most affecting galleries of the vast Musée de l'Armée cover the two world wars, beginning with Prussia's annexation of Alsace-Lorraine in 1871 and ending with the defeat of the Third Reich. The battles, the resistance and the slow liberation are documented through imaginatively displayed war memorabilia combined with stirring contemporary newsreels, most of which have an English-language option. The simplest artefacts – a rag doll found on a battlefield, plaster casts of mutilated faces, an overcoat caked in mud from the trenches – tell a stirring human story, while

un-narrated footage, from the Somme, Dunkirk and a bomb attack on a small French town, flicker across bare walls in grim silence. The collection of medieval and Renaissance armour in the west wing of the royal courtyard is also worth admiring. Highlights include highly decorative seventeenth-century Italian suits, and two dimly lit chambers of beautifully worked Chinese and Japanese weaponry.

MUSÉE DES PLANS-RELIEFS

Same hours and ticket as the Musée de l'Armée. MAP P.56–57, POCKET MAP D8

Up under the roof of the east wing, the Musée des Plans-Reliefs displays an extraordinary collection of super-scale models of French ports and fortified cities. Essentially giant three-dimensional maps, they were created in the seventeenth and eighteenth centuries to plan defences or plot potential artillery positions. The eerie green glow of their landscapes only just illuminates the long, tunnel-like attic; the effect is rather chilling.

EGLISE DES SOLDATS

Entrance from main courtyard of Les Invalides. Same hours as the Musée de l'Armée. Free. MAP P.56–57, POCKET MAP D8

The lofty "Soldiers' Church" is the spiritual home of the French army, its proud simplicity standing in stark contrast to the elaborate Eglise du Dôme, which lies on the other side of a dividing glass wall – an innovation that allowed worshippers to share the same high altar without the risk of coming into social contact. The walls are hung with almost one hundred enemy standards captured on the battlefield, part of a collection of some three thousand that once adorned Notre-Dame.

EGLISE DU DÔME

Entrance from south side of Les Invalides.
Same hours and ticket as the Musée de
l'Armée. MAP P.56–57, POCKET MAP D8

Some find the lavish Eglise
du Dôme, or "royal church",
gloriously sumptuous – others
find it overbearing. A perfect
example of the architectural
pomposity of Louis XIV's day,
with grandiose frescoes and
an abundance of Corinthian
columns and pilasters, it is now
a monument to Napoleon.

NAPOLEON'S TOMB

Eglise du Dôme. Same hours and ticket as
the Musée de l'Armée. MAP P.56–57,
POCKET MAP D8

On December 14, 1840,
Napoleon was finally laid to
rest in the crypt of the Eglise
du Dôme. Brought home from
St Helena twenty years after
his death, his remains were
carried through the streets
from the newly completed
Arc de Triomphe to the
Invalides. As many as half
a million people came out
to watch the emperor's last
journey, and Victor Hugo
commented that "it felt as if
the whole of Paris had been
poured to one side of the city,

like liquid in a vase which has
been tilted". He now lies in a
giant sarcophagus of smooth
red porphyry, encircled with
Napoleonic quotations of
staggering but largely truthful
conceit, and overshadowing
the nearby tombs of two of his
brothers, as well as his son,
the King of Rome, whose body
was brought here on Hitler's
orders in 1940. Another chapel
upstairs holds Marshal Foch,
the Supreme Commander of
Allied forces in World War I.

MUSÉE RODIN

79 rue de Varenne Ⓜ Varenne
☎ 01.44.18.61.10, Ⓦ www.musee-rodin
.fr. Tues–Sun 10am–5.45pm; garden closes
6pm (March–Sept), 5pm (Oct–March). House
and gardens €7; garden only €1. MAP P.56–57,
POCKET MAP D8

The setting of the Musée Rodin
is superbly elegant, a beautiful
eighteenth-century mansion
which the sculptor leased from
the state in return for the gift
of all his work upon his death.
Bronze versions of major
projects like *The Burghers of
Calais*, *The Thinker*, *The Gate of
Hell* and *Ugolino* are exhibited
in the large gardens – the last-
named forms the centrepiece
of the ornamental pond.

Things get even better inside – the vigorous energy of the sculptures contrasting with the worn wooden panelling of the *boiseries* and the tarnished mirrors and chandeliers. It's usually very crowded with visitors eager to see much-loved works like *The Hand of God* and the touchingly erotic *The Kiss*, which was originally designed to portray Paolo and Francesca da Rimini, from Dante's *Divine Comedy*, in the moment before they were discovered and murdered by Francesca's husband. Rodin once self-deprecatingly referred to it as "a large sculpted knick-knack following the usual formula"; art critics today like to think of it as the last master-work of figurative sculpture before the whole art form was reinvented – largely by Rodin himself. Paris's *Kiss* is one of only four marble versions of the work, but hundreds of smaller bronzes were turned out as money-spinners.

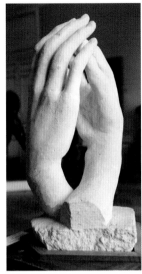

SCULPTURE AT THE MUSÉE RODIN

It's well worth lingering over the museum's vibrant, impressionistic clay works, small studies that Rodin took from life. In fact, most of the works here are in clay or plaster, as these are considered to be Rodin's finest achievements – after completing his apprenticeship, he rarely picked up a chisel, in line with the common nineteenth-century practice of delegating the task of working up stone and bronze versions to assistants. Instead, he would return to his plaster casts again and again, modifying and refining them and sometimes deliberately leaving them "unfinished".

Don't miss the room devoted to Camille Claudel, Rodin's pupil, model and lover. Among her works is the painfully allegorical *The Age of Maturity*, symbolizing her ultimate rejection by Rodin, and a bust of the artist himself. Claudel's perception of her teacher was so akin to Rodin's own that he considered it his self-portrait.

COURTYARD STATUE AT THE MUSÉE RODIN

Cafés

CAFÉ CARLU

Palais de Chaillot, 1 place du Trocadéro ⓂTrocadéro. Mon, Wed & Fri–Sun 11am–7pm, Thurs 11am–9pm. MAP P.56–57, POCKET MAP A7

It's well worth the slightly inflated prices at this modern little museum café to enjoy the phenomenal close-up views of the Eiffel Tower from the outdoor terrace – you could sit here all day grazing on light snacks, coffees and juices.

CAFÉ DU MARCHÉ

38 rue Cler ⓂLa-Tour-Maubourg. Mon–Sat 7am–midnight, Sun 7am–4pm. MAP P.56–57, POCKET MAP C8

Big, busy café-brasserie in the rue Cler market serving reasonably priced meals, with hearty salads (€9.50) and market-fresh *plats du jour* for €11. Outdoor seating, with a covered terrace in winter.

Restaurants

L'ARPÈGE

84 rue de Varenne ⓂVarenne ☎ 01.47.05.09.06. Mon–Fri noon–2.30pm & 7.30–10.30pm. MAP P.56–57, POCKET MAP E8

Elite chef Alain Passard puts the spotlight on vegetables at this Michelin-starred restaurant – grilled turnips with chestnuts, or beetroot baked in salt crust are astonishingly good – but you'll also find plenty of other exhilarating dishes. Lunch *menu* €130, with an incredible *menu dégustation* at over €350. Reserve well in advance and dress up.

AU BON ACCUEIL

14 rue de Monttessuy ⓂDuroc/Vaneau ☎ 01.47.05.46.11. Mon–Fri noon–2.30pm & 7–10.30pm. MAP P.56–57, POCKET MAP C8

Practically in the shadow of the Eiffel Tower, this relaxed but upbeat wine-*bistrot* offers fresh, well-considered dishes, such as a delicate salad of prawns and lemon verbena, and veal liver with Jerusalem artichoke purée. There are a few outside tables. Expect to pay €50 with wine.

LA FONTAINE DE MARS

129 rue Saint-Dominique ⓂLa Tour-Maubourg ☎ 01.47.05.46.44. Daily noon–3pm & 7.30–11pm. MAP P.56–57, POCKET MAP C8

Pink checked tablecloths, leather banquettes, tiled floor, outside tables, attentive service: this is quintessential France – the Obama family certainly enjoyed it. The food is meaty, southwestern French fare: think snails, *magret de canard* and *boudin* sausages. Starters at €10–15, *plat du jour* around €20.

LE JULES VERNE

Eiffel Tower ⓂBir-Hakeim ☎ 01.45.55.61.44. Daily noon–2pm & 7–10pm. MAP P.56–57, POCKET MAP B8

It's not only the food that's elevated here, but the restaurant

L'ARPÈGE

too: Alain Ducasse's newest gastronomic venture is 125m up the Eiffel Tower. Best at dinner (€200), but the weekday lunch is a more bearable €85. Reserve well in advance.

AUX MARCHÉS DU PALAIS

5 rue de la Manutention Ⓜ Iéna/ Alma-Marceau ☎ 01.47.23.52.80. Daily noon–2.30pm & 7.30–10.30pm; closed two weeks in Aug.

MAP P.56–57, POCKET MAP B7

This cheery, traditional *bistrot* makes a good lunch stop, with sunny tables on the pavement opposite the side wall of the Palais de Tokyo, and a menu of substantial, quintessentially French dishes. You can eat very well for around €35.

AU PETIT TONNEAU

20 rue Surcouf Ⓜ Invalides ☎ 01.47.53.05.59. Wed–Sun noon–3pm & 7–11.30pm. Closed Aug. MAP P.56–57, POCKET MAP D7

Mme Boyer runs this friendly *bistrot*-style restaurant with panache, cooking delicious French cuisine. Wild mushrooms are a speciality, as is the *tarte Tatin*. All prices are *à la carte*: under €10 for starters, €15–20 for mains.

LE P'TIT TROQUET

28 rue de l'Exposition Ⓜ Ecole Militaire ☎ 01.47.05.80.39. Tues–Fri noon–2.30pm & 6.30–10.30pm, Sat 6.30–10.30pm. MAP P.56–57, POCKET MAP C8

This tiny, discreet family restaurant has a nostalgic feel with its marble tables, tiled floor and ornate zinc bar. Serving refined cuisine to the diplomats of the *quartier*, the well-judged, traditional menu changes seasonally; on a summer *menu du marché* (€33) for example, you might find tabbouleh with herbs, grapefruit and prawns, followed by rabbit with mustard.

LUNCH AT TOKYO EAT

TOKYO EAT

Site de Création Contemporaine, Palais de Tokyo Ⓜ Iéna/Alma-Marceau ☎ 01.47.20.00.29. Tues–Sat noon–3pm & 8–11.30pm, Sun noon–5.30pm & 8–10.30pm. MAP P.56–57, POCKET MAP B7

The restaurant inside this cutting-edge gallery is a self-consciously hip hangout – all bucket chairs, primary colours, nightclub lighting and clashing shapes. The food – modern Mediterranean and Asian fusion, in dishes like lamb cutlets with edamame beans and aubergine confit – isn't bad, with a lunch *formule* for €20, and mains starting at around €18, but you're here more to see and be seen than to enjoy an intimate meal. Downstairs, the pared-down snack bar, *Tokyo Self* (open museum hours) is good for a quick drink or a creative pre-made salad.

The Grands Boulevards and *passages*

Built on the old city ramparts, the Grands Boulevards are the eight broad streets that extend in a long arc from the Eglise de la Madeleine eastwards. In the nineteenth century, the boulevards, with their fashionable cafés, street theatre and puppet shows, were where "Paris vivant" was to be found. A legacy from this heyday, brasseries, cafés, theatres and cinemas (notably the splendid Art Deco cinemas Le Grand Rex and Max Linder; see p.184) still abound. To the south of the Grands Boulevards lies the city's main commercial and financial district, while just to the north, beyond the glittering Opéra Garnier, are the large department stores Galeries Lafayette and Printemps. Rather more well-heeled shopping is concentrated on the rue St-Honoré in the west and the streets around aristocratic place Vendôme, lined with top couturiers, jewellers and art dealers. Scattered around the whole area are the delightful *passages* – nineteenth-century arcades that hark back to shopping from a different era.

THE OPÉRA GARNIER

MUSÉE GRÉVIN

Bd Montmartre Ⓜ Grands-Boulevards.
Mon–Fri 10am–6.30pm, Sat & Sun
10am–7pm. €21.50, children €14. MAP
P.68–69, POCKET MAP G5

A remnant from the fun-loving
times on the Grands Boulevards
are the waxworks in the Musée
Grévin, comprising mainly
French personalities and the
usual bunch of Hollywood
actors. The best thing about the
museum is the original rooms:
the magical Palais des Mirages
(Hall of Mirrors), built for the
Exposition Universelle in 1900;
the theatre with its sculptures
by Bourdelle; and the 1882
Baroque-style Hall of Columns.

OPÉRA GARNIER

Ⓜ Opéra. Daily 10am–4.30pm. €9; see p.77
for booking information. MAP P.68–69, POCKET
MAP F5

The ornate Opéra Garnier,
built by Charles Garnier for
Napoleon III, exemplifies the
Second Empire in its show of
wealth and hint of vulgarity.
The theatre's facade is a concoc-
tion of white, pink and green
marble, colonnades, rearing
horses and gleaming gold busts.
No less opulent is the interior
with its spacious gilded-marble
and mirrored lobbies. The
auditorium is all red velvet and
gold leaf, hung with a six-tonne
chandelier; the colourful ceiling

was painted by Chagall in
1964 and depicts scenes from
well-known operas and ballets
jumbled up with Parisian
landmarks. You can visit the
interior and auditorium outside
of rehearsals (your best chance
is 1–2pm).

PLACE VENDÔME

Ⓜ Opéra. MAP P.68–69, POCKET MAP A13

Built by Versailles architect
Hardouin-Mansart, place
Vendôme is one of the city's
most impressive set pieces.
It's a pleasingly symmetrical,
eight-sided square, enclosed
by a harmonious ensemble of
elegant mansions, graced with
Corinthian pilasters and steeply
pitched roofs. Once the grand
residences of tax collectors
and financiers, they now house
such luxury establishments as
the Ritz hotel, Cartier, Bulgari
and other top-flight jewellers,
lending the square a decidedly
exclusive air. No. 12, now
occupied by Chaumet jewellers,
is where Chopin died, in 1849.

Somewhat out of proportion
with the rest of the square,
the centrepiece is a towering
triumphal column, surmounted
by a statue of Napoleon dressed
as Caesar. It was raised in
1806 to celebrate the Battle of
Austerlitz and features bronze
reliefs of scenes of the battle
spiralling their way up.

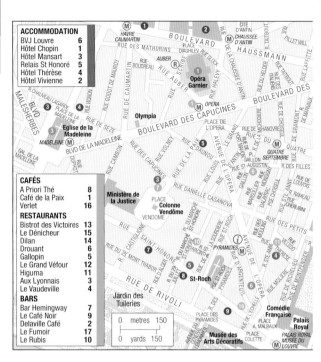

ACCOMMODATION

BVJ Louvre	6
Hôtel Chopin	1
Hôtel Mansart	3
Relais St Honoré	5
Hôtel Thérèse	4
Hôtel Vivienne	2

CAFÉS

A Priori Thé	8
Café de la Paix	1
Verlet	16

RESTAURANTS

Bistrot des Victoires	13
Le Dénicheur	15
Dilan	14
Drouant	6
Gallopin	5
Le Grand Véfour	12
Higuma	11
Aux Lyonnais	3
Le Vaudeville	4

BARS

Bar Hemingway	7
Le Café Noir	9
Delaville Café	2
Le Fumoir	17
Le Rubis	10

EGLISE DE LA MADELEINE

Ⓜ Madeleine. Mon–Sat 7.30am–7pm, Sun 8am–1pm & 4–7pm. MAP P.68–69, POCKET MAP E6

Originally intended as a monument to Napoleon's army, the imperious-looking Eglise de la Madeleine is modelled on the Parthenon, surrounded by Corinthian columns and fronted by a huge pediment depicting The Last Judgement. Inside, the wide single nave is decorated with Ionic columns and surmounted by three huge domes – the only source of natural light. A theatrical stone sculpture of the Magdalene being swept up to heaven by two angels draws your eye to the high altar, and above is a half-dome with a fresco commemorating the concordat signed between the Church and Napoleon, healing the rift after the Revolution.

PLACE DE LA MADELEINE

Ⓜ Madeleine. Flower market Tues–Sat 8am–7.30pm. MAP P.68–69, POCKET MAP E6

Place de la Madeleine is home to some of Paris's top gourmet food stores, the best known being Fauchon and Hédiard (see p.72). On the east side is one of the city's oldest flower markets dating to 1832, while nearby, some rather fine Art Nouveau public toilets are worth inspecting.

RUE ST-HONORÉ

MAP P.68–69, POCKET MAP A13–D15

Rue St-Honoré – especially its western end and the Faubourg St-Honoré – hosts top fashion designers and art galleries. Admire the beautiful silk scarves at Hermès at no.24 or join the style-conscious Parisians at the Colette concept store at no. 213 (see p.72).

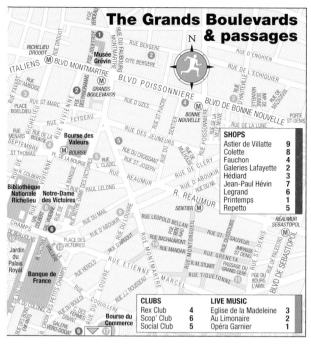

The map contains the following labels:

The Grands Boulevards & passages

N

SHOPS	
Astier de Villatte	9
Colette	8
Fauchon	4
Galeries Lafayette	2
Hédiard	3
Jean-Paul Hévin	7
Legrand	6
Printemps	1
Repetto	5

CLUBS		LIVE MUSIC	
Rex Club	4	Eglise de la Madeleine	3
Scop' Club	6	Au Limonaire	2
Social Club	5	Opéra Garnier	1

PALAIS ROYAL

Ⓜ Palais Royal-Musée du Louvre. Gardens daily
dawn–dusk. Free. MAP P.68-69, POCKET MAP B14-C14
The Palais Royal was built for
Cardinal Richelieu in 1624,
though little now remains of
the original palace. The current
building, mostly dating from
the eighteenth century, houses
various governmental bodies
and the Comédie Française,
long-standing venue for the
classics of French theatre. To
the rear lie sedate gardens
with fountains and avenues
of clipped limes, bounded
by stately eighteenth-century
mansions built over arcades
housing quirky antique and
designer shops. You'd hardly
guess that for a time these
peaceful arcades and gardens
were a site of gambling dens,
brothels and funfair attractions
until the prohibition on public
gambling in 1838 put an end
to the fun. Folly, some might
say, has returned – in the form
of contemporary artist Daniel
Buren's black-and-white striped
pillars. They're rather like sticks
of Brighton rock of varying
heights, dotted about the main
courtyard in front of the palace.

THE PALAIS ROYAL

The *passages*

Conceived by town planners in the early nineteenth century to protect pedestrians from mud and horse-drawn vehicles, the *passages*, elegant glass-roofed shopping arcades, were for decades left to crumble and decay, but many have been renovated and restored to something approaching their former glory, and chic boutiques have moved in alongside the old-fashioned traders and secondhand dealers. Most are closed at night and on Sundays.

GALERIE VÉRO-DODAT

Between rue Croix-des-Petits-Champs and rue Jean-Jacques Rousseau Ⓜ Palais Royal-Musée du Louvre. MAP P.68-69, POCKET MAP C14

With its tiled floors, ceiling decorations and mahogany shop fronts divided by faux marble columns, Galerie Véro-Dodat is one of the most attractive and homogeneous *passages*. Fashionable new shops rub shoulders with older businesses, such as R.F. Charle at no. 17, specializing in the repair and sale of vintage stringed instruments.

GALERIE VIVIENNE

Links rue Vivienne with rue des Petits-Champs Ⓜ Bourse. MAP P.68-69, POCKET MAP C13-14

The flamboyant decor of Grecian and marine motifs in charming Galerie Vivienne establishes the perfect ambience in which to buy Jean-Paul Gaultier gear, or you can browse in the antiquarian bookshop, Librairie Jousseaume, which dates back to the arcade's earliest days.

PASSAGE CHOISEUL

Links rue des Petits Champs and rue St Augustin Ⓜ Pyramides. MAP P.68-69, POCKET MAP B13

Evocatively described by Louis-Ferdinand Céline in his autobiographical *Death on Credit*, the alluringly dark and dingy-looking passage Choiseul harbours takeaway food shops, discount clothes and book stores, bars, art galleries and Lavrut, at no. 52, selling top-quality artists' materials.

PASSAGE DES PANORAMAS

Off rue Vivienne Ⓜ Grands-Boulevards. MAP P.68-69, POCKET MAP G6

The grid of arcades collectively known as the passage des Panoramas has an appealing old-fashioned chic. Standing out among the bric-a-brac shops and secondhand postcard dealers are a restaurant, *L'Arbre à Cannelle*, with fantastic carved wood panelling, and a fine old printshop, Stern.

THE GALERIE VIVIENNE

ceiling sheltering antiquarian books and old prints.

PASSAGE DU GRAND-CERF

Between rue St-Denis and rue Dessoubs ⓂEtienne-Marcel. MAP P.68-69, POCKET MAP D14-E14

The lofty, three-storey passage du Grand-Cerf arcade is stylistically the best of all. The wrought-iron work, glass roof and plain-wood shop fronts have all been cleaned, attracting stylish contemporary design, jewellery and fairtrade boutiques. There's always something quirky and original on display in the window of Le Labo (no. 4), specializing in lamps and other lighting fixtures made from recycled objects, while As'Art, opposite, is a treasure trove of home furnishings and objects from Africa.

BIBLIOTHÈQUE NATIONALE RICHELIEU

58 rue de Richelieu Ⓜ Bourse Ⓦ www.bnf .fr. Exhibitions Tues–Sat 10am–7pm, Sun noon–7pm; €7. Cabinet des Monnaies, Médailles et Antiques Mon–Fri 9–6pm, Sat 9–5pm; free. MAP P.68-69, POCKET MAP C13

The Bibliothèque Nationale Richelieu, the French National Library, is a huge, forbidding-looking building, dating back to the 1660s. It's currently undergoing major renovation, due to be completed in 2017. Parts of the library will remain open for exhibitions, but it's best to check the website for the latest information. You can see a rich display of coins and ancient treasures in the Cabinet des Monnaies, Médailles et Antiques. There's no restriction on entering the library, nor on peering into the atmospheric reading rooms, though many of the books have now been transferred to the new François Mitterrand site in the 13ᵉ (see p.138).

PASSAGES JOUFFROY AND VERDEAU

Off bd Montmartre Ⓜ Grands-Boulevards. MAP P.68-69, POCKET MAP G5

Across boulevard Montmartre, passage Jouffroy is full of the kind of stores that make shopping an adventure rather than a chore. M & G Segas sells eccentric walking canes and theatrical antiques opposite a shop stocking every conceivable fitting and furnishing for a doll's house, while near the romantic *Hôtel Chopin* (see p.168), Paul Vulin spreads his secondhand books along the passageway, and Ciné-Doc appeals to cinephiles with its collection of old film posters. Crossing rue de la Grange-Batelière, you enter the equally enchanting passage Verdeau, perhaps the lightest of the arcades, with its high glass

Shops

As well as the shops below, be sure to check out the *passages*, fertile hunting ground for curios and one-off buys.

ASTIER DE VILLATTE

173 rue St-Honoré Ⓜ Palais Royal. Mon–Sat 11am–7.30pm. MAP P.68–69, POCKET MAP B14

An atmospheric old shop full of oak cabinets displaying stylish ceramic dinnerware. The pieces (starting from around €35) manage to seem elegant and rustic at the same time, with their milky white glaze and slightly unfinished look.

COLETTE

213 rue St-Honoré Ⓜ Tuileries. Mon–Sat 11am–7pm. MAP P.68–69, POCKET MAP A14

Style-conscious young Parisians peruse the latest Anya Hindmarch handbags and Prada offerings at this cutting-edge concept store, combining high fashion and design. Coolest of all is the downstairs Water Bar, offering eighty different kinds of bottled H_2O.

FAUCHON

24–30 place de la Madeleine Ⓜ Madeleine. Mon–Sat 9am–8pm. MAP P.68–69, POCKET MAP E6

A cornucopia of extravagant and beautiful groceries, charcuterie and wines. Just the place for presents of tea, jam, truffles, chocolates, exotic vinegars and mustards.

GALERIES LAFAYETTE

40 bd Haussmann Ⓜ Chaussée d'Antin. Mon–Sat 9.30am–8pm, Thurs until 9pm. MAP P.68–69, POCKET MAP F5

This venerable department store's forte is high fashion, with two floors given over to the latest creations by leading designers and nearly a whole floor devoted to lingerie. Then

there's a host of big names in men's and women's accessories and a huge parfumerie – all under a superb 1900 dome. Just down the road at no. 35 is Lafayette Maison, five floors of quality kitchenware, linen and furniture.

HÉDIARD

21 place de la Madeleine Ⓜ Madeleine. Mon–Sat 9am–8.30pm. MAP P.68–69, POCKET MAP E6

Since the 1850s, Hédiard has been the aristocrat's grocer, selling superlative-quality food, an especially good range of fruit and veg, as well as over 70 kinds of spices and over 200 types of tea.

JEAN-PAUL HÉVIN

231 rue St-Honoré Ⓜ Tuileries. Mon–Sat 10am–7.30pm, closed 1 week in Aug. MAP P.68–69, POCKET MAP A14

Jean-Paul Hévin is one of Paris's best chocolatiers. His sleek shop displays an array of elegantly presented tablets of chocolate, bearing little descriptions of their aroma and characteristics as though they were choice wines; try for example the São Tomé, with its "grande intensité aromatique". Upstairs is a cosy *salon de thé*, with chocolate-coloured wood panelling and white furnishings, where you can choose from around fifteen different chocolate cakes.

LEGRAND

1 rue de la Banque Ⓜ Bourse. Mon 11am–7pm, Tues–Fri 10am–7.30pm, Sat 10am–7pm. MAP P.68-69, POCKET MAP C14

This beautiful old wine shop is the place to stock up on your favourite vintages and discover some little-known ones too. There's also a bar (noon–7pm) for drinks, *saucisson* and pâté.

PRINTEMPS

64 bd Haussmann Ⓜ Havre-Caumartin. Mon–Sat 9.35am–8pm, Thurs until 10pm. MAP P.68-69, POCKET MAP F5

Books, records, a parfumerie and an excellent fashion department for men and women, plus a sixth-floor restaurant underneath the beautiful Art Nouveau glass dome. The store underwent a major revamp: its fine decor is fully restored and it stocks more luxury brands.

REPETTO

22 rue de la Paix Ⓜ Opéra. Mon–Sat 9.30am–7.30pm. MAP P.68-69, POCKET MAP B13

This long-established supplier of ballet shoes has branched out to produce attractive ballerina pumps in assorted colours, much coveted by the fashion crowd, from €170.

Cafés

A PRIORI THÉ

35 Galerie Vivienne Ⓜ Bourse. Mon–Sat 9am–6pm, Sun noon–6.30pm. MAP P.68-69, POCKET MAP C13

An attractive little *salon de thé* in a charming *passage*, with some tables spilling into the arcade. You can get crumbly home-made scones and tea, plus more substantial dishes at lunch for €14–18.

CAFÉ DE LA PAIX

Cnr of place de l'Opéra and bld de Capuchines Ⓜ Opéra. Daily 9am–11.30pm. MAP P.68-69, POCKET MAP F5

This grand café counts Zola, Tchaivkovsky and Oscar Wilde among its illustrious past *habitués*. Sit in the sumptuous interior or watch the world go by from the *terrasse*. Espresso €6.

VERLET

256 rue St-Honoré Ⓜ Palais Royal–Musée du Louvre. Mon–Sat 9.30am–6.30pm; closed Aug. MAP P.68-69, POCKET MAP B14

A heady aroma of freshly ground coffee greets you as you enter this old-world coffee merchant and café. Choose from around thirty varieties, such as Mokka Harar d'Ethiopie. There's also a selection of teas and cakes.

REPETTO

AUX LYONNAIS

Restaurants

BISTROT DES VICTOIRES

6 rue de la Vrillère Ⓜ Bourse
☎ 01.42.61.43.78. Daily noon–3pm & 7–11pm.
MAP P.68–69, POCKET MAP C14

Located just behind the chic place des Victoires, but very reasonably priced for the area, this charming, old-fashioned *bistrot*, with zinc bar, mustard-coloured walls and globe lamps, serves good old standbys such as *confit de canard* and *poulet rôti* for around €10, as well as huge salads and hearty *tartines* – recommended is the *savoyarde* with bacon, potatoes and gruyère. Sunday brunch for €15.50.

LE DÉNICHEUR

4 rue Tiquetonne Ⓜ Etienne-Marcel
☎ 01.42.21.31.03. Tues–Sat noon–3pm & 6.30–11.30pm, Sun noon–5pm. MAP P.68–69.
POCKET MAP E14

This small, chic, gay-friendly café-restaurant is a hotch-potch of wacky decor: bright-blue globes above, garden gnomes, and bin-shaped lampshades dotted around. Salads are the main event here, though you can find lasagne, ravioli, gazpacho and *tartines* too, all at reasonable prices. Mains around €13.

DILAN

13 rue Mandar Ⓜ Les Halles/Sentier
☎ 01.40.26.81.04. Mon–Sat noon–2.30pm & 7.30–11pm. MAP P.68–69, POCKET MAP D14

An excellent-value, popular Kurdish restaurant, with kilims strewn liberally across the benches and taped Kurdish music playing in the background. You can't really go wrong whatever you choose from the menu, but you could do worse than start with the melt-in-your mouth *babaqunuc* (stuffed aubergines), followed by delicious *beyti* (spiced minced beef wrapped in pastry, with yoghurt, tomato sauce and bulgar wheat). Mains cost around €13.

DROUANT

16–18 rue Gaillon Ⓜ Opéra ☎ 01.42.65.15.16.
Daily noon–3pm & 7pm–midnight.
MAP P.68–69, POCKET MAP B13

Legendary restaurant *Drouant*, the setting for the annual Goncourt prize, has shaken off its slightly fusty image with a sleek makeover and a new chef, Michelin-starred Antoine Westermann, who has injected fun and creativity into the cuisine. The starters and desserts are the stars of the show – you get four of each served in small portions and grouped around a theme, such as "four corners of the world". Starters cost €25, mains €30 (€20 at lunch), desserts €13, and there's a lunchtime *menu* for €44, as well as a €35 brunch on weekends.

GALLOPIN

40 rue Notre-Dame-des-Victoires
Ⓜ Bourse ☎ 01.42.36.45.38. Daily noon–midnight. MAP P.68–69, POCKET MAP C13

An utterly endearing old brasserie, with all its original brass and mahogany fittings and a beautiful painted glass roof in the back room. The classic French dishes, especially the *foie gras maison*, are well above par; lunch set menus from €19.90, evening from €38.

LE GRAND VÉFOUR

17 rue de Beaujolais Ⓜ Pyramides/Bourse
☎ 01.42.96.56.27. Mon–Thurs 12.30–2pm & 7.30–10pm, Fri 12.30–2pm. Closed Aug.
MAP P.68–69, POCKET MAP C14

The carved wooden ceilings, frescoes, velvet hangings and late eighteenth-century

DROUANT

chairs haven't changed since Napoleon brought Josephine here. Considering the luxury of the cuisine, the lunchtime *menu* for €96 is good value. The evening is à la carte only – reckon on €320, with wine.

HIGUMA

32bis rue Ste Anne Ⓜ Pyramides
☎ 01.47.03.38.59. Daily 11.30am–10pm.
MAP P.68–69, POCKET MAP B14

The pick of the numerous Japanese canteens in this area, Higuma serves up cheap, filling staples like pork katsu curry and yaki udon. Sit at the counter and watch the chefs at work, or cram onto one of the tiny tables further back. It's popular and you may have to queue at lunchtime. *Menus* €11–12.50.

AUX LYONNAIS

32 rue St-Marc Ⓜ Bourse/Richelieu-Drouot
☎ 01.42.96.65.04. Tues–Fri noon–2pm & 7.30–11pm, Sat 7.30–11pm. MAP P.68–69,
POCKET MAP G6

This revamped, attractive old *bistrot*, overseen by top chefs Alain Ducasse and Thierry de la Brosse, sports *belle époque* tiles and mirrored walls, and serves up delicious Lyonnais fare, such as *quenelles* (light, delicate fish dumplings). The lunch set menu costs €30. In the evening count on €60–70, including wine.

LE VAUDEVILLE

29 rue Vivienne Ⓜ Bourse ☎ 01.40.20.04.62.
Daily noon–3pm & 7pm–1am; breakfast Mon–Sat 7–11am. MAP P.68–69, POCKET MAP C13

There's often a queue to get a table at this lively, late-night Art Deco brasserie, attractively decorated with marble and mosaics. Dishes include tuna steak with chorizo and lamb with *boulangère* potatoes. *Menus* at €26–32 are available for lunch and in the evening.

THE REX CLUB

or late-night drinks, when the music and ambience hot up and it's standing room only at the bar. DJ Thurs and Fri.

DELAVILLE CAFÉ

34 bd de la Bonne Nouvelle
Ⓜ Bonne-Nouvelle. Daily 11am–2am.
MAP P.68–69, POCKET MAP H6

This ex-bordello, with grand staircase, gilded mosaics and marble columns, draws in crowds of pre-clubbers who sling back a mojito or two before going on to one of the area's nightclubs. DJs reign till the early hours on Thurs, Fri and Sat from 10pm. For the day after, there's a range of international dishes, and a famous brunch.

LE FUMOIR

6 rue de l'Amiral de Coligny Ⓜ Louvre-Rivoli.
Daily 11am–2am. MAP P.68–69, POCKET MAP C15

Animated chatter rises above a mellow jazz soundtrack and the sound of cocktail shakers in this coolly designed and relaxing bar-restaurant, situated just by the Louvre. You can browse the international press and there's also a restaurant at the back complete with library. Cocktails around €10.

LE RUBIS

10 rue du Marché-St-Honoré Ⓜ Pyramides.
Mon–Fri 7.30am–10pm, Sat 9am–3pm; closed mid-Aug. MAP P.68–69, POCKET MAP B14

This very small and crowded wine bar is one of the oldest in Paris, known for its excellent wines and home-made *rillettes* (a kind of pork pâté). The faded sign and peeling paint just add to the charm.

Bars

BAR HEMINGWAY

Ritz Hotel, place Vendôme Ⓜ Tuileries/
Opéra. Mon–Sat 6.30pm–2am. MAP P.68–69,
POCKET MAP A13

Hidden away at the back of the Ritz, this discreetly elegant bar with leather armchairs and deferential white-suited bar staff was once Hemingway's regular haunt, and the walls are covered with photos of him. His favourite drink, dry martini, is on the menu, but if you're feeling adventurous go for one of the more unusual cocktails (around €30) concocted by award-winning barman Colin Field.

LE CAFÉ NOIR

65 rue Montmartre Ⓜ Les Halles/Sentier.
Mon–Fri 8.30am–2am, Sat 4pm–2am.
MAP P.68–69, POCKET MAP D13

Despite the name, it's the colour red that predominates in this cool little corner café-bar, with papier-mâché red lightshades and other bits of eccentric decor. It's great for an aperitif

Clubs

REX CLUB

5 bd Poissonnière Ⓜ Bonne-Nouvelle
☎ 01.42.36.28.83, Ⓦ www.rexclub.com.

Wed–Sat 11.30pm–6am. Entry up to €20.
MAP P.68–69, POCKET MAP H6

The clubbers' club: serious about its music, which is strictly electronic, notably techno, played through a top-of-the line sound system. Attracts big-name DJs.

SCOP' CLUB

5 av de l'Opéra Ⓜ Pyramide/Palais Royal ☎ 01.42.60.64.45, ⓦ lescopclub .com. Wed–Sat 7pm–5am. MAP P.68–69, POCKET MAP B14

Currently one of the cooler clubs in town, pulling in a designer-scruffy Parisian crowd. The entrance fee varies, with gigs earlier on, and lots of free nights.

SOCIAL CLUB

142 rue Montmartre Ⓜ Bourse ☎ 01.43.35.25.48, ⓦ www.parissocialclub .com. Wed 11.30pm–3am, Thurs–Sat 11pm–6am. Entry price up to €20. MAP P.68–69, POCKET MAP D13

This unpretentious, grungey club is packed with a mixed clientele, from local students to lounge lizards. Here, it's all about the music, with everything from electro to jazz to hip-hop to ska on the playlist. Calvin Harris, Mr Scruff and Hot Chip's Alexis Taylor have all taken to the decks recently.

Live music

EGLISE DE LA MADELEINE

Ⓜ Madeleine ☎ 01.42.50.96.18, ⓦ www .eglise-lamadeleine.com. MAP P.68–69, POCKET MAP E6

A grand, regular venue for organ recitals and choral concerts, the church has a long and venerable musical tradition. Gabriel Fauré, who was organist here for a time, wrote his famous Requiem for the church. It also premiered here in 1888. Tickets €22–44.

AU LIMONAIRE

18 Cité Bergère Ⓜ Grands-Boulevards ☎ 01.45.23.33.33, ⓦ http://limonaire.free.fr. Tues–Sat. MAP P.68–69, POCKET MAP H5

This tiny backstreet place is the perfect intimate and informal venue for Parisian *chanson*, often showcasing committed young singers or zany music/ poetry/performance acts trying to catch a break. Dinner beforehand (traditional, fairly inexpensive and usually quite good) guarantees a seat for the show at 10pm, otherwise you'll be crammed up against the bar – if you can get in at all.

OPÉRA GARNIER

Ⓜ Opéra ☎ 08.36.69.78.68, ⓦ www.opera -de-paris.fr. MAP P.68–69, POCKET MAP F5

The Opéra Garnier is generally used for ballets and smaller-scale opera productions than those put on at the Opéra Bastille. For programme and booking details consult their website or phone the box office. Tickets can cost as little as €9 if you don't mind being up in the gods, though most are in the €30–90 range.

PERFORMER AT AU LIMONAIRE

Beaubourg and Les Halles

One of the city's most recognizable and popular landmarks, the Pompidou Centre, or Beaubourg as the building is known locally, draws large numbers of visitors to its excellent modern art museum and high-profile exhibitions. Its groundbreaking architecture provoked a storm of controversy on its opening in 1977, but since then it has won over critics and public alike. By contrast, nearby Les Halles, a shopping complex built at around the same time as the Pompidou Centre to replace the old food market that once stood there, has never really endeared itself to the city's inhabitants and is probably the least inspired of all the urban developments undertaken in Paris in the last thirty years. The good news is that it's currently undergoing a major revamp. It's also worth seeking out some of Les Halles' surviving old *bistrots* and food stalls, which preserve traces of the old market atmosphere.

THE POMPIDOU CENTRE

Ⓜ Rambuteau/Hotel-de-Ville
☎ 01.44.78.12.33, ⓦ www.cnac-gp.fr.
MAP P.80, POCKET MAP E15

At the heart of one of Paris's oldest districts stands the resolutely modern Centre Pompidou. Wanting to move away from the traditional idea of galleries as closed treasure chests and create something more open and accessible, the architects Renzo Piano and Richard Rogers stripped the "skin" off the building and made all the "bones" visible. The infrastructure was put on the outside: escalator tubes and utility pipes, brightly colour-coded according to their function, climb around the exterior in a crazy snakes-and-ladders fashion. The centre's main draw is its modern art museum and exhibitions, but there are also two cinemas and performance spaces. One of the added treats of the museum is that you get to ascend the transparent escalator on the outside of the building, affording superb views.

THE POMPIDOU CENTRE

MUSÉE NATIONAL D'ART MODERNE

Pompidou Centre Ⓜ Rambuteau/Hotel-de-Ville. Daily except Tues 11am–9pm. €13, under-18s & EU residents aged 18–25 free (pick up a pass at the ticket office), free for everyone on first Sun of the month. MAP P.80, POCKET MAP E15

The Musée National d'Art Moderne collection, spread over floors four and five of the Pompidou Centre, is one of the finest of its kind in the world, and is so large that only a fraction of the 50,000-plus works are on show at any one time (they're frequently rotated).

The section covering the years 1905 to 1960 is a near-complete visual essay on the history of modern art: Fauvism, Cubism, Dada, abstract art, Surrealism and Abstract Expressionism are all well represented. There's a particularly rich collection of Matisses, ranging from early Fauvist works to his late masterpieces – a standout is his *Tristesse du Roi*, a moving meditation on old age and memory. Other highlights include a number of Picasso's and Braque's early Cubist paintings and a substantial collection of Kandinskys. A whole room is devoted to the characteristically colourful paintings of Robert and Sonia Delaunay, while the mood darkens in later rooms with unsettling works by Surrealists Magritte, Dalí and Ernst.

In the Pop Art section is Andy Warhol's easily recognizable *Ten Lizes*, in which the actress Elizabeth Taylor sports a Mona Lisa-like smile. Elsewhere, Yves Klein prefigures performance art with his *Grande anthropophagie bleue, Hommage à Tennessee Williams*, one in a series of "body prints" in which the artist turned female models into human paintbrushes, covering them in paint to create his artworks.

Established contemporary artists you might see include Claes Oldenburg, Christian Boltanski and Daniel Buren, whose works are easy to spot with their trademark stripes, exactly 8.7cm in width. Some space is dedicated to video art, with changing installations by artists such as Jean-Luc Vilmouth, Dominique Gonzalez-Foerster, Melik Ohanian, Rineke Dijkstra and Pierre Huyghe.

ATELIER BRANCUSI

Pompidou Centre Ⓜ Rambuteau/
Hôtel-de-Ville. Daily except Tues 2–6pm.
Free. MAP P.80, POCKET MAP E15

The Atelier Brancusi is the reconstructed home and studio of sculptor Constantin Brancusi. He bequeathed the contents of his atelier to the state on condition that the rooms be arranged exactly as he left them, and they provide a fascinating insight into how the artist lived and worked. Studios one and two are crowded with Brancusi's trademark abstract bird and column shapes in highly polished brass and marble, while studios three and four comprise the artist's private quarters.

QUARTIER BEAUBOURG

Ⓜ Rambuteau/Hôtel-de-Ville. MAP P.80,
POCKET MAP E15

The lively quartier Beaubourg around the Pompidou Centre also offers much in the way of visual art. The colourful, swirling sculptures and fountains, in the pool in front of the Eglise St-Merri on the south side of the Pompidou Centre, were created by Jean Tinguely and Niki de Saint Phalle. North of the Pompidou Centre, numerous commercial galleries take up the contemporary art theme on rue Quincampoix, a narrow, pedestrianized street lined with fine old houses.

LES HALLES

Ⓜ Les-Halles/RER Châtelet-Les-Halles.
Mon–Sat 10am–8pm. MAP P.80, POCKET MAP D15

Described by Zola as "le ventre (stomach) de Paris", Les Halles was Paris's main food market for over eight hundred years until, despite widespread opposition, it was

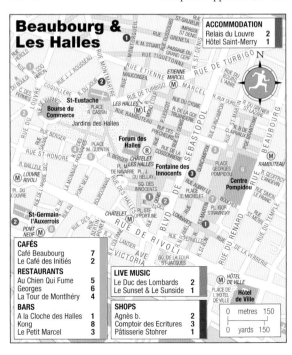

spread over four levels. The overground section comprises aquarium-like arcades of shops, arranged around a sunken patio, and landscaped gardens. The shops are mostly devoted to high-street fashion, though there's also a large FNAC bookshop and the Forum des Créateurs, an outlet for young fashion designers.

Little now remains of the old working-class quarter, but you can still catch a flavour of the old market atmosphere in some of the surrounding bars and *bistrots* and on pedestrianized **rue Montorgueil** to the north, where traditional grocers, horse butchers and fishmongers still ply their trade.

ST-EUSTACHE

Ⓜ Les-Halles/RER Châtelet-Les-Halles.
MAP P.80, POCKET MAP D14

For an antidote to the steel and glass troglodytism of Les Halles, head for the soaring vaults of the beautiful church of St-Eustache. Built between 1532 and 1637, it's Gothic in structure, with lofty naves and graceful flying buttresses, and Renaissance in decoration – all Corinthian columns, pilasters and arcades. Molière was baptized here, and Rameau and Marivaux are buried here.

FONTAINE DES INNOCENTS

Ⓜ Les-Halles/RER Châtelet-Les-Halles.
MAP P.80, POCKET MAP D15

The Fontaine des Innocents, a perfectly proportioned Renaissance fountain, decorated with reliefs of water nymphs, is Paris's oldest surviving fountain, dating from 1549. On warm days shoppers sit around its edge, drawn to the cool of its cascading waters. It is named after the cemetery that used to occupy this site, the Cimetière des Innocents.

moved out to the suburbs in 1969. It was replaced by a large underground shopping and leisure complex, known as the **Forum des Halles**, as well as a major métro/RER interchange (métro Châtelet-les Halles). Unsightly and run-down, the complex is now widely acknowledged as an architectural disaster and work is under way to give it a major facelift. A vast glass roof is being suspended over the forum, allowing light to flood in, and a wide promenade on the model of Barcelona's Ramblas is being created. Work is expected to be complete by 2014.

The Forum des Halles centre stretches underground from the Bourse du Commerce rotunda to rue Pierre-Lescot and is

Shops

AGNÈS B.

2–4 & 6 rue du Jour Ⓜ Les-Halles/RER Châtelet-Les-Halles. Mon–Sat 10.30am–7pm. MAP P.80, POCKET MAP D14

Agnès b. pays scant regard to fashion trends, creating chic, timeless, understated clothes for men, women and children. Her best-known staples are the snap cardigan and well-made T-shirts that don't lose their shape.

COMPTOIR DES ECRITURES

35 rue Quincampoix Ⓜ Les-Halles/RER Châtelet-Les-Halles. Tues–Fri 11am–7pm, Sat 11am–6pm. MAP P.80, POCKET MAP E15

A delightful shop entirely devoted to the art of calligraphy, with an extensive collection of paper, pens, brushes and inks.

PÂTISSERIE STOHRER

51 rue Montorgueil Ⓜ Sentier. Daily 7.30am–8.30pm; closed first two weeks of Aug. MAP P.80, POCKET MAP D14

Discover what *pain aux raisins* should really taste like at this wonderful patisserie, in business since 1730 and preserving its lovely old decor.

AGNÈS B.

Cafés

CAFÉ BEAUBOURG

43 rue St-Merri Ⓜ Rambuteau/Hôtel-de-Ville. Mon–Wed & Sun 8am–1am, Thurs–Sat 8am–2am. MAP P.80, POCKET MAP E15

A seat under the expansive awnings of this stylish café, bearing the trademark sweeping lines of designer Christian Portzamparc, is one of the best places for people-watching on the Pompidou Centre's piazza. It's also good for a relaxed Sunday brunch – €24 for the full works, including eggs, hash browns and sausage. Drinks from €6.50.

LE CAFÉ DES INITIÉS

3 place des Deux-Ecus Ⓜ Châtelet-Les-Halles/Louvre. Mon–Fri 7.30–2am, Sat & Sun 9–2am. MAP P.80, POCKET MAP C14

A smart yet intimate and comfortable café, with dark-red leather banquettes, wooden floor and arty photos on the wall. Locals gather round the zinc bar or tuck into tasty dishes such as grilled king prawns and steak tartare (around €16) and home-made apple crumble. It's also a good spot for an evening drink.

Restaurants

AU CHIEN QUI FUME

33 rue du Pont Neuf Ⓜ Châtelet-Les Halles ☎ 01.42.36.07.42. Daily noon–2am. MAP P.80, POCKET MAP D15

Named after a local poodle who allegedly smoked a cigar, this popular brasserie has been around for centuries. Tuxedoed waiters serve house favourites like fresh oysters, *langoustines fricassée volaille* (prawn fricassee) and *cuisse de canard en marmite et lentilles* (leg of duck with lentils). Set menus from €26.90.

GEORGES

Pompidou Centre, top floor Ⓜ Rambuteau/
Hôtel-de-Ville ☎ 01.44.78.47.99.
Daily noon–midnight except Tues.
MAP P.80, POCKET MAP E15

This ultra-minimalist restaurant commands stunning views over the rooftops of Paris. The French-Asian fusion cuisine is somewhat overpriced (mains around €30–45) – but that's not really why you come.

LA TOUR DE MONTLHÉRY (CHEZ DENISE)

5 rue des Prouvaires Ⓜ Louvre-Rivoli/
Châtelet ☎ 01.42.36.21.82. Mon–Fri
noon–3pm & 7.30pm–5am; closed mid-July to
mid-Aug. MAP P.80, POCKET MAP D15

An old-style Les Halles *bistrot*, packed with diners at long tables tucking into substantial meaty French dishes, such as *daube* of beef with perfectly cooked chips. Mains around €25.

Bars

A LA CLOCHE DES HALLES

28 rue Coquillière Ⓜ Châtelet-Les Halles/
Louvre. Noon–10pm; closed Sat eve & Sun.
MAP P.80, POCKET MAP C14

The bell hanging over this wine bar once marked the end of trading in the market, and the great ambience is due to local vendors who spend their off-duty hours here. Fine wines are best sampled with the *jambon d'Auvergne* or one of their delectable cheeses, all reasonably priced.

KONG

5th floor, 1 rue du Pont Neuf Ⓜ Pont Neuf
☎ 01.40.39.09.00. Daily 12.30pm–2am, club
Fri & Sat 11pm–3am. MAP P.80, POCKET MAP C15

A lift whisks you up to this cool, Philippe Starck-designed bar-restaurant atop the flagship Kenzo building. The decor is

KONG

new Japan meets old: geisha girls and manga cartoons. Happy hour daily 6–8pm. Cocktails €10–16.

LE PETIT MARCEL

63 rue Rambuteau Ⓜ Rambuteau.
Daily 10am–1am. MAP P.80, POCKET MAP E15

A bustling place with tiled floors, a jazz soundtrack and about eight square metres of drinking space. The dining area serves cheap, filling dishes such as sausages with mustard. Mains €11–14.

Live music

LE DUC DES LOMBARDS

42 rue des Lombards Ⓜ Châtelet
☎ 01.42.33.22.88, Ⓦ www.ducdeslombards.com.
Mon–Sat until 3am. MAP P.80, POCKET MAP D15

Stylish jazz club with nightly performances from 9pm of gypsy jazz, blues, ballads and fusion. Most gigs €25–30.

LE SUNSET & LE SUNSIDE

60 rue des Lombards Ⓜ Châtelet
☎ 01.40.26.46.20, Ⓦ www.sunset-sunside.com.
Daily 8pm–2.30am. MAP P.80, POCKET MAP D15

Two clubs in one: *Le Sunside* on the ground floor features mostly traditional jazz; while the downstairs *Sunset* is a venue for electric and fusion jazz. Admission €20–28.

The Marais

Full of splendid old mansions, narrow lanes and buzzing bars and restaurants, the Marais is one of the most seductive areas of central Paris, known for its sophistication and artsy leanings, and for being the neighbourhood of choice for gay Parisians. The quarter also boasts a concentration of fine museums, not least among them the Musée d'Art et d'Histoire du Judaïsme, the Maison Européenne de la Photographie and the Carnavalet history museum, all set in handsome Renaissance buildings.

MUSÉE D'ART ET D'HISTOIRE DU JUDAÏSME

71 rue du Temple Ⓜ Rambuteau
☎ 01.53.01.86.53, ⓦ www.mahj.org. Mon–Fri 11am–6pm, Sun 10am–6pm. €6.80.
MAP P.86–87, POCKET MAP F15

Housed in the attractively restored Hôtel de Saint-Aignan, the Musée d'Art et d'Histoire du Judaïsme traces Jewish culture and history, mainly in France. The result is a comprehensive collection, as educational as it is beautiful.

Highlights include a Gothic-style Hanukkah lamp, one of the very few French-Jewish artefacts to survive from the period before the expulsion of the Jews from France in 1394; an Italian gilded circumcision chair from the seventeenth century; and a completely intact late-nineteenth-century Austrian Sukkah, a temporary dwelling for the celebration of the harvest.

The museum also holds the Dreyfus archives, with one room devoted to the notorious Dreyfus affair. The wrongful conviction of Captain Alfred Dreyfus caused deep divisions in French society, stoking up anticlerical, socialist sympathies on the one hand and conservative, anti-Semitic feelings on the other.

The last few rooms contain a significant collection of paintings and sculpture by Jewish artists – Marc Chagall, Samuel

WEDDING RINGS, MUSÉE D'ART ET D'HISTOIRE DU JUDAÏSME

EXHIBIT AT THE MUSÉE PICASSO

Hirszenberg, Chaïm Soutine and Jacques Lipchitz – who came to live in Paris at the beginning of the twentieth century. The Holocaust is only briefly touched on, since it's dealt with in depth by the Mémorial de la Shoah (see p.90).

HÔTEL SOUBISE ET HÔTEL DE ROHAN

60 rue des Francs-Bourgeois Ⓜ Rambuteau/ St-Paul Ⓦ www.archivesnationales.culture .gouv.fr. Mon & Wed–Fri 10am–12.30pm & 2–5.30pm, Sat & Sun 2–5.30pm. €4. MAP P.86–87, POCKET MAP F15

The entire block enclosed by rue des Quatre Fils, rue des Archives, rue Vieille-du-Temple and rue des Francs-Bourgeois, was once filled by a magnificent early eighteenth-century palace complex. Only half remains, but it is utterly splendid, especially the colonnaded courtyard of the Hôtel Soubise, with its Rococo interiors and vestigial fourteenth-century towers on rue des Quatre Fils. The hôtel houses the city archives and mounts changing exhibitions. The adjacent Hôtel de Rohan is also often used for exhibitions from the archives and has more fine interiors, including the Chinese-inspired Cabinet des Singes, whose walls are painted with monkeys acting out various aristocratic scenes.

MUSÉE PICASSO

5 rue de Thorigny Ⓜ Chemin Vert/St-Paul Ⓣ 01.42.71.25.21, Ⓦ www.musee-picasso.fr. Daily except Tues: April–Sept 9.30am–6pm; Oct–March 9.30am–5.30pm. €8.50, under-18s free, free for everyone first Sun of month. MAP P.86–87, POCKET MAP G15

Behind the elegant classical facade of the seventeenth-century Hôtel Salé lies the Musée Picasso, closed until spring 2013 for a major renovation. The museum is home to the largest collection of Picassos anywhere, representing almost all the major periods of the artist's life from 1905 onwards.

Many of the works were owned by Picasso and on his death in 1973 were seized by the state in lieu of taxes owed. The result is an unedited body of work, which, although perhaps not among the most recognizable of Picasso's masterpieces, provides an insight into the person behind the myth. Some of the most engaging works on display are his more personal ones, for example the contrasting portraits of his lovers Dora Maar and Marie-Thérèse.

The museum also holds a substantial number of Picasso's ceramics and sculptures, some of which he created from recycled household objects.

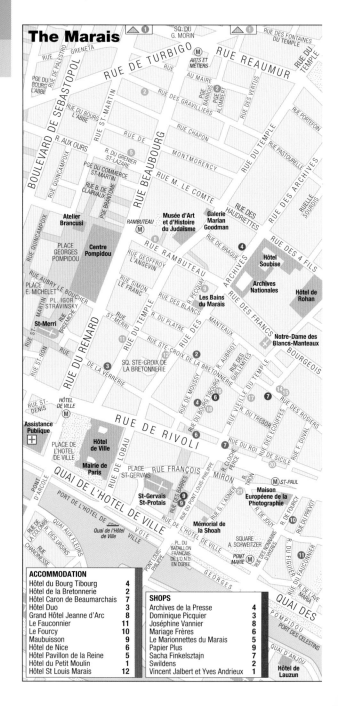

The Marais

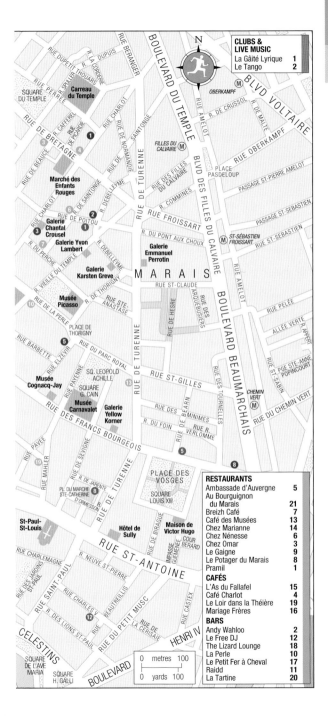

CLUBS & LIVE MUSIC

La Gâîté Lyrique	1
Le Tango	2

RESTAURANTS

Ambassade d'Auvergne	5
Au Bourguignon du Marais	21
Breizh Café	7
Café des Musées	13
Chez Marianne	14
Chez Nénesse	6
Chez Omar	3
Le Gaigne	9
Le Potager du Marais	8
Pramil	1

CAFÉS

L'As du Fallafel	15
Café Charlot	4
Le Loir dans la Théière	19
Mariage Frères	16

BARS

Andy Wahloo	2
Le Free DJ	12
The Lizard Lounge	18
La Perle	10
Le Petit Fer à Cheval	17
Raidd	11
La Tartine	20

MUSÉE COGNACQ-JAY

8 rue Elzévir ⓂSt-Paul ☎01.40.27.07.21.
Tues–Sun 10am–6pm. Free.
MAP P.86–87, POCKET MAP G16

The compact Musée Cognacq-Jay occupies the fine Hôtel Donon. The Cognacq-Jay family built up the Samaritaine department store and were noted philanthropists and lovers of European art. Their collection of eighteenth-century pieces on show includes a handful of works by Canaletto, Fragonard, Rubens and Rembrandt, as well as an exquisite still life by Chardin, displayed in beautifully carved wood-panelled rooms filled with Sèvres porcelain and Louis XV furniture.

MUSÉE CARNAVALET

23 rue de Sévigné ⓂSt-Paul
☎01.44.59.58.58, ⓦwww.carnavalet
.paris.fr. Tues–Sun 10am–6pm. Free.
MAP P.86–87, POCKET MAP G16

The fascinating Musée Carnavalet charts the history of Paris from its origins up to the *belle époque* through a huge and extraordinary collection of paintings, sculptures, decorative arts and archeological finds, occupying over 140 rooms. The museum's setting in two beautiful Renaissance mansions, Hôtel Carnavalet and Hôtel Le Peletier,

surrounded by attractive formal gardens, is worth a visit in itself.

Among the highlights on the ground floor, devoted largely to the early history of Paris, is the orangery, housing a significant collection of Neolithic finds, including a number of wooden pirogues unearthed during the redevelopment of the Bercy riverside area in the 1990s.

On the first floor, decorative arts feature strongly, with numerous re-created salons and boudoirs full of richly sculpted wood panelling and tapestries from the time of Louis XII to Louis XVI. Room 21 is devoted to the famous letter-writer Madame de Sévigné, who lived in the Carnavalet mansion and wrote a series of letters to her daughter, which vividly portray her privileged lifestyle under the reign of Louis XIV. Rooms 128 to 148 are largely devoted to the *belle époque*, evoked through numerous paintings of the period and some wonderful Art Nouveau interiors, among which is the sumptuous peacock-green interior designed by Alphonse Mucha for Fouquet's jewellery shop in the rue Royal. Also well preserved is José-Maria Sert's Art Deco ballroom, with its extravagant gold-leaf decor and grand-scale

Hammams

Hammams, or Turkish baths, are one of the unexpected delights of Paris. Much more luxurious than the standard Swedish sauna, these are places to linger and chat, and you can usually pay extra for a massage and a gommage – a rubdown with a rubber glove – followed by mint tea to recover. One of the most attractive is to be found at **Les Bains du Marais** (31–33 rue des Blancs-Manteaux ⓜ Rambuteau/St-Paul ⓣ 01.44.61.02.02, ⓦ www.lesbainsdumarais.com), as much a posh health club as a hammam, with a chichi clientele and glorious interior. Sauna and steam room entry costs €35 for two hours; massage/gommage is €35 extra. There are exclusive sessions for women (Mon 10am–8pm, Tues 10am–11pm, Wed 10am–7pm) and men (Thurs 10am–11pm, Fri 10am–8pm), as well as mixed sessions (Wed 7–11pm, Sat 10am–8pm, Sun 10am–11pm), for which you have to bring a swimsuit.

paintings, including one of the Queen of Sheba with a train of elephants. Nearby is a section on literary life at the beginning of the twentieth century, including a reconstruction of Proust's cork-lined bedroom (room 147). The second floor has rooms full of mementoes of the French Revolution.

THE JEWISH QUARTER: RUE DES ROSIERS

ⓜ St-Paul. MAP P.86–87, POCKET MAP F16

The narrow, pedestrianized rue des Rosiers has been the city's Jewish quarter ever since the twelfth century. Despite the incursion of trendy boutiques, it just about manages to retain a Jewish flavour, with the odd

delicatessen, kosher food shop and Hebrew bookstore, as well as a number of falafel takeaways – testimony to the influence of the North African Sephardim, who, since the end of World War II, have sought refuge here from the uncertainties of life in the former French colonies.

PLACE DES VOSGES

ⓜ St-Paul. MAP P.86–87, POCKET MAP G16

A grand square of handsome pink brick and stone mansions built over arcades, the place des Vosges is a masterpiece of aristocratic elegance and the first example of planned development in the history of Paris. It was built by Henri IV and inaugurated in 1612 for the wedding of Louis XIII and Anne of Austria; a replica of Louis' statue stands hidden by chestnut trees in the middle of the grass-and-gravel gardens at the square's centre.

Today, well-heeled Parisians pause in the arcades to browse art, antique and clothing shops, and lunch alfresco in the restaurants while buskers play classical music. Unusually for Paris, you're allowed to sprawl on the grass in the garden.

STATUE OF LOUIS XIV AT THE MUSÉE CARNAVALET

MAISON DE VICTOR HUGO

Place des Vosges Ⓜ St-Paul
☎ 01.42.72.10.16. Tues–Sun 10am–6pm,
closed hols. Free. MAP P.86–87, POCKET MAP G17

Among the many celebrities
who made their homes in place
des Vosges was Victor Hugo;
his house, at no. 6, where he
wrote much of *Les Misérables*,
is now a museum, the Maison
de Victor Hugo. Hugo's life is
evoked through a sparse collection of memorabilia, portraits
and photographs. What the
museum conveys, though,
is an idea of his prodigious
creativity: as well as being
a prolific writer, he enjoyed
drawing and designed his own
furniture. Some of his sketches
and Gothic-style furniture are
on display, and a Chinese-style
dining room that he designed
for his house in Guernsey is
re-created in its entirety.

HÔTEL DE SULLY

62 rue St-Antoine Ⓜ St-Paul Tues–Fri
noon–7pm, Sat & Sun 10am–7pm. €5.
MAP P.86–87, POCKET MAP G17

The exquisite Renaissance
Hôtel de Sully is the sister site
to the Jeu de Paume (see p.50),
and mounts temporary
photographic exhibitions,
usually on social, historical or
anthropological themes. In the
mansion's formal garden is a
newly opened branch of the
Angélina tea room.

THE QUARTIER ST-PAUL-ST-GERVAIS

Ⓜ St-Paul. MAP P.86–87, POCKET MAP E16–F17

The southern section of the
Marais, below rues de Rivoli
and St-Antoine, is quieter
than the northern part and
has some picturesque corners.
One of these is cobbled rue
des Barres, perfumed with the
scent of roses from nearby
gardens and the occasional waft
of incense from the church
of St-Gervais-St-Protais, a
late Gothic construction that
looks somewhat battered on
the outside owing to a direct
hit from a shell fired from a
Big Bertha howitzer in 1918.
Its interior contains some
lovely stained glass, carved
misericords and a seventeenth-
century organ – Paris's oldest.

MÉMORIAL DE LA SHOAH

17 rue Geoffroy l'Asnier Ⓜ St-Paul/
Pont-Marie ☎ 01.42.77.44.72. Ⓦ www
.memorialdelashoah.org. Mon–Fri & Sun
10am–6pm, Thurs until 10pm. Free.
MAP P.86–87, POCKET MAP F17

Since 1956 this has been the
site of the Mémorial du Martyr
Juif Inconnu (Memorial to an

MAISON DE VICTOR HUGO

Unknown Jewish Martyr), a sombre crypt containing a large black marble star of David. In 2005 President Chirac opened a new museum here and unveiled a Wall of Names: four giant slabs of marble engraved with the names of the 76,000 Jews sent to death camps from 1942 to 1944.

The excellent museum gives an absorbing account of the history of Jews in France, and especially Paris, during the German occupation. There are last letters from deportees to their families, videotaped testimonies from survivors, numerous ID cards and photos. The museum ends with the Mémorial des Enfants, an overwhelming collection of photos of 2500 French children, each with the dates of their birth and their deportation.

MAISON EUROPÉENNE DE LA PHOTOGRAPHIE

5–7 rue de Fourcy Ⓜ St-Paul
☎ 01.44.78.75.00, ⓦ www.mep-fr.org.
Wed–Sun 11am–8pm. €7, free Wed after 5pm.
MAP P.86–87, POCKET MAP F16

A gorgeous Marais mansion, the early eighteenth-century Hôtel Hénault de Cantobre, has been turned into a vast and serene space dedicated to the art of contemporary photography. Temporary shows are combined with a revolving exhibition of the Maison's permanent collection; young photographers and news photographers get a look-in, as well as artists using photography in multimedia creations or installation art.

HÔTEL DE VILLE

Ⓜ Rambuteau/Hotel-de-Ville.
MAP P.86–87, POCKET MAP E16

The Hôtel de Ville, the seat of the city's mayor, is a mansion of gargantuan proportions

THE HÔTEL DE VILLE

in florid neo-Renaissance style, modelled pretty much on the previous building burned down during the Commune in 1871. The huge square in front of the Hôtel de Ville, a notorious guillotine site during the Revolution, becomes the location of a popular **ice-skating rink** from December to February; it's particularly magical at night. It's open till midnight at weekends, and skate hire is around €5.

THE HAUT MARAIS

MAP P.86–87, POCKET MAP F14/15–G14/15

The northern part of the Marais, the "haut Marais", is currently the favoured strolling ground of bobo (bourgeois-bohemian) Parisians, drawn by the contemporary art galleries, chichi design shops and fashion boutiques, especially along rue Charlot and rue de Poitou. The main thoroughfare is rue de Bretagne, with its bustling cafés and traditional shops such as cheesemongers, bakeries and coffee merchants. The adjacent Marché des Enfants-Rouges, one of the smallest and oldest food markets in Paris (Tues–Sat 8.30am–1pm and 4–7.30pm, Sun 8.30am–2pm), dating back to 1616, makes a good lunchtime stop.

Shops

ARCHIVES DE LA PRESSE

51 rue des Archives Ⓜ Rambuteau.
Tues–Fri 10.30am–7pm, Mon & Sat 2–7pm.
MAP P.86–87, POCKET MAP F15

A fascinating shop for a browse, trading in old French newspapers and magazines – vintage *Vogues* and the like.

DOMINIQUE PICQUIER

10 rue Charlot Ⓜ Filles du Calvaire.
Tues–Fri 11am–7.30pm, Mon & Sat 2.30–7.30pm. MAP P.86–87, POCKET MAP F15

"A tribute from the town to the country" is how this textile designer describes her beautiful hand-printed fabrics of swirling orchids, delicate mimosas and daisies. She also does a stylish range of accessories, such as tote bags, purses and travel bags, starting from around €40.

JOSÉPHINE VANNIER

4 rue du Pas de la Mule Ⓜ Bastille.
Tues–Sat 11am–1pm & 2–7pm, Sun & Mon 2.30–7pm. MAP P.86–87, POCKET MAP H16

This inventive chocolatier sells chocolate-shaped accordions, violins, books, Eiffel Towers and Arcs de Triomphe – exquisite creations, almost too perfect to eat. Prices are reasonable, from around €12.

MARIAGE FRÈRES

30 rue du Bourg-Tibourg Ⓜ Hôtel-de-Ville.
Shop daily 10.30am–7.30pm. MAP P.86–87,
POCKET MAP F16

Hundreds of teas, neatly packed in tins, line the floor-to-ceiling shelves of this venerable tea emporium and *salon de thé* (see p.96).

LES MARIONNETTES DU MARAIS

15 rue Elzevir Ⓜ St-Paul. Mon–Sat 11.30am–7.30pm. MAP P.86–87, POCKET MAP F15

A tiny shop, selling irresistible brightly coloured hand-knitted

MARIAGE FRÈRES

children's finger puppets, such as the complete cast of characters for Little Red Riding Hood, including bespectacled grandma and slavering wolf.

PAPIER PLUS

9 rue du Pont-Louis-Philippe Ⓜ Hôtel-de-Ville. Mon–Sat noon–7pm. MAP P.86–87, POCKET MAP F16

Fine-quality colourful stationery, including notebooks, photo albums and artists' portfolios, with prices starting from around €20.

SACHA FINKELSZTAJN

27 rue des Rosiers Ⓜ Hôtel-de-Ville. Daily except Tues 10am–7pm; closed mid-July to mid-Aug. MAP P.86–87, POCKET MAP F16

A marvellous Jewish deli for takeaway snacks and goodies: Eastern European breads, apple strudel, *gefilte* fish, aubergine purée, tarama, *blinis* and *borscht*.

SWILDENS

22 rue de Poitou Ⓜ Saint-Sébastien Froissart. Mon–Sat 10am–7.30pm. MAP P.86–87, POCKET MAP G15

Womenswear designer Juliette Swildens makes well-cut, affordable clothes, with a hint of rock'n'roll. Typical pieces are off-the-shoulder smocks, slouchy sweatshirts, baggy harem pants and layered knits.

Galleries

The Marais, and the Haut Marais in particular, is where most of the city's commercial art galleries are concentrated. Many occupy handsome old houses, set back from the road and reached via a cobbled courtyard. The following are some of the highlights; entry to all is free. Typical opening hours are Tues–Sat 11am–7pm.

Galerie Chantal Crousel 10 rue Charlot ⓜ Filles du Calvaire; ☎ 01.42.77.38.87, ⓦ www.crousel.com. Displays the work of emerging (notably video) artists from France and abroad.

Galerie Emmanuel Perrotin 76 rue de Turenne ⓜ St-Sébastien Froissart; ☎ 01.42.16.79.79, ⓦ www.galerieperrotin. Idiosyncratic gallery that has exhibited French artists like Sophie Calle as well as international names such as Takashi Murakami.

Galerie Karsten Greve 5 rue Debelleyme ⓜ St-Sébastien Froissart; ☎ 01.42.77.19.37, ⓦ www.artnet.com/kgreve.html. Paris branch of the German gallery, showing the work of world-class artists like Louise Bourgeois.

Galerie Marian Goodman 79 rue du Temple ⓜ Rambuteau; ☎ 01.48.04.70.52, ⓦ www.mariangoodman.com. This offshoot of the famed New York gallery recently exhibited Gerhard Richter and photographer David Goldblatt.

Galerie Yellow Korner 8 rue des Francs Bourgeois ⓜ St-Paul; ☎ 01.49.96.50.23, ⓦ www.yellowkorner.com. Contemporary photography gallery with outposts throughout Europe, showcasing both established and up-and-coming talent.

Galerie Yvon Lambert 108 rue Vieille du Temple ⓜ Filles du Calvaire; ☎ 01.42.71.09.33, ⓦ www.yvon-lambert.com. A major player for more than 30 years: the likes of Andres Serrano, Giulio Paolini and Andy Warhol have all been exhibited here in recent years.

VINCENT JALBERT ET YVES ANDRIEUX

55 rue Charlot ⓜ Filles du Calvaire. Mon–Fri 10am–1pm & 2–7pm, Sat 11am–7pm.
MAP P.86–87, POCKET MAP G14

SWILDENS BOUTIQUE

It's hard to believe these beautiful clothes (each piece is unique and costs from around €400) were made from recycled army uniforms from the 1950s. The tailored jackets and long coats are particularly stylish and pair well with the flouncy skirts made from recycled parachutes and tents. A more affordable range of attractive bags is also available, as well as panama hats in 1960s fabrics.

Restaurants

AMBASSADE D'AUVERGNE

22 rue du Grenier St-Lazare Ⓜ Rambuteau
☎ 01.42.72.31.22. Daily noon–2pm &
7.30–10pm; closed three weeks in Aug.
MAP P.86–87, POCKET MAP E14

Suited, moustachioed waiters
serve scrumptious Auvergnat
cuisine that would have made
Vercingetorix proud. There's a
set menu for €28, but you may
well be tempted by some of the
house specialities such as the
roast Marvejols lamb. Among
the after-dinner treats are a
cheese plate and divine
profiteroles.

AU BOURGUIGNON DU MARAIS

52 rue François Miron Ⓜ St-Paul
☎ 01.48.87.15.40. Tues–Sat noon–11pm;
closed two weeks in Aug. MAP P.86–87,
POCKET MAP F16

A relaxed restaurant with
attractive contemporary decor
and tables outside in summer,
serving excellent Burgundian
cuisine (snails with parsley and
garlic, boeuf bourguignon, pike
perch with pinot noir) with
wines to match.Allow around
€60 a head, with wine.

AMBASSADE D'AUVERGNE

BREIZH CAFÉ

109 rue Vieille du Temple Ⓜ St-Paul
☎ 01.42.72.13.77. Wed–Sun noon–11pm;
closed three weeks in Aug. MAP P.86–87,
POCKET MAP G15

A Breton café, serving the best
crêpes in the Marais (and
arguably the city), with
traditional fillings like ham and
cheese, as well as more exotic
options such as smoked
herring, which you can wash
down with one of twenty
different ciders. Leave room for
dessert, as Valrhona chocolate
is used in the sweet crêpes. It's
very popular, so book ahead.

CAFÉ DES MUSÉES

49 rue de Turenne Ⓜ Chemin Vert
☎ 01.42.72.96.17. Daily noon–3pm & Sun
7–11pm, also open for breakfast Mon–Fri
8am–noon, Sat & Sun 10.30am–noon. MAP
P.86–87, POCKET MAP G16

An attractive old *bistrot* (with
a less appealing basement
room) popular with locals
drawn by the reasonably
priced, hearty fare, such as
steak-frites, terrines and *crème
caramel*. There's always a
vegetarian dish on the menu,
too. The evening set menu is a
bargain €20, otherwise mains
cost around €19.

CHEZ MARIANNE

2 rue des Hospitalières-Saint-Gervais
Ⓜ St-Paul ☎ 01.42.72.18.86. Daily
noon–10.30pm. MAP P.86–87, POCKET MAP F16

This homely place with cheery
red awnings and a cosy,
bustling dining room
specializes in Middle Eastern
and Jewish delicacies, with
plenty of vegetarian options. A
platter of mezze (from €12)
might include tabbouleh,
aubergine purée, chopped liver
and hummus, and there's a
good selection of wines. You
can sit outside in fine weather,
and the place stays open
throughout the summer.

CHEZ NÉNESSE

17 rue Saintonge Ⓜ Filles-du-Calvaire
☎ 01.42.78.46.49. Mon–Fri noon–2.30pm &
8–10.30pm; closed Aug. MAP P.86–87, POCKET
MAP G15

Steak in bilberry sauce, scallops with endive and figs stuffed with cream of almonds are just some of the unique delights on offer at this welcoming restaurant, along with home-made chips on Thursday lunchtimes. Look out for the restaurant's own comic strip in the window. Mains around €18.

CHEZ OMAR

47 rue de Bretagne Ⓜ Temple/
Filles-du-Calvaire ☎ 01.42.72.36.26. Mon–Sat
noon–2.30pm & 7–11.30pm, Sun 7–11.30pm;
no credit cards. MAP P.86–87, POCKET MAP G14

No reservations are taken at this popular North African couscous restaurant, but it's no hardship to wait for a table at the bar, taking in the handsome old brasserie decor, fashionable crowd and spirited atmosphere. Portions are copious and the couscous light and fluffy. The *merguez* (spicy sausage) is good, or go all out for the *royal* (€26), though don't expect to have any room left afterwards for the sticky cakes.

LE GAIGNE

12 rue Pecquay Ⓜ Rambuteau ☎ 01.44.
59.86.72. Tues–Sat 12.15–2pm &
7.30–10.30pm. MAP P.86–87, POCKET MAP F15

Run by young chef Mickaël Gaignon, this small contemporary bistrot with only nine tables set against a muted decor of pale browns and mauves, serves beautifully presented inventine cuisine, with a slant towards fish. Considering the quality of the food, it's very good value at €45 for the five-course tasting menu, or €64 with specially chosen accompanying wines.

LE POTAGER DU MARAIS

LE POTAGER DU MARAIS

22 rue Rambuteau Ⓜ Rambuteau
☎ 01.42.74.24.66. Daily except Tues
noon–4pm & 7–10.30pm. MAP P.86–87, POCKET
MAP E15

Come early or book in advance for a place at this organic vegetarian restaurant, with only 25 covers at a long communal table. There's plenty for vegans, too. Dishes include goat's cheese with honey and "crusty" quinoa burger. Set menu €25.

PRAMIL

9 rue du Vertbois Ⓜ Temple/Arts-et-Métiers
☎ 01.42.72.03.60. Tues–Sat noon–2pm &
7.30–10pm, Sun 7.30–10pm. MAP P.86–87,
POCKET MAP F13

An elegant restaurant with simple decor, serving a short but appetizing menu of classic French and more unusual dishes, such as cauliflower "cake", squash soup with a dollop of foie gras ice cream, and raspberry and red pepper tart. The set dinner for €30 (lunch €20) is excellent value.

Cafés

L'AS DU FALLAFEL

34 rue des Rosiers Ⓜ St-Paul. Mon–Thurs &
Sun noon–midnight. MAP P.86–87, POCKET MAP F16

The sign above the doorway of
this falafel shop in the Jewish
quarter reads "*Toujours imité,
jamais égalé*" ("always copied,
but never equalled"), a boast
that few would challenge, given
the queues outside. Falafels to
take away cost €5, or pay a bit
more and sit in the buzzing
little dining room.

CAFÉ CHARLOT

38 rue de Bretagne Ⓜ Filles du Calvaire.
Daily 7am–2am. MAP P.86–87, POCKET MAP G14

You'll need to fight for a
seat on the terrace of this
white-tiled retro-chic café,
which bursts at the seams on
weekends with local hipsters
and in-the-know tourists. The
food – a mix of French and
American standards – is not
that special, but it's a great
place for a drink and a spot of
people-watching.

LE LOIR DANS LA THÉIÈRE

3 rue des Rosiers Ⓜ St-Paul. Mon–Fri
11am–7pm, Sat & Sun 10am–7pm.
MAP P.86–87, POCKET MAP F16

A characterful *salon de thé*
decorated with antique toys and
Alice in Wonderland murals.
It's a popular spot for meeting
friends and lounging about on
battered sofas, while feasting
on delicious home-made cakes
or excellent vegetarian quiches.
Sunday brunch (from €19.50) is
particularly busy.

MARIAGE FRÈRES

30 rue du Bourg-Tibourg Ⓜ Hôtel-de-Ville.
Daily noon–7pm. MAP P.86–87, POCKET MAP F16

A classy, colonial-style *salon de
thé* in the Mariages Frères tea
emporium, with a choice of
over five hundred brews.

ANDY WAHLOO

Bars

ANDY WAHLOO

69 rue des Gravilliers Ⓜ Arts-et-Métiers.
Tues–Sat 6pm–2am. MAP P.86–87, POCKET MAP E14

Great little bar decked out in
colourful Arabic Pop
Art-inspired decor, and playing
a wide range of dance music.
Delicious mezze appetizers are
served until midnight, and
cocktails include the Wahloo
Special (rum, lime, ginger,
banana and cinnamon; €10).

LE FREE DJ

35 rue Ste-Croix de la Bretonnerie
Ⓜ Hôtel-de-Ville. Mon–Wed & Sun
6pm–3am, Fri & Sat 6pm–4am. MAP P.86–87,
POCKET MAP F16

This stylish gay bar draws the
young and très *looké* –
beautiful types. It's friendly,
though, and features some big
sounds (house, disco-funk) in
the basement club.

THE LIZARD LOUNGE

18 rue du Bourg-Tibourg Ⓜ Hôtel-de-Ville/
St-Paul. Daily noon–2am. MAP P.86–87, POCKET
MAP F16

A loud, lively, stone-walled bar
on two levels; American-run
and popular with young expats.
Choose from around fifty
reasonably priced cocktails.

LA PERLE

78 rue Vieille du Temple Ⓜ St-Paul. Mon–Fri
6am–2am, Sat & Sun 8am–2am. MAP P.86–87,
POCKET MAP F15

An Emperor's New Clothes
kind of place that maintains a
très cool reputation. Always
packed with an arty indie
crowd drinking cheap beer,
despite being somewhat
scruffy and playing generic
dance music.

LE PETIT FER À CHEVAL

30 rue Vieille-du-Temple Ⓜ St-Paul.
Mon–Fri 9am–2am, Sat & Sun 11am–2am;
food served noon–midnight. MAP P.86–87,
POCKET MAP F16

An attractive, tiny bar with
original fin-de-siècle decor,
including a marble-topped
bar in the shape of a
horseshoe (*fer à cheval*).
Snack on sandwiches or
light meals in the little back
room furnished with old
wooden métro seats.

RAIDD

23 rue du Temple Ⓜ Hôtel-de-Ville.
Mon–Thurs 5pm–4am, Sat & Sun 5pm–5am.
MAP P.86–87, POCKET MAP E15

A popular gay bar, famous
for its sculpted, topless
waiters and go-go boys'
shower shows. Straights and
non-beautiful people need
not apply.

LA TARTINE

24 rue de Rivoli Ⓜ St-Paul. Daily 8am–2am.
MAP P.86–87, POCKET MAP F16

This traditional bar's been
given a fresh lick of paint,
while retaining a distinctive
Art Nouveau feel. It draws
a refreshing mix of students,
pensioners, fashionistas
and workmen. Glasses of
wine from €3.50, plus light
meals including, of course,
tartines.

Clubs and live music

LA GÂITÉ LYRIQUE

3 bis rue Papin Ⓜ Réaumur-Sébastopol/
Arts-et-Métiers Ⓦ gaiete-lyrique.net. Tues–Sat
2–8pm, Sun 2–6pm. MAP P.86–87, POCKET MAP E13

New centre for digital arts and
contemporary music, housed in
a venerable theatre. After years
of closure, it has been given a
radical makeover –the architects have restored the facade
and splendid marble foyer and
entrance hall, while opening
up the interior to accom-
modate various performance
spaces, including a state-of-
the-art concert hall. The busy
programme of events includes
exhibitions, dance, theatre and
art installations.

LE TANGO

13 rue au Maire Ⓜ Arts-et-Métiers Ⓦ www
.boite-a-frissons.fr. Fri & Sat 10.30pm–5am,
Sun 6–11pm. MAP P.86–87, POCKET MAP F14

Unpretentious gay and lesbian
club with a Sunday-afternoon
tea dance, with proper slow
dances as well as tangos. Friday
and Saturday nights start with
anything from camp 1980s
disco classics to world music,
turning into a full-on club
around midnight.

LE PETIT FER À CHEVAL

Bastille and eastern Paris

Traditionally working-class areas, with a history of radical and revolutionary activity, Bastille and the districts of Belleville and Ménilmontant further east, are nowadays some of the most diverse and vibrant parts of the city, home to sizeable ethnic populations, as well as students and artists. The area's most popular attractions are Père-Lachaise cemetery, the final resting place of numerous famous artists and writers; the Canal St-Martin, with its trendy cafés and bars; and the vast, postmodern Parc de la Villette. To the south lies Bercy, once the largest wine market in the world, its warehouses now converted into restaurants and bars.

PLACE DE LA BASTILLE

Ⓜ Bastille. MAP P.100, POCKET MAP H17

The huge and usually traffic-clogged place de la Bastille is where Parisians congregate to celebrate Bastille Day on July 14, though hardly anything survives of the prison – the few remains have been transferred to square Henri-Galli at the end of boulevard Henri-IV. At the centre of the place is a column (Colonne de Juillet) surmounted by a gilded Spirit of Liberty, erected to commemorate not the surrender of the prison, but the July Revolution of 1830 that replaced the autocratic Charles X with the "Citizen King" Louis-Philippe.

PLACE D'ALIGRE MARKET

Ⓜ Ledru-Rollin. Tues–Sun 7.30am–1pm. MAP P.100, POCKET MAP L9

The place d'Aligre market, between avenue Daumesnil and rue du Faubourg St-Antoine, is a lively, raucous affair, particularly at weekends. The square itself is given over to clothes and bric-a-brac stalls, selling anything from old gramophone players to odd bits of crockery. It's along the adjoining rue d'Aligre where the market really comes to life though, with the vendors, many of Algerian origin, doing a frenetic trade in fruit and veg.

THE PROMENADE PLANTÉE

Ⓜ Bastille. MAP P.100, POCKET MAP L10

The Promenade Plantée is a stretch of disused railway line, much of it along a viaduct,

THE COLONNE DE JUILLET, PLACE DE LA BASTILLE

THE PARC FLORAL, BOIS DE VINCENNES

ingeniously converted into an elevated walkway and planted with trees and flowers. Starting near the beginning of avenue Daumesnil, just south of the Bastille opera house, it is reached via a flight of stone steps – or lifts – with a number of similar access points all the way along. It takes you to the Parc de Reuilly, then descends to ground level and continues nearly as far as the *périphérique*, from where you can follow signs to the Bois de Vincennes. The whole walk is around 4.5km long, but if you don't feel like doing the whole thing you could just walk the first, most attractive stretch, along the viaduct.

THE VIADUC DES ARTS

Ⓜ Bastille. MAP P.100, POCKET MAP L9–10

The arches of the Promenade Plantée's viaduct have been converted into attractive spaces for artisans' studios and craft shops, collectively known as the Viaduc des Arts, and include furniture and tapestry restorers, interior designers, cabinet-makers, violin- and flute-makers, embroiderers and fashion and jewellery designers.

THE BOIS DE VINCENNES

Ⓜ Château de Vincennes. Daily dawn till dusk. POCKET MAP M11

The Bois de Vincennes is one of the city's largest green spaces, but it is crisscrossed with roads. There are some pleasant corners, including Paris's best gardens, the **Parc Floral** (daily 9.30am–8pm, winter till dusk; free except Wed, Sat & Sun June–Sept when entry is €5; Ⓦ www .parcfloraldeparis.com; Ⓜ Château-de-Vincennes, then bus #112 or a fifteen-minute walk). Flowers are always in bloom in its **Jardin des Quatre Saisons**, where you can picnic beneath the pines. Between April and September there are art and horticultural exhibitions, free music concerts, an adventure ground for children and a mini-golf of Parisian monuments.

You can go boating on the **Lac Daumesnil,** near the Porte Dorée entrance and métro station (line 8), and to the north, at 53 avenue de St-Maurice, is the city's largest **zoo**, closed for renovation until 2014.

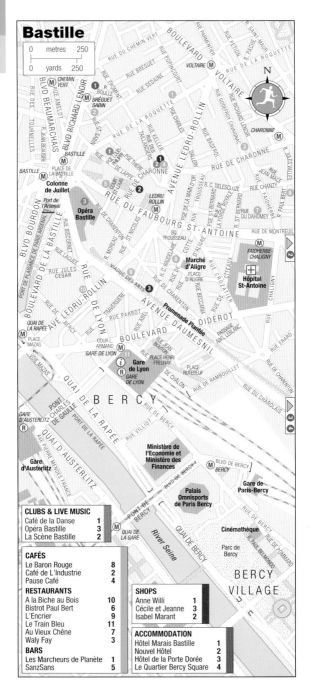

Bastille

CLUBS & LIVE MUSIC	
Café de la Danse	1
Opéra Bastille	3
La Scène Bastille	2

CAFÉS	
Le Baron Rouge	8
Café de L'Industrie	2
Pause Café	4

RESTAURANTS	
A la Biche au Bois	10
Bistrot Paul Bert	6
L'Encrier	9
Le Train Bleu	11
Au Vieux Chêne	7
Waly Fay	3

BARS	
Les Marcheurs de Planète	1
SanzSans	5

SHOPS	
Anne Willi	1
Cécile et Jeanne	3
Isabel Marant	2

ACCOMMODATION	
Hôtel Marais Bastille	1
Nouvel Hôtel	2
Hôtel de la Porte Dorée	3
Le Quartier Bercy Square	4

CHÂTEAU DE VINCENNES

Ⓜ Château-de-Vincennes ☎ 01.48.08.31.20. Daily: May–Aug 10am–6pm; Sept–April 10am–5pm; €8.50. POCKET MAP M10

On the northern edge of the *bois* is the Château de Vincennes – erstwhile royal medieval residence, then state prison, porcelain factory, weapons dump and military training school. It presents a rather austere aspect on first sight, but is worth visiting for its beautiful Flamboyant-Gothic **Chapelle Royale**, completed in the mid-sixteenth century and decorated with superb Renaissance stained-glass windows. Nearby, in the renovated fourteenth-century *donjon* (keep), you can see some fine vaulted ceilings and Charles V's bedchamber, as well as graffiti left by prisoners.

BERCY VILLAGE

Ⓜ Cour St-Emilion. MAP P.100, POCKET MAP M12

Bercy village is a complex of rather handsome old wine warehouses stylishly converted into shops, restaurants and, appropriately enough, wine bars – popular places to come before or after a film at the giant Bercy multiplex cinema at the eastern end of Cour Saint Emilion.

PARC DE BERCY

Ⓜ Bercy/Cour St-Emilion. MAP P.100, POCKET MAP M12

The contemporary-style Parc de Bercy incorporates elements of the old warehouse site, such as disused railway tracks and cobbled lanes. The western section of the park is a fairly unexciting expanse of grass, but the area to the east has arbours, rose gardens, lily ponds and an orangerie.

LA CINÉMATHÈQUE FRANÇAISE

51 rue de Bercy Ⓜ Bercy ☎ 01.71.19.33.33, Ⓦ www.cinematheque.fr. MAP P.100, POCKET MAP M11–12

The Cinémathèque, a striking glass, zinc and stone building designed by Guggenheim architect Frank Gehry and resembling a falling pack of cards, houses a huge archive of films dating back to the earliest days of cinema. Regular retrospectives of French and foreign films are screened in its four cinemas and it also has an engaging **museum** (Mon and Wed–Sat noon–7pm, Sun 10am–8pm; €5), with lots of early cinematic equipment, silent film clips and costumes such as the dress worn by Vivienne Leigh in *Gone With the Wind*.

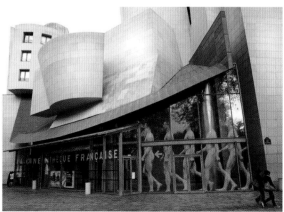

THE CINÉMATHÈQUE

THE CANAL ST-MARTIN

MAP P.104, POCKET MAP K4–6

Built in 1825 to enable river traffic to shortcut the great western loop of the Seine around Paris, the Canal St-Martin possesses a great deal of charm, especially along its southern reaches: plane trees line the cobbled *quais,* and elegant, high-arched footbridges punctuate the spaces between the locks, from where you can still watch the odd barge slowly rising or sinking to the next level. In the last decade or so the area has been colonized by the new arts and media intelligentsia, bringing in their wake trendy bars, cafés and boutiques. The area is particularly lively on Sunday afternoons when the *quais* are closed to traffic; pedestrians, cyclists and roller-bladers take over the streets, and people hang out along the canal's edge.

LE 104

104 rue d'Aubervilliers Ⓜ Riquet
☎ 01.53.35.50.00, Ⓦ www.104.fr.
Tues–Fri noon–7pm, Sat & Sun 11am–7pm;
free entry to the main hall. MAP P.104,
POCKET MAP K2–L2

THE CANAL ST-MARTIN

Located in one of the poorest parts of the 19^e, in a former grand nineteenth-century funeral parlour, Le 104 is a huge arts centre, with an impressive glass-roofed central hall (*nef curial*) and numerous artists' studios. It hosts exhibitions and installations, dance and theatre, with an emphasis on presenting "avant-premieres" of new plays and extended runs of sell-out performances from other theatres. The complex also houses a good bookshop, charity and fair-trade shops, a café and restaurant.

THE PARC DE LA VILLETTE

Ⓜ Porte-de-Pantin/Porte-de-la-Villette
☎ 01.40.03.75.75, Ⓦ www.villette.com. Daily
6am–1am. Free. MAP P.104, POCKET MAP M2

Built in 1986 on the site of what was once Paris's largest abattoir and meat market, the Parc de la Villette's landscaped grounds include a state-of-the-art science museum, a superb music museum, a series of themed gardens and a number of jarring, bright-red "follies". The effect of these numerous, disparate elements can be quite disorienting – all in line with the creators' aim of eschewing meaning and "deconstructing" the whole into its parts. All very well, but on a practical level you'll probably want to pick up a map at the information centre at the southern entrance to help you make sense of it all.

The extensive park grounds contain ten themed gardens, aimed mainly at children. In the Jardin des Miroirs, for example, steel monoliths hidden amongst the trees and scrub cast strange reflections, while, predictably, dune-like shapes, sails and windmills make up the Jardin des Dunes

INSIDE THE PARC DE LA VILLETTE

(for under-13s only and accompanying adults). Also popular with children is the eighty-metre-long Dragon Slide.

In front of the Cité des Sciences floats the Géode (hourly shows: Tues–Sat 10.30am–8.30pm, Mon 10.30am–6.30pm; €10.50), a bubble of reflecting steel that looks as though it's been dropped from an intergalactic boules game into a pool of water. Inside is a screen for Omnimax films, not noted for their plots, but a great visual experience.

CITÉ DES SCIENCES ET DE L'INDUSTRIE

Parc de la Villette ⓂPorte-de-la-Villette
Ⓦwww.cite-sciences.fr. Tues–Sat 10am–6pm, Sun 10am–7pm. €8. Planetarium shows hourly 11am–5pm; 35min; €3. Cité des Enfants ☎08.92.69.70.72; sessions Tues–Fri 10am, 11.45am, 1.30pm & 3.15pm; Sat & Sun 10.30am, 12.30pm, 2.30pm & 4.30pm; €6. MAP P.104, POCKET MAP M1

The Cité des Sciences et de l'Industrie is one of the world's finest science museums, set in a huge building four times the size of the Pompidou Centre. Its walls are made of glass and

the centre of the museum is left open to the full extent of the roof, 40m high. An excellent programme of temporary exhibitions complements the permanent exhibition, called Explora, covering subjects such as sound, robotics, energy, light, ecology, maths, medicine, space and language. As the name suggests, the emphasis is on exploring, and there are numerous interactive computers, videos, holograms, animated models and games. You can have your head spun further by a session in the planetarium.

The Cité has a special section for children called the Cité des Enfants, with areas for 2- to 7-year-olds and 5- to 12-year-olds; all children must be accompanied by an adult and a session lasts ninety minutes. Among the numerous engaging activities, children can play about with water, construct buildings on a miniature construction site (complete with cranes, hard hats and barrows), experiment with sound and light and manipulate robots.

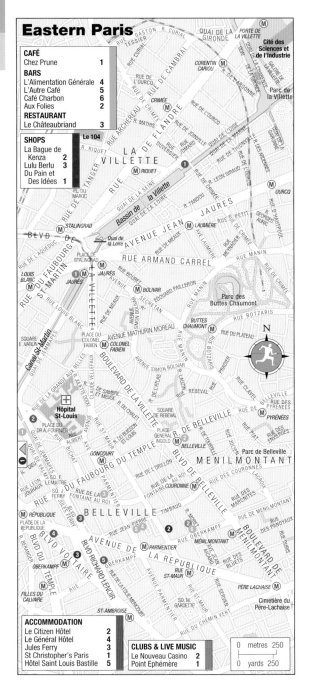

Eastern Paris

CAFÉ
Chez Prune   **1**

BARS
L'Alimentation Générale   **4**
L'Autre Café   **5**
Café Charbon   **6**
Aux Folies   **2**

RESTAURANT
Le Châteaubriand   **3**

SHOPS   Le 104
La Bague de Kenza   **2**
Lulu Berlu   **3**
Du Pain et Des Idées   **1**

ACCOMMODATION
Le Citizen Hôtel   **2**
Le Général Hôtel   **4**
Jules Ferry   **3**
St Christopher's Paris   **1**
Hôtel Saint Louis Bastille   **5**

CLUBS & LIVE MUSIC
Le Nouveau Casino   **2**
Point Ephémère   **1**

0 metres 250
0 yards 250

MUSÉE DE LA MUSIQUE

Cité de la Musique complex, Parc de la
Villette ⓜ Porte-de-Pantin ☎ 01.44.84.45.00,
ⓦ www.cite-musique.fr. Tues–Sat noon–6pm,
Sun 10am–6pm. €8. POCKET MAP M3

The Musée de la Musique
presents the history of
music from the end of the
Renaissance to the present
day, both visually, exhibiting
some 4500 instruments, and
aurally, via headsets (available
in English; free). Glass cases
hold gleaming instruments,
each presented in the context
of a key work in the history of
Western music: as you step past
each case, the headphones are
programmed to emit a short
scholarly narration, followed by
a delightful concert.

PÈRE-LACHAISE CEMETERY

Main entrance on bd de Ménilmontant
ⓜ Père-Lachaise/Philippe Auguste.
Mon–Fri 8am–5.30pm, Sat 8.30am–5.30pm,
Sun 9am–5.30pm. Free. MAP P.104, POCKET
MAP A20/21–B20/21

Final resting place of a host of
French and foreign notables,
Père-Lachaise covers some
116 acres, making it one of
the world's largest cemeteries.
It's surely also one of the
most atmospheric – an eerily
beautiful haven, with terraced
slopes and magnificent old
trees spreading their branches
over the moss-grown tombs.
Free maps are available at the
entrance, but it's worth buying
a more detailed one, as some
of the graves are tricky to track
down; you can buy maps (and
souvenirs) at the Père-Lachaise
shop at 45 boulevard de
Ménilmontant near the main
entrance.

   Père-Lachaise was opened in
1804 to ease the strain on the
city's overflowing cemeteries
and churchyards. The civil
authorities had Molière,
La Fontaine, Abélard and

PÈRE-LACHAISE CEMETERY

Héloïse reburied here, and to
be interred in Père-Lachaise
quickly acquired cachet.
Among the most visited graves
is that of Chopin (Division 11),
often attended by Poles bearing
red-and-white wreaths and
flowers. Fans also flock to the
grave of ex-Doors singer Jim
Morrison (Division 6), who
died in Paris at the age of 27.

   One of the most impressive of
the individual tombs is Oscar
Wilde's (Division 89), topped
with a sculpture by Jacob
Epstein of a mysterious Phara-
onic winged messenger. *Femme
fatale* Colette's tomb, close to
the main entrance in Division
4, is very plain, though always
covered in flowers, whereas
Marcel Proust lies in his
family's conventional black
marble tomb (Division 85).

   On a more sombre note,
in Division 97 you'll find
memorials to the victims of the
Nazi concentration camps and
to executed Resistance fighters.

PARC DES BUTTES-CHAUMONT

Ⓜ Buttes-Chaumont/Botzaris. MAP P.104, POCKET MAP L5-M4

The Parc des Buttes-Chaumont was constructed under Haussmann in the 1860s to camouflage what until then had been a desolate warren of disused quarries, rubbish dumps and shacks. Out of this rather unlikely setting, a fairy-tale-like park was created – there's a grotto with a cascade and artificial stalactites, and a picturesque lake from which a huge rock rises up, topped with a delicate Corinthian temple. From the temple you get fine views of the Sacré-Coeur and beyond, and you can also go boating on the lake in summer.

BELLEVILLE

Ⓜ Belleville/Pyrénées. MAP P.104, POCKET MAP L5/6-M5/6

Absorbed into Paris in the 1860s and subsequently built up with high-rise blocks to house migrants from rural areas and the ex-colonies, Belleville might not exactly be "belle", but it's worth seeing this side of the city. The main street, rue de Belleville, abounds with Vietnamese, Thai and Chinese shops and restaurants, which spill south along boulevard de Belleville and rue du Faubourg-du-Temple. African and Oriental fruits, spices, music and fabrics attract shoppers to the boulevard de Belleville market on Tuesday and Friday mornings. From the Parc de Belleville, with its terraces and waterfalls, you get great views across the city, especially at sunset.

MÉNILMONTANT

Ⓜ Ménilmontant. MAP P.104, POCKET MAP L7-M6

Ménilmontant has a similar history to that of Belleville, and aligns itself along one straight, steep, long street, the rue de Ménilmontant and its lower extension rue Oberkampf. Although run-down in parts, its popularity with students and artists has brought a cutting-edge vitality to the area. Alternative shops and trendy bars and restaurants have sprung up among the grocers and cheap hardware stores, especially along rue Oberkampf, one of the city's premier after-dark hangouts.

THE PARC DE BELLEVILLE

ANNE WILLI

Shops

ANNE WILLI

13 rue Keller Ⓜ Ledru-Rollin/Voltaire.
Mon 2–6pm, Tues–Sat 11am–7pm.
MAP P.100, POCKET MAP L9

Completely original pieces
of clothing in gorgeous,
luxurious fabrics, from layered,
casual-chic sets to one-piece
geometric studies of the body.
Prices from €70 upwards. There
are also cute clothes for kids.

LA BAGUE DE KENZA

106 rue St-Maur Ⓜ St-Maur. Mon–Sat
10am–8pm. MAP P.104, POCKET MAP M6

An Algerian pâtisserie full
of enticing cakes made of
dates, orange, pistachios, figs,
almonds and other tasty
ingredients. There's also a little
salon de thé attached.

CÉCILE ET JEANNE

49 av Daumesnil Ⓜ Gare-de-Lyon.
Mon–Sat 10am–7pm. MAP P.100,
POCKET MAP L10

Reasonably priced and
innovative jewellery from local
artisans in one of the Viaduc
des Arts showrooms. Many
pieces under €100.

DU PAIN ET DES IDÉES

34 rue Yves Toudic Ⓜ Jacques Bonsergent.
Mon–Fri 6.45am–8pm. MAP P.104, POCKET MAP K6

Named best bakery in Paris by
Gault et Miliau in recent years,
and a visit quickly reveals why:
heavenly baguettes, brioches
and the signature *pain des amis*,
a nutty flatbread.

ISABEL MARANT

16 rue de Charonne Ⓜ Ledru-Rollin.
Mon–Sat 10.30am–7.30pm. MAP P.100,
POCKET MAP L9

Marant has established an
international reputation for her
feminine and flattering clothes
in quality fabrics such as silk
and cashmere. Prices are above
average, but not exorbitant.

LULU BERLU

2 rue Grand Prieuré Ⓜ Oberkampf. Mon–Sat
11am–7.30pm. MAP P.104, POCKET MAP H14

This shop is crammed with
twentieth-century toys and
curios, most with their original
packaging. There's a particularly good collection of
1970–90s favourites, including
Doctor Who, Star Wars, Planet
of the Apes and Batman pieces,
plus a good range of new toys.

Cafés

LE BARON ROUGE

1 rue Théophile-Roussel Ⓜ Ledru-Rollin.
Tues–Fri 10am–2pm & 5–10pm, Sat
10am–10pm, Sun 10.30am–3.30pm.
MAP P.100, POCKET MAP L9

This *bar à vins* is as close as
you'll get to the spit-on-the-
floor, saloon stereotype of
the old movies. Stallholders
and shoppers from the place
d'Aligre market gather for
a light lunch or an apéritif
during the day, especially
on Sundays, with a younger
crowd appearing later on. Join
the locals on the pavement
lunching on *saucisson*, mussels
or Cap Ferrat oysters washed
down with a glass of Muscadet.

CAFÉ DE L'INDUSTRIE

16 rue St-Sabin Ⓜ Bastille. Daily
10am–2am; closed 3 weeks in Aug.
MAP P.100, POCKET MAP H16

One of the best Bastille cafés
(actually two cafés, across the
road from each other), packed
out every evening. Rugs on the
floor around solid old wooden
tables, mounted rhinoceros
heads, old black-and-white
photos on the walls and an
unpretentious crowd.

CHEZ PRUNE

36 rue Beaurepaire Ⓜ Jacques-Bonsergent
☎ 01.42.41.30.47. Mon–Sat 8am–2am, Sun
10am–2am. MAP P.104, POCKET MAP K5

Named after the owner's grand-
mother (a bust of whom can
be found inside), *Chez Prune*
is popular with an arty media
crowd, but remains friendly
and laid-back, with pleasant
outdoor seating overlooking
the canal. Lunchtime dishes
around €14; evening snacks like
platters of cheese or charcuterie
around €11; beer €3.

PAUSE CAFÉ

41 rue de Charonne, cnr rue Keller
Ⓜ Ledru-Rollin. Tues–Sat 8am–2am, Sun to
9pm. MAP P.100, POCKET MAP L9

Or maybe "Pose Café" – given
its popularity with the *quartier's*
young and fashionable
(sunglasses are worn at all
times) who bag the pavement
tables at lunch and apéritif
time. Service is predictably
insouciant. *Plats du jour*
around €14.

Restaurants

A LA BICHE AU BOIS

45 av Ledru-Rollin Ⓜ Gare de Lyon
☎ 01.43.43.34.38. Mon 7–11pm, Tues–Fri
noon–2pm & 7–10.30pm; closed four weeks
July–Aug. MAP P.100, POCKET MAP H18

The queues leading out
through the conservatory at
the front are a strong indicator
of the popularity of this
restaurant, which mixes
charming service with keenly
priced, well-produced food.
The house speciality is a rich
coq au vin, and you can start
off with a pâté or terrine.
Three-course lunch and
dinner *menu* with cheese to
finish €28.50.

LE BARON ROUGE

BISTROT PAUL BERT

18 rue Paul Bert Ⓜ Faidherbe-Chaligny
☎ 01.43.72.24.01. Tues–Sat noon–2pm &
7.30–11pm; closed Aug. MAP P.100, POCKET MAP M9

A quintessential Parisian *bistrot*, with little wooden tables and white tablecloths, tobacco-stained ceiling and old posters. A mix of locals and visitors flock here for the cosy ambience and high-quality simple fare, such as *poulet rôti*, as well as more sophisticated dishes such as guineafowl with morel mushrooms. Save room for the perfectly cooked Grand Marnier soufflé. Dinner is around €60 a head, with wine.

LE CHÂTEAUBRIAND

129 av Parmentier Ⓜ Goncourt
☎ 01.43.57.45.95. Tues–Sat 7.30–10.30pm.
Bookings taken 3–7pm up to 2 weeks in advance. MAP P.104, POCKET MAP H13

Innovative Basque chef, Inaki Aizpitarte, has turned this vintage *bistrot* into an avant-garde dining room that's booked out every evening. Dishes include mackerel ceviche with pear sorbet, and oyster soup with red fruits and beetroot. Around €55 a head. Second sitting at 9.30pm –just turn up and be prepared to queue.

L'ENCRIER

55 rue Traversière Ⓜ Ledru-Rollin
☎ 01.44.68.08.16. Mon–Fri noon–2.15pm &
7.30–11pm, Sat 7.30–11pm; usually closed Aug. MAP P.100, POCKET MAP L10

The interior of exposed brick walls and wood beams complements the homely fare served up by pleasant staff in this restaurant near the Viaduc des Arts. The food has a southwestern influence and might include goose breast in honey. Lunch *menu* from €14.50, evening *menus* from €19.30.

LE TRAIN BLEU

LE TRAIN BLEU

Gare de Lyon Ⓜ Gare de Lyon
☎ 01.43.43.09.06. Daily 11.30am–3pm &
7–11pm. MAP P.100, POCKET MAP L10

The *Train Bleu*'s decor is straight out of a bygone era – everything drips with gilt, and chandeliers hang from frescoed ceilings. The French cuisine is good, if a tad overpriced. *Menu* €56, including half a bottle of wine; for à la carte reckon on €80.

AU VIEUX CHÊNE

7 rue du Dahomey Ⓜ Faidherbe-Chaligny
☎ 01.43.71.67.69. Mon–Fri noon–2pm &
8–10.30pm; closed one week in July and two in Aug. MAP P.100, POCKET MAP M9

Outstanding restaurant with packed bookshelves and smart service. Try smoked haddock on a bed of carrots, followed by a perfect *tarte Tatin*. The *menus* – lunch from €15, dinner €33 – are a steal.

WALY FAY

6 rue Godefroy-Cavaignac Ⓜ Charonne/
Faidherbe-Chaligny ☎ 01.40.24.17.79.
Mon–Sat 7–11pm. MAP P.100, POCKET MAP M8

West African restaurant with a cosy, stylish atmosphere. Smart young Parisians come here to dine on richly spiced stews and other West African delicacies at a moderate cost (mains €13–18).

Bars

L'ALIMENTATION GÉNÉRALE

64 rue Jean-Pierre Timbaud ⓂParmentier Ⓦalimentation-generale.net. Daily 6pm–2am. MAP P.100, POCKET MAP L6

One of Oberkampf's hottest nightlife spots, with a global line-up of live music ranging from Afro-rock to Italian folk. A DJ usually takes over later on and there's room for dancing. Sometimes a cover charge of €10 that includes the first drink.

L'AUTRE CAFÉ

62 rue Jean-Pierre Timbaud ⓂParmentier Daily 8am–2am. MAP P.100, POCKET MAP L6

Amid the heaving throng of bars on this popular nightlife stretch, this high-ceilinged *fin-de-siècle* café-bar-restaurant stands slightly apart, perhaps because it seems to welcome all comers and has no trace of precision, and yet still a great vibe. Drinks are reasonably priced, and the food isn't bad either, especially if you stick to the blackboard specials (around €10).

CAFÉ CHARBON

CAFÉ CHARBON

109 rue Oberkampf ⓂSaint-Maur/ Parmentier. Sun–Thurs 9am–2am, Fri & Sat 9am–4am. MAP P.104, POCKET MAP L6

The place that pioneered the rise of the Oberkampf bar scene in the mid-90s is still going strong and continues to draw in a fashionable crowd. Part of its allure is the attractively restored twentieth-century decor, with comfy booths and dangling lights. Meals €13–18, cocktails from €7.50, beer from €3.50.

AUX FOLIES

8 rue de Belleville ⓂBelleville. Daily 6.30–1am. MAP P.104, POCKET MAP L5

Once a *café-théâtre* where Edith Piaf and Maurice Chevalier sang, *Aux Folies* offers a slice of Belleville life; its outside terrace and long brass bar, with mirrored tiles, pinball machine and broken window panes held together with sticking tape, are packed day and night with a cosmopolitan crowd, enjoying beer, cocktails and mint tea.

LES MARCHEURS DE PLANÈTE

73 rue de la Roquette ⓂVoltaire. Tues–Sat 5.30pm–2am, Sun 11am–11pm. MAP P.100, POCKET MAP L8

Good old-fashioned Parisian atmosphere, with an effortlessly cool, vaguely retro vibe, with chess tables, posters and a wild-haired owner. More than 100 wines (from €2.70 a glass) are on offer, plus excellent cheeses and charcuterie dishes.

SANZSANS

49 rue du Faubourg St-Antoine ⓂBastille. Mon–Sat 9am–5am. MAP P.100, POCKET MAP H17

The gothic get-up of red velvet, oil paintings and chandeliers makes this bar popular with a young crowd, especially on Friday and Saturday evenings, when DJs play rare groove and funky/Brazilian house.

Clubs

LE NOUVEAU CASINO

109 rue Oberkampf ⓂParmentier
☎ 01.43.57.57.40, Ⓦ www.nouveaucasino.
net. Thurs–Sat midnight–5am. MAP P.104,
POCKET MAP L6

Right behind *Café Charbon*
(see opposite) lies this excellent
venue. An experimental line-up
of gigs from 8pm makes way
for a relaxed, dancey crowd
later on, with music ranging
from electro-pop or house to
rock. Entry price up to €12,
depending on who's playing.

LA SCÈNE BASTILLE

2bis rue des Taillandiers ⓂBastille
☎ 01.48.06.50.70 (restaurant reservations:
☎ 01.48.06.12.13), Ⓦ www.la-scene.com.
Mon–Thurs 7.30pm–midnight, Fri–Sun till
6am; closed Aug. MAP P.100, POCKET MAP L9

Club, concert venue and
restaurant all rolled into one,
in a snazzily refurbished
warehouse, playing rock,
electro and funk, with regular
gay nights. Entry €12–25.

Live music

CAFÉ DE LA DANSE

5 passage Louis-Philippe ⓂBastille
☎ 01.47.00.57.59, Ⓦ www.cafedeladanse.com.
Open nights of concerts only. MAP P.100, POCKET
MAP H17

Rock, pop, world and folk
music played in an intimate
and attractive space.

LA FLÈCHE D'OR

102bis rue de Bagnolet ⓂPorte-de-
Bagnolet/Alexandre-Dumas (15min walk
from both) ☎ 01.44.64.01.02, Ⓦwww.
flechedor.fr. Mon–Thurs 8pm–2am, Fri & Sat
8pm–6am. POCKET MAP C21

Housed in the old Bagnolet
station on the defunct *petite
ceinture* railway, this bar and
live music venue is one of the
hottest tickets in town (gigs

PERFORMER AT LA SCÈNE BASTILLE

up to €15), programming
indie-pop, ska, rock, chanson
and punk.

OPÉRA BASTILLE

120 rue de Lyon ⓂBastille
☎ 08.36.69.78.68, Ⓦ www.opera-de-paris.fr.
MAP P.100, POCKET MAP H17

Opened in 1989 to a rather
mixed reception, the
amorphous glass and steel opera
house building still inspires
a fair amount of controversy,
but its performances are nearly
always a sell-out. Tickets start
from €9, but most are in the
€40–90 range.

POINT EPHÉMÈRE

200 quai de Valmy ⓂJaurès/Louis Blanc
☎ 01.40.34.02.48, Ⓦ www.pointephemere.org.
Mon–Sat noon–2am, Sun 1–9pm (later if
there's a concert). MAP P.104, POCKET MAP K4

A great, energetic atmosphere
pervades this creative space
for music, dance and visual
arts, set in a former canal
boathouse. Bands play rock,
indie, jazz and more, while
the rotating art exhibitions
run from the quotidian to
the abstract. Enjoy a decent
cheeseburger or bagel in the
restaurant looking out onto
the canal.

The Quartier Latin

The Quartier Latin has been associated with students ever since the Sorbonne was established in the thirteenth century. The name derives from the Latin spoken at the medieval university, which perched on the slopes of the Montagne Ste-Geneviève. Many colleges remain in the area to this day, along with some fascinating vestiges of the medieval city, such as the Gothic church of St-Séverin and the Renaissance Hôtel de Cluny, site of the national museum of the Middle Ages. Some of the quarter's student chic may have worn thin in recent years – notably around the now too-famous place St-Michel – and high rents have pushed scholars and artists out of their garrets, but the cafés, restaurants and arty cinemas are still packed with students, making this one of the most relaxed areas of Paris for going out.

THE RIVERBANK

Ⓜ St-Michel. MAP P.114–115, POCKET MAP D17–E18

The riverbank *quais* east of place St-Michel are ideal for wandering and enjoying a good browse among the old books, postcards and prints sold from the **bouquinistes**, whose green kiosks line the parapets. There are wonderful views across the

CAFÉ TERRACE IN THE QUARTIER LATIN

river to Notre-Dame from square Viviani, a welcome patch of grass around the corner from the celebrated English-language bookshop **Shakespeare and Co** (see p.118). The mutilated church behind the square is **St-Julien-le-Pauvre** (daily 9.30am–1pm and 3–6.30pm; Ⓜ St-Michel/Maubert Mutualité). The same age as Notre-Dame, it used to be the venue for university assemblies until rumbustious students tore it apart in 1524. For the most dramatic view of Notre-Dame, walk along the riverbank as far as the tip of the Ile St-Louis and the Pont de Sully.

THE HUCHETTE QUARTER

Ⓜ St-Michel. MAP P.114–115, POCKET MAP D17

The touristy bustle is at its worst around **rue de la Huchette**, just east of the place St-Michel, but look beyond the cheap bars and overpriced Greek kebab-and-disco tavernas and you'll find some evocative

remnants of medieval Paris. Connecting rue de la Huchette to the riverside is the narrow rue du Chat-qui-Pêche, a tiny slice of how Paris looked before Baron Haussmann flattened the old alleys to make room for his wide boulevards. One block south of rue de la Huchette, just west of rue St-Jacques, is the mainly fifteenth-century church of **St-Séverin**, whose entrance is on rue des Prêtres St-Séverin (Mon–Sat 11am–7.30pm, Sun 9am–8.30pm; Ⓜ St-Michel/Cluny–La Sorbonne). It's one of the city's more intense churches, its windows filled with edgy stained glass by the modern French painter Jean Bazaine.

MUSÉE NATIONAL DU MOYEN AGE

6 place Paul-Painlevé Ⓜ Cluny-La Sorbonne 📞 01.53.73.78.16, 🌐 www.musee-moyenage .fr. Daily except Tues 9.15am–5.45pm. €8.50. Medieval music concerts throughout the week –phone for details; €6. MAP P.114–115, POCKET MAP D18

The walls of the third-century **Roman baths** are visible in the garden of the **Hôtel de Cluny**, a sixteenth-century mansion built by the abbots of the Cluny monastery as their Paris

pied-à-terre. It now houses the rewarding Musée National du Moyen Age, a treasure trove of medieval art. There's a feast of medieval sculpture throughout, along with wonderful stained glass, books and curious objets d'art, but the real beauties are the **tapestries** that hang in most rooms, including vivid depictions of a grape harvest, a lover making advances and a woman in a bath that overflows into a duck pond. The greatest of all is the stunning **La Dame à la Licorne** ("The Lady with the Unicorn") series, displayed in its own chapel-like chamber. Made in the late fifteenth century, the set depicts the five senses – along with an ambiguous image that may represent the virtue in control-ling them – in six luxuriantly detailed allegoric scenes, each featuring a richly dressed woman flanked by a lion and a unicorn. On the ground floor, the vaults of the Roman baths are preserved intact.

The museum also has a busy progamme of medieval music **concerts**; look out for the regular "heure musicale".

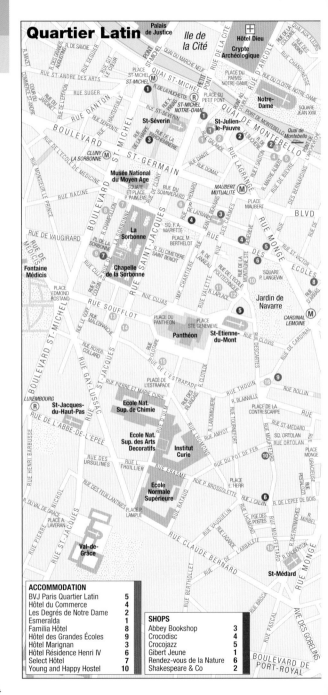

Quartier Latin

ACCOMMODATION

BVJ Paris Quartier Latin	5
Hôtel du Commerce	4
Les Degrés de Notre Dame	2
Esmeralda	1
Familia Hôtel	8
Hôtel des Grandes Écoles	9
Hôtel Marignan	3
Hôtel Résidence Henri IV	6
Select Hôtel	7
Young and Happy Hostel	10

SHOPS

Abbey Bookshop	3
Crocodisc	4
Crocojazz	5
Gibert Jeune	1
Rendez-vous de la Nature	6
Shakespeare & Co	2

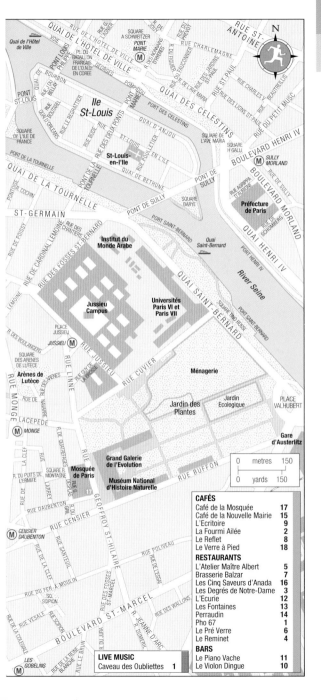

CAFÉS

Café de la Mosquée	17
Café de la Nouvelle Mairie	15
L'Ecritoire	9
La Fourmi Ailée	2
Le Reflet	8
Le Verre à Pied	18

RESTAURANTS

L'Atelier Maître Albert	5
Brasserie Balzar	7
Les Cinq Saveurs d'Anada	16
Les Degrés de Notre-Dame	3
L'Ecurie	12
Les Fontaines	13
Perraudin	14
Pho 67	1
Le Pré Verre	6
Le Reminet	4

BARS

Le Piano Vache	11
Le Violon Dingue	10

LIVE MUSIC

Caveau des Oubliettes	1

THE SORBONNE

Ⓜ Cluny–La Sorbonne/RER Luxembourg.
MAP P.114–115, POCKET MAP C18–D18

The traffic-free place de la Sorbonne is a great place to sit back and enjoy the Quartier Latin atmosphere. Frowning over it are the high walls of the Sorbonne, which was once the most important of the medieval colleges huddled atop the Montagne Ste-Geneviève. More recently it was a flashpoint in the student riots of 1968 – and again in the spring of 2006. The frontage is dominated by the Chapelle Ste-Ursule, built in the 1640s by the great Cardinal Richelieu, whose tomb it contains.

THE PANTHÉON

Ⓜ Cardinal-Lemoine/RER Luxembourg
☎ 01.44.32.18.00, Ⓦ http://pantheon
.monuments-nationaux.fr. Daily: April–Sept
10am–6.30pm; Oct–March 10am–6pm. €8.50.
MAP P.114–115, POCKET MAP D19

Crowning the Montagne Ste-Geneviève, the largest and most visible of Paris's domes graces the bulky Panthéon, Louis XV's thank-you to Ste-Geneviève, patron saint of Paris, for curing him of illness. Completed only in 1789, after the Revolution it was transformed into a mausoleum, emblazoned with the words *"Aux grands hommes la patrie reconnaissante"* ("The nation honours its great men") beneath the pediment of the giant portico. The remains of giants of French culture, including Voltaire, Rousseau, Hugo and Zola, are entombed in the vast, barrel-vaulted crypt, along with Marie Curie (the sole woman), and Alexandre Dumas, who was "panthéonized" in 2002. The bombastically Classical nave displays a working model of **Foucault's Pendulum** swinging from the dome. French physicist

Léon Foucault devised the experiment, conducted here in 1851, to demonstrate that while the pendulum appeared to rotate over a 24-hour period, it was in fact the earth beneath it turning.

ST-ETIENNE-DU-MONT

Ⓜ Cardinal Lemoine. MAP P.114–115, POCKET
MAP D19

The remains of Pascal and Racine, two seventeenth-century literary giants who didn't make it into the Panthéon, and a few relics of Ste-Geneviève, lie in the church of St-Étienne-du-Mont. The main attraction, however, is the fabulously airy interior, formed of a Flamboyant Gothic choir joined to a Renaissance nave, the two parts linked by a sinuous catwalk that runs around the interior, arching across the nave in the form of a carved rood screen – an extremely rare survival, as most French screens fell victim to Protestant iconoclasts, reformers or revolutionaries.

INSTITUT DU MONDE ARABE

1 rue des Fossés St-Bernard Ⓜ Jussieu/
Cardinal-Lemoine ☎ 01.40.51.38.38,
Ⓦ www.imarabe.org. Tues–Sun 10am–6pm.
Museum €6. MAP P.114–115, POCKET MAP F18

A bold slice of glass and steel,
the stunning exterior of the
Institut du Monde Arabe
betrays architect Jean Nouvel's
obsession with light – its
broad southern facade, which
mimics a *moucharabiyah*, or
traditional Arab latticework, is
made up of thousands of tiny
metallic shutters. Originally
designed to be light-sensitive,
they now open and close
just once an hour, and the
exhibition spaces are consequently quite gloomy. Inside, a
museum winds down from the
seventh floor as it traces the
evolution of art in the Islamic
world; impressive temporary
exhibitions (extra admission)
go into more detail.

THE PARIS MOSQUE AND HAMMAM

Entrance on rue Daubenton Ⓜ Jussieu
☎ 01.45.35.97.33, Ⓦ www.mosquee-de
-paris.org. Daily except Fri & Muslim hols
9am–noon & 2–6pm. €3. MAP P.114–115,
POCKET MAP J11

Even in this quiet area,
the Paris mosque, built by
Moroccan craftsmen in the
early 1920s, feels like an oasis
of serenity behind its crenel-
lated walls. You can walk in
the sunken garden and patios
with their polychrome tiles and
carved ceilings, and relax at
the laid-back café (see p.119),
but non-Muslims are asked not
to enter the prayer room. The
hammam (women Mon, Wed,
Thurs and Sat 10am–9pm, Fri
2–9pm; men Tues 2–9pm, Sun
10am–9pm. €15; towels extra)
is one of the most atmospheric
in the city, with its vaulted
cooling-off room and marble-
lined steam chamber.

JARDIN DES PLANTES

Entrances at the corners of the park
and opposite rue Jussieu Ⓜ Jussieu/
Censier Daubenton. Daily: April–Aug
7.30am–7.45pm; Sept–March 8am–5.30pm.
Free. MAP P.114–115, POCKET MAP F19–G19

Behind the mosque the Jardin
des Plantes, a medicinal herb
garden from 1626, now hosts
Paris's botanical gardens,
with avenues of trees, lawns,
hothouses, museums and an
old-fashioned **menagerie**, also
France's oldest zoo.

GRANDE GALERIE DE L'EVOLUTION

Jardin des Plantes; entrance off rue Buffon
Ⓜ Censier-Daubenton/Gare d'Austerlitz.
Daily except Tues 10am–6pm. €7.
MAP P.114–115, POCKET MAP J11

Magnificent floral beds make a
fine approach to the collection
of buildings that forms the
**Muséum National d'Histoire
Naturelle** (Ⓦ www.mnhn.fr).
Skip the musty displays of
palaeontology, anatomy,
mineralogy and palaeobotany
in favour of the Grande Galerie
de l'Évolution, housed in a
restored nineteenth-century
glass-domed building. It
doesn't actually tell the story of
evolution, but it does feature a
huge cast of life-sized animals,
some of them striding dramatically across the space.

STROLLING IN THE JARDIN DES PLANTES

Shops

ABBEY BOOKSHOP

29 rue de la Parcheminerie ⓂSt-Michel.
Mon–Sat 10am–7pm. MAP P.114–115, POCKET
MAP D17

An overstuffed warren of a
bookshop with lots of used
British and North American
fiction and travel guides, plus
knowledgeable, helpful staff –
and free coffee.

CROCODISC

40–42 rue des Ecoles ⓂMaubert-
Mutualité. Tues–Sat 11am–7pm. Closed
first two weeks of Aug.MAP P.114–115,
POCKET MAP D18

Everything from folk and
Afro-Antillais to salsa and
movie soundtracks, new and
used, at good prices.

CROCOJAZZ

64 rue de la Montagne-Ste-Geneviève
ⓂMaubert-Mutualité. Tues–Sat 11am–1pm
& 2–7pm. MAP P.114–115, POCKET MAP D19

Mainly new jazz and blues
imports, with some inexpensive
used titles.

GIBERT JEUNE

5 place St-Michel and around ⓂSt-Michel.
Mon–Sat 9.30am–7.30pm; closed first two
weeks of Aug. MAP P.114–115, POCKET MAP D17

A Latin Quarter institution for
student/academic books, with
nine stores on and around
place St-Michel. There's a
secondhand selection at
no. 2 and foreign-language
titles at no. 10.

SHAKESPEARE & CO

RENDEZ-VOUS DE LA NATURE

96 rue Mouffetard ⓂCensier-Daubenton.
Tues–Sat 9.30am–7.30pm, Sun 9.30am–1pm.
MAP P.114–115, POCKET MAP H11

One of the city's largest and
most comprehensive
health-food stores, with
everything from organic
produce to herbal teas.

SHAKESPEARE & CO

37 rue de la Bûcherie ⓂMaubert-Mutualité.
Mon–Fri 10am–11pm; Sat & Sun 11am–11pm.
MAP P.114–115, POCKET MAP D17

A Latin Quarter institution,
this cosy, crowded literary
haunt, run by Americans and
staffed by earnest young
Hemingway wannabes, sells
the best selection of English-
language books in town. Day
and evening readings in the
week; check website for
details.

Latin Quarter markets

The narrow, half-kilometre run of "La Mouff", the city's famed rue
Mouffetard market, is now mostly given over to classy food shops, but the
Quartier Latin still offers some of the city's classic food markets.
Maubert place Maubert ⓂMaubert-Mutualité. Tues &
Thurs 7am–2.30pm, Sat 7am–3pm.
Monge place Monge ⓂMonge. Wed and Fri 7am–2.30pm, Sun 7am–3pm.

Cafés

CAFÉ DE LA MOSQUÉE

39 rue Geoffroy-St-Hilaire ⓂMonge. Daily 9am–11pm. MAP P.114–115, POCKET MAP J11

Drink mint tea and eat sweet cakes beside the courtyard fountain and fig trees of the Paris mosque – a haven of calm (except on weekend lunchtimes when it's a popular spot for festive families). The indoor salon has a beautiful Arabic interior, where tasty tagines and couscous are served for €15 and up.

CAFÉ DE LA NOUVELLE MAIRIE

19 rue des Fossés-St-Jacques ⓂCluny-La Sorbonne/RER Luxembourg. Mon–Fri 8am–midnight. MAP P.114–115, POCKET MAP D19

Sleek café/wine bar with some pavement seating and a relaxed feel generated by its older, university clientele. Serves good, modern food and plates of cheese or charcuterie (all around €10).

LUNCH AT THE CAFÉ DE LA NOUVELLE MAIRIE

L'ECRITOIRE

3 place de la Sorbonne ⓂCluny-La Sorbonne/RER Luxembourg. Daily 7am–midnight. MAP P.114–115, POCKET MAP C18

This classic university café is right beside the Sorbonne, and has outside tables by the fountain.

LA FOURMI AILÉE

8 rue du Fouarre ⓂMaubert-Mutualité. Daily noon–11pm; food served noon–3pm & 7–10pm. MAP P.114–115, POCKET MAP D17

Simple, classically French food and speciality teas are served in this former feminist bookshop, now a relaxed *salon de thé* with a pretty, tiled exterior. The high, cloud-painted ceiling, book-lined walls and background jazz contribute to the atmosphere. Around €12 for a *plat du jour*.

LE REFLET

6 rue Champollion ⓂCluny-La Sorbonne. Daily 11am–2am. MAP P.114–115, POCKET MAP C18

This artsy cinema café has a strong flavour of the nouvelle vague, with its scruffy black paint scheme, lights rigged up on a gantry and rickety tables packed with film-goers and chess players. Perfect for a drink either side of a film at one of the art cinemas on rue Champollion, perhaps accompanied by a steak, quiche or salad from the short list of blackboard specials.

LE VERRE À PIED

118bis rue Mouffetard ⓂMonge. Tues–Sat 9am–9.30pm, Sun 9am–4pm. MAP P.114–115, POCKET MAP H11

Wonderfully old-fashioned little market bar where traders take their morning glass of wine at the bar, or sit down to eat a delicious *plat du jour* for €11 and engage in lively conversation. Simple *menus* €13.

Restaurants

L'ATELIER MAÎTRE ALBERT

1 rue Maitre Albert ⓜ Maubert-Mutualité
☎ 01.56.81.30.01. Mon–Wed noon–2.30pm &
6.30–11pm, Thurs & Fri noon–2.30pm &
6.30pm–1am, Sat 6.30pm–1am, Sun
6.30–11pm. MAP P.114–115, POCKET MAP E18

One of chef-entrepreneur
Guy Savoy's ventures, this
contemporary rôtisserie
specializes in top-notch spit-
roast meats, though you can
also find lighter dishes like cod
casseroled with seasonal veg
or a delicious starter of prawns
stuffed with citrus butter.
Expect to pay around €55
à la carte without wine.

BRASSERIE BALZAR

49 rue des Ecoles ⓜ Maubert-Mutualité
☎ 01.43.54.13.67. Daily 8am–11.45pm.
MAP P.114–115, POCKET MAP D18

Classic, high-ceilinged
brasserie, long frequented by
the literary intelligentsia of the
Latin Quarter – along with
hordes of delighted tourists.
It's not cheap: steak tartare,
roast chicken or sauerkraut
garnished with sausage cost
around €18, but there are
menus from €24.

BRASSERIE BALZAR

LES CINQ SAVEURS D'ANADA

72 rue du Cardinal-Lemoine ⓜ Cardinal-
Lemoine ☎ 01.43.29.58.54. Tues–Sun
noon–2.30pm & 7–10.30pm. MAP P.114–115,
POCKET MAP E19

Bare-bones restaurant serving
macrobiotic, vegetarian food.
Salads are tasty, along with
creative meat-substitute dishes
(around €14–18), such as tofu
soufflé.

LES DEGRÉS DE NOTRE-DAME

10 rue des Grands Degrés ⓜ Maubert-
Mutualité ☎ 01.55.42.88.88. Mon–Sat
7am–10.30pm. MAP P.114–115, POCKET MAP E17

Linked to the hotel of the
same name, serving reliable,
substantial and home-made
French food – plus lots of
couscous dishes and tagines –
in a cosy *bistrot* setting or out
on the *terrasse*. Lunch *menu*
€12.50; dinner *menu* €26.50.

L'ECURIE

58 rue de la Montagne Ste-Geneviève
ⓜ Maubert-Mutualité/Cardinal-Lemoine
☎ 01.46.33.68.49. Mon & Wed–Sat
noon–2.30pm & 7pm–11.30pm, Tues & Sun
7pm–11.30pm. MAP P.114–115, POCKET MAP D19

Shoe-horned into a former
stables on a lovely corner, this
quirky, family-run restaurant
serves well-cooked grilled meat
dishes with chips for less than
€20. Book ahead.

LES FONTAINES

9 rue Soufflot. RER Luxembourg
☎ 01.43.26.42.80. Daily 7.30–1am; food
served noon–3.30pm & 7–10.30pm. MAP
P.114–115, POCKET MAP C19

The dated brasserie-cum-diner
decor looks unpromising from
the outside, but the welcome
inside this family-run place is
warm, the atmosphere friendly,
and the food – honest, seasonal
French meat and fish dishes
– is great, with a nice mix
of innovation and tradition.
Three-course menu €15 at
lunch, €28 in the evening.

PERRAUDIN

157 rue St-Jacques. RER Luxembourg
☎ 01.46.33.15.75. Daily noon–2.30pm &
7.30–10.30pm. MAP P.114–115, POCKET MAP D19

Quintessential Left Bank *bistrot* featuring solid cooking and an atmosphere thick with Parisian chatter floating above packed tables. *Menus* €18 (lunch) and €28 (dinner).

PHO 67

59 rue Galande ⓜ Maubert-Mutualité
☎ 01.43.25.56.69. Daily except Mon lunchtime
11.30am–3pm & 6.30–11pm. MAP P.114–115,
POCKET MAP D17

The Vietnamese proprietors work in an open kitchen, preparing a range of inexpensive dishes, including sour pig ears; the less adventurous should go for the delicious *pho* soup (€8–11), or one of the four good-value *menus* (€10–20).

LE PRÉ VERRE

8 rue Thénard ⓜ Maubert-Mutualité
☎ 01.43.54.59.47. Tues–Sat noon–2pm &
7.30–10.30pm. MAP P.114–115, POCKET MAP D18

Unusually relaxed, contemporary *bistrot* offering adventurous food such as swordfish on a bed of quinoa. Stunning value *menus*: evening €28.50: lunchtime two-courser €13.50.

LE REMINET

3 rue des Grands-Degrés ⓜ Maubert-
Mutualité ☎ 01.44.07.04.24. Daily
noon–2.30pm & 7–10.30pm. MAP P.114–115,
POCKET MAP E17

This tiny *bistrot* is effortlessly stylish, with gilded mirrors and brass candlesticks at every table, and French windows opening out onto a leafy square. The classy food incorporates quality French ingredients and imaginative sauces. The weekday only €14.50 lunch *menu* is an astonishing bargain. Pricier in the evenings when the crowds arrive.

LE PIANO VACHE

Bars

LE PIANO VACHE

8 rue Laplace ⓜ Cardinal-Lemoine. Mon–Fri
noon–2am, Sat 6pm–2am. MAP P.114–115,
POCKET MAP D18

Left Bank favourite crammed with students at little tables, with cool music and a laid-back atmosphere.

LE VIOLON DINGUE

46 rue de la Montagne-Ste-Geneviève
ⓜ Maubert-Mutualité. Daily from 7pm (from
10pm in Aug), happy hour 7–10pm. MAP
P.114–115, POCKET MAP D18

A long, dark student pub that's noisy and popular with young travellers. English-speaking bar staff and cheap drinks. The cellar bar stays open until 4.30am on busy nights.

Live music

CAVEAU DES OUBLIETTES

52 rue Galande ⓜ Cluny-La Sorbonne
☎ 01.46.34.23.09, ⓦ www.caveaudes
oubliettes.fr. Tues–Sun 5pm–4am; music from
10pm. Free. MAP P.114–115, POCKET MAP D17

Lively jazz jams – blues, Latin, African – in a gloomy, smoky dungeon setting, once a medieval prison.

St-Germain

St-Germain, the westernmost section of Paris's Left Bank, has long been famous as the haunt of bohemians and intellectuals. A few famous cafés preserve a strong flavour of the old times, but the dominant spirit these days is elegant, relaxed and seriously upmarket. At opposite ends of the quarter are two of the city's busiest and best-loved sights: to the east, bordering the Quartier Latin, spreads the huge green space of the Jardin du Luxembourg, while to the west stands the jaw-dropping Musée d'Orsay, a converted railway station with a world-beating collection of Impressionist paintings. Between the two, you can visit the churches of St-Sulpice and St-Germain-des-Prés, or intriguing museums dedicated to the artists Delacroix and Maillol, but really, shopping is king. The streets around place St-Sulpice swarm with international fashion brands, while on the north side of boulevard St-Germain, antique shops and art dealers dominate.

PONT DES ARTS

Ⓜ Pont Neuf. MAP P.124–125, POCKET MAP C16

The delicate and much-loved Pont des Arts was installed in Napoleon's time. It offers a classic upstream view of the Ile de la Cité, and also provides a grand entrance to St-Germain under the watchful eye of the Institut de France, an august academic institution whose members are known as "Immortals".

MUSÉE D'ORSAY

1 rue de la Légion d'Honneur Ⓜ Solférino/
RER Musée-d'Orsay ☎ 01.40.49.48.14,
Ⓦ www.musee-orsay.fr. Tues–Sun
9.30am–6pm, Thurs till 9.45pm. €9,
free on first Sun of the month & to under-18s
MAP P.124–125, POCKET MAP A15

Along the riverfront, on
the western edge of
St-Germain, the Musée
d'Orsay dramatically fills a
vast former railway station
with paintings and sculptures
dating between 1848 and
1914, including an unparal-
leled Impressionist and
Post-Impressionist collection.

The museum's **ground
floor**, spread out under a
giant glass arch, is devoted to
pre-1870 work, contrasting
Ingres, Delacroix and other
serious-minded painters
and sculptors acceptable to
the mid-nineteenth century
salons with the relatively
unusual works of Puvis de
Chavannes, Gustave Moreau
and the younger Degas. The
influential Barbizon school
and the Realists are also
showcased, with works by
Daumier, Corot and Millet
preparing the ground for the
early controversies of Monet's
violently light-filled *Femmes
au Jardin* (1867) and Manet's
provocative *Olympia* (1863),
which heralded the arrival of
Impressionism. Impressionism
proper packs the attic-like
upper level. Here, you'll have
to fight a persistent sense of
familiarity – Manet's waterlilies,
Degas' *Au Café du L'Absinthe*,
Renoir's *Bal du Moulin de
la Galette*, Monet's *Femme à
l'Ombrelle* – to appreciate the
movement's vibrant, experimental vigour. You'll also find
Degas' ballet dancer sculptures
and small-scale landscapes
and outdoor scenes by Renoir,
Sisley, Pissarro and Monet that

VAN GOGH PAINTING AT THE MUSÉE D'ORSAY

owed much of their brilliance
to the novel practice of setting
up easels in the open. Berthe
Morisot, the first woman to
join the early Impressionists, is
represented by her famous *Le
Berceau* (1872), among others.
There are more heavyweight
masterpieces in the form of
Van Gogh and Cézanne, and
Monet and Renoir in their
middle and late periods.
Beyond Toulouse-Lautrec's
smoky nightclub caricatures, a
dimly lit, melancholy chamber
is devoted to pastels by
Redon, Mondrian and others,
while the final rooms have
an edgier feel, beginning
with Rousseau's dreamlike *La
Charmeuse de Serpents* (1907)
and continuing past Gauguin's
ambivalent Tahitian paintings
to Pointillist works by Seurat,
Signac and others.

Down on the **middle level** a
disparate group of paintings
includes the Art Nouveau
Nabis, notably Bonnard and
Vuillard, and some inter-
national Symbolist works.
Bridging the sculpture terraces,
the **Rodin terrace** puts almost
everything else to shame. If
you've energy to spare, don't
skip the last few rooms, which
contain superb Art Nouveau
furniture and objets d'art.

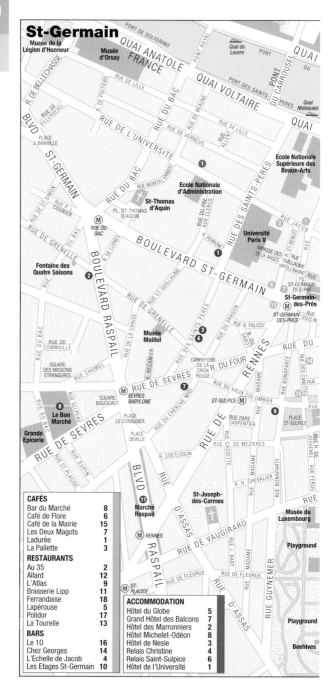

St-Germain

CAFÉS

Bar du Marché	8
Café de Flore	6
Café de la Mairie	15
Les Deux Magots	7
Ladurée	1
La Pallette	3

RESTAURANTS

Au 35	2
Allard	12
L'Atlas	9
Brasserie Lipp	11
Ferrandaise	18
Lapérouse	5
Polidor	17
La Tourelle	13

BARS

Le 10	16
Chez Georges	14
L'Echelle de Jacob	4
Les Etages St-Germain	10

ACCOMMODATION

Hôtel du Globe	5
Grand Hôtel des Balcons	7
Hôtel des Marronniers	2
Hôtel Michelet-Odéon	8
Hôtel de Nesle	3
Relais Christine	4
Relais Saint-Sulpice	6
Hôtel de l'Université	1

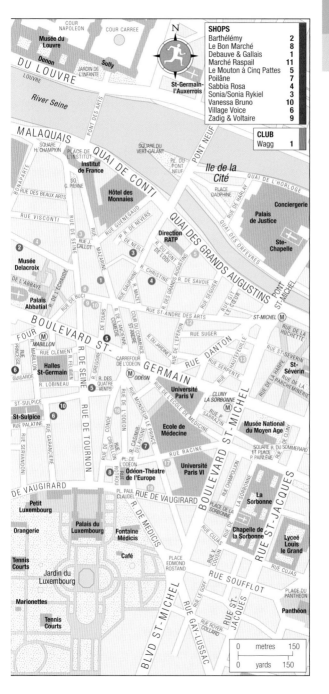

SHOPS
Barthélémy 2
Le Bon Marché 8
Debauve & Gallais 1
Marché Raspail 11
Le Mouton à Cinq Pattes 5
Poilâne 7
Sabbia Rosa 4
Sonia/Sonia Rykiel 3
Vanessa Bruno 10
Village Voice 6
Zadig & Voltaire 9

CLUB
Wagg 1

MUSÉE DELACROIX

6 rue de Furstenberg Ⓜ Mabillon/
St-Germain-des-Prés ☎ 01.44.41.86.50,
Ⓦ www.musee-delacroix.fr. Daily except Tues
9.30am–5pm. €5. MAP P.124–125, POCKET MAP B17

The Musée Delacroix is tucked
away halfway down rue de
Furstenberg, opposite a tiny
square and backing onto a
secret garden. Although the
artist's major work is exhibited
permanently at the Louvre (see
p.42) and the Musée d'Orsay
(see p.123), this museum,
housed in the studio where the
artist lived and worked from
1857 until his death in 1863,
displays a refreshingly intimate
collection, including a scattering
of personal belongings and
minor exhibitions of his work.

PLACE ST-GERMAIN-DES-PRÉS

Ⓜ St-Germain-des-Prés. MAP P.124–125,
POCKET MAP B17

Place St-Germain-des-Prés is
the hub of the *quartier*, with the
Deux Magots café (see p.129)
on the corner of the square,
Flore (see p.129) adjacent and
Lipp (see p.130) across the
boulevard St-Germain. All are
renowned for the number of
philosophico-politico-literary
backsides that have shone –
and continue to shine – their
seats, along with plenty of

celebrity-hunters. Picasso's bust
of a woman, dedicated to the
poet Apollinaire, recalls the
district's creative heyday.

ST-GERMAIN-DES-PRÉS

Place St-Germain-des-Prés Ⓜ St-Germain-
des-Prés. Daily 7.30am–7.30pm.
MAP P.124–125, POCKET MAP B17

The ancient tower overlooking
place St-Germain-des-Prés
belongs to the church of
St-Germain, all that remains
of an enormous Benedictine
monastery. Inside, the transfor-
mation from Romanesque to
early Gothic is just about visible
under the heavy green and gold
nineteenth-century paintwork.
The last chapel on the south
side contains the tomb of the
philosopher René Descartes.

ST-SULPICE

Place St-Sulpice Ⓜ St-Sulpice. Daily
7am–7.30pm. MAP P.124–125, POCKET MAP B18

The enormous, early
eighteenth-century church
of St-Sulpice is an austerely
Classical building with Doric
and Ionic colonnades and
Corinthian pilasters in the
towers. The north tower is
under reconstruction work
until 2011, spoiling the aspect
of the square somewhat;
perhaps fittingly, on the south

tower you'll see centuries-old uncut masonry blocks protruding from the top, still awaiting the sculptor's chisel. There are three Delacroix murals in the first chapel on the right, but most visitors come to see the gnomon, a kind of solar clock whose origins and purpose were so compellingly garbled by *The Da Vinci Code*.

JARDIN DU LUXEMBOURG

Ⓜ Odéon/RER Luxembourg. Daily dawn to dusk. MAP P.124-125, POCKET MAP B18/19-C18/19

Fronting onto rue de Vaugirard, the Jardin du Luxembourg is the chief green space of the Left Bank, its atmosphere a beguiling mixture of the formal and the relaxed. At the centre, the round pond and immaculate floral parterres are overlooked by the haughty Palais du Luxembourg, seat of the French Senate. Students sprawl on the garden's famous metal chairs, children sail toy yachts, watch the puppets at the *guignol*, or run about in the playgrounds, and old men play boules or chess. In summer, the most contested spots are the shady Fontaine de Médicis in the northeast corner, and the lawns of the southernmost strip – one of the few areas where you're allowed to lie on the grass. The southwest corner is dotted with the works of famous sculptors.

MUSÉE DU LUXEMBOURG

19 rue de Vaugirard Ⓜ Odéon/RER Luxembourg ☎ 01.42.34.25.95. Ⓦ www .museeduluxembourg.fr. Mon, Fri-Sun 9am-10pm, Tues-Thurs 10am-8pm. Around €10-15. MAP P.124-125, POCKET MAP B18

The Musée du Luxembourg, at the top end of rue de Vaugirard, hosts temporary art exhibitions that rank among the most ambitious in Paris – recent shows have included Vlaminck and Andy Warhol.

MUSÉE MAILLOL

61 rue de Grenelle Ⓜ Rue du Bac ☎ 01.42.22.59.58. Ⓦ www.museemaillol.com. Daily 10.30am-7pm, Fri 10.30am-9.30pm. €11. MAP P.124-125, POCKET MAP A17

Occupying a handsome eighteenth-century house, the Musée Maillol is stuffed with Aristide Maillol's sculpted female nudes, of which the curvaceous *Mediterranean* is his most famous. Other rooms house work by Matisse, Bonnard, Camille Bombois, and the odd minor work by Picasso, Degas, Cézanne, Gauguin and Suzanne Valadon. The museum also organizes excellent exhibitions of contemporary art.

OUTDOOR GAMES IN THE JARDIN DU LUXEMBOURG

Shops

BARTHÉLÉMY

51 rue de Grenelle ⓂRue du Bac.
Tues–Fri 8.30am–1pm & 4–7.15pm, Sat
8.30am–1.30pm & 3–7pm; closed Aug.
MAP P.124–125, POCKET MAP E8

This aromatic nook sells
carefully ripened seasonal
cheeses to the rich and
powerful, with attendants on
hand to offer expert advice.

LE BON MARCHÉ

38 rue de Sèvres ⓂSèvres-Babylone.
Mon–Wed & Sat 10am–8pm, Thurs & Fri
10am–9pm. MAP P.124–125, POCKET MAP E9

The world's oldest department
store, founded in 1852, is
a beautiful building and a
classy place to shop – despite
its name, this is a luxury
emporium – with a legendary
food hall.

DEBAUVE & GALLAIS

30 rue des Saints-Pères ⓂSt-Germain-des-
Prés/Sèvres-Babylone. Mon–Sat 9am–7pm.
MAP P.124–125, POCKET MAP A16

A beautiful, ancient shop
specializing in expensive,
ambrosial chocolates.

SONIA RYKIEL

MARCHÉ RASPAIL

Bd Raspail, between rue du Cherche-Midi
& rue de Rennes ⓂRennes. Tues, Fri & Sun
7am–2.30pm. MAP P.124–125, POCKET MAP A18

The Sunday organic market
which takes over the broad
central reservation of the
boulevard is one of the classic
experiences of bourgeois Paris.
Come to people-watch as well
as to browse, taste and shop.

LE MOUTON À CINQ PATTES

138 bd St-Germain ⓂOdéon/Mabillon.
Mon–Fri 10.30am–7.30pm, Sat 10.30am–8pm.
MAP P.124–125, POCKET MAP C17

Superb used/end-of-line
clothes store. You might find
a Helmut Lang or a Gaultier
among the racks of bargains.
Other branches at 8 rue
St-Placide and 18 rue St-Placide
(both Mon–Sat 10am–7pm;
ⓂSèvres-Babylone).

POILÂNE

8 rue du Cherche-Midi ⓂSèvres-Babylone.
Mon–Sat 7.15am–8.15pm. MAP P.124–125,
POCKET MAP A17

This delicious-smelling bakery
is the ultimate source of
traditional sourdough *pain
Poilâne*, and great for other
baked treats.

SABBIA ROSA

71–73 rue des Saints-Pères ⓂSt-Germain-
des-Près. Mon–Sat 10am–7pm. MAP P.124–125,
POCKET MAP A17

Supermodels' knickers – they
all shop here – at supermodel
prices in this famed store.
Exquisite lingerie in buttery
silk and Calais lace.

SONIA/SONIA RYKIEL

61 rue des Saints-Pères ⓂSèvres-Babylone.
Mon–Sat 10.30am–7pm. MAP P.124–125, POCKET
MAP A17

Sonia Rykiel has been an area
institution since opening a
store on bd St-Germain in
1968; this is a younger, less
expensive offshoot.

VANESSA BRUNO

25 rue St-Sulpice Ⓜ Odéon. Mon–Sat 10.30am–7.30pm. MAP P.124–125, POCKET MAP B17

Prices start in the hundreds for these effortlessly beautiful women's fashions with a hint of hippy chic.

VILLAGE VOICE

6 rue Princesse Ⓜ Mabillon. Mon 2–7.30pm, Tues–Sat 10am–7.30pm, Sun noon–6pm. MAP P.124–125, POCKET MAP B17

Welcoming neighbourhood bookstore with a good selection of contemporary titles and British and American classics.

ZADIG & VOLTAIRE

1 & 3 rue du Vieux Colombier Ⓜ St-Sulpice. Mon–Sat 10.30am–7.30pm. MAP P.124–125, POCKET MAP B18

The clothes at this pricey Parisian chain have a wayward flair. There are two shops next door to each other selling clothes for women, men and children, the other only womenswear.

Cafés

BAR DU MARCHÉ

75 rue de Seine Ⓜ Mabillon. Daily 8am–1.45am. MAP P.124–125, POCKET MAP B17

Buzzing café in the heart of the Buci market bustle, with *serveurs* kitted out in flat caps and market-trader dungarees. *Plats* €13, *tartines* from €5.

CAFÉ DE FLORE

172 bd St-Germain Ⓜ St-Germain-des-Prés. Daily 7.30am–1.30am. MAP P.124–125, POCKET MAP B17

The rival and neighbour of *Les Deux Magots*, with a trendier and more local clientele. Sartre, De Beauvoir, Camus et al used to hang out here – and there's still the odd reading or debate. Come for the famous morning hot chocolate. Prices are high.

CAFÉ DE FLORE

CAFÉ DE LA MAIRIE

8 place St-Sulpice Ⓜ St-Sulpice. Mon–Sat 7am–1am. MAP P.124–125, POCKET MAP B17

A pleasant, ever-popular café on the sunny north side of the square, opposite the church.

LES DEUX MAGOTS

170 bd St-Germain Ⓜ St-Germain-des-Prés. Daily 7.30am–1am. MAP P.124–125, POCKET MAP B17

This historic Left Bank intellectual hangout has fallen victim to its own fame. Prices are ridiculous, but it's irresistible for people-watching. Come for breakfast (€20).

LADURÉE

21 rue Bonaparte Ⓜ St-Germain-des-Prés. Mon–Fri 8.30am–7.30pm, Sat 8.30am–8.30pm; Sun 10am–7.30pm. MAP P.124–125, POCKET MAP B16

Elegant outpost of *Ladurée*'s mini-empire, with a conservatory at the back and a decadent Second Empire lounge upstairs. The famous *macarons* are out of this world, but they also do a good, if pricey, brunch.

LA PALETTE

43 rue de Seine Ⓜ Odéon. Mon–Sat 9am–1am. MAP P.124–125, POCKET MAP B16

This venerable art-student hangout is now frequented more by art dealers, though it's still very relaxed, and the decor of paint-spattered palettes is superb. There's a roomy *terrasse* outside.

Restaurants

AU 35

35 rue Jacob ⓜ St-Germain-des-Prés
☎ 01.42.60.23.24. Daily noon–2.30pm &
7.30–11pm. MAP P.124–125, POCKET MAP B16

This adorable, intimate *bistrot*,
filled with Art Deco lamps,
murals, mirrors and old
posters, serves superb food:
try a rich *pastilla de poulet*
(chicken in pastry with honey
and spices) or a simple salmon
tartare. Lunch *menus* €18 and
€22; around €40 à la carte
without wine.

ALLARD

41 rue St-André-des-Arts ⓜ Odéon
☎ 01.43.26.48.23. Daily noon–2.30pm &
7–11.30pm; closed occasionally in Aug.
MAP P.124–125, POCKET MAP C17

Proudly unreconstructed
restaurant serving meaty, rich
standards. If it wasn't for the
almost exclusively inter-
national clientele, you could
be dining in another century.
Menus from €22 (lunch) and
€34 (dinner).

L'ATLAS

11 rue de Buci ⓜ Mabillon ☎ 01.40.51.26.30.
Daily 7am–midnight. MAP P.124–125, POCKET MAP C17

Art Deco details are the only
fuss at this unpretentious
market brasserie, which serves
good seafood and simple meaty
dishes from €14.

BRASSERIE LIPP

151 bd St-Germain ⓜ St-Germain-des-Prés
☎ 01.45.48.53.91. Daily noon–12.30am. MAP
P.124–125, POCKET MAP B17

One of the most celebrated of
the classic Paris brasseries, the
haunt of the successful and
famous, *Lipp* has a wonderful
1900s wood-and-glass interior.
Decent *plats*, including the
famous *choucroute* (sauerkraut),
start at €20, but exploring the
carte gets expensive.

BRASSERIE LIPP

FERRANDAISE

8 rue de Vaugirard ⓜ St-Germain-des-
Prés ☎ 01.43.26.36.36. Mon 7–10.30pm,
Tues–Thurs noon–2.30pm & 7–10.30pm, Fri
noon–2.30pm & 7–11pm, Sat 7–11pm.
MAP P.124–125, POCKET MAP C18

Arty photos of cows line the
flagstoned walls, and beef
dominates the menu – though
you'll also find dishes such as
minced cod with ratatouille,
oven-steamed pike-perch or
spiced strawberries in red
wine. Lunch *menu* €15;
€32/€44 at dinner.

LAPÉROUSE

51 quai des Grands Augustins ⓜ St-Michel
☎ 01.56.79.24.31. Mon–Sat 11.30am–2.30pm
& 7.30–10.30pm, Sat 7–11.30pm. MAP .124–125,
POCKET MAP C16

The food is unexceptionally
traditional, the prices inflated
and the service patchy, but
come for the experience: the
eighteenth-century building on
the Seine, the red plush seats,
gilt pannelling and endless
tarnished mirrors. Above all,
come for the private dining
rooms (lunch from €35, dinner
at €130), where you summon
the waiter with a push button.

POLIDOR

41 rue Monsieur-le-Prince Ⓜ Odéon
☎ 01.43.26.95.34. Mon–Sat noon–2.30pm &
7pm–midnight, Sun noon–2.30pm & 7–11pm.
MAP P.124–125, POCKET MAP C18

A Left Bank classic, open since
1845, this bright, easy-going
place bustles with aproned
middle-aged waitresses and
gets packed elbow-to-elbow
with noisy diners. Good, solid
French classics like *confit de
canard* or guinea fowl, with
plats from €13. *Menus* €28.

LA TOURELLE

5 rue Hautefeuille Ⓜ St-Michel
☎ 01.46.33.12.47. Mon–Fri noon–1.45pm &
7–10pm, Sat 7–10pm; closed Aug.
MAP P.124–125, POCKET MAP C17

This little *bistrot*, named after
the stone tower outside, is
packed into a low-ceilinged,
stone-walled, convivial room.
The cuisine is fresh, simple and
traditional, and service is great.
Menus €12 and €16 at lunch, €23
in the evening. No bookings.

Bars

LE 10

10 rue de l'Odéon Ⓜ Odéon. Daily
5.30pm–2am. MAP P.124–125, POCKET MAP C18
Classic Art Deco-era posters
line the walls of this small,
dark, studenty bar. The vaulted
cellar bar gets noisy in the
small hours.

CHEZ GEORGES

11 rue des Canettes Ⓜ Mabillon. Tues–Sat
2pm–2am; closed Aug. MAP P.124–125, POCKET
MAP B17

This delapidated wine bar,
with its venerable zinc counter,
is one of the few authentic
addresses in an area ever-more
dominated by theme pubs. The
young, studenty crowd gets
good-naturedly rowdy later on
in the cellar bar.

L'ECHELLE DE JACOB

12 rue Jacob Ⓜ St-Germain-des-Prés.
Tues–Sat 10am–5pm; closed Aug.
MAP P.124-125, POCKET MAP B16

Named the "Jacob's ladder" for
the staircase leading up to the
intimate mezzanine bar, this is
one for the exceptionally
well-styled "Germainopratins"
of the area, who squeeze onto
velvet loungers for flavoured
Martinis and pre-club sounds.

LES ETAGES ST-GERMAIN

5 rue de Buci Ⓜ Mabillon. Daily 2pm–2am.
MAP P.124–125, POCKET MAP C17

Bastion of boho trendiness at
the edge of the Buci street
market, with pop-retro
banquettes outside and
dog-eared armchairs inside.
Great for a coffee while watching
the street bustle and for people-
watching over a cocktail.

Club

WAGG

62 rue Mazarine Ⓜ Odéon ☎ 01.55.42.22.01.
Ⓦ www.wagg.fr. From 11pm; closed Aug. MAP
P.124–125, POCKET MAP C17

The *WAGG* pulls in a yuppie
Left Bank crowd for Eighties
music, Latin beats, and the
Seventies-themed "Carwash"
nights on Fri. Entry €12.

WAGG

Montparnasse and southern Paris

Montparnasse divides the well-heeled opinion-formers of St-Germain and the 7e from the relatively anonymous populations to the south. Long a kind of borderland of theatres, cinemas and cafés, Montparnasse still trades on its association with the wild characters of the interwar years. The artistic and literary glitterati have mostly ended up in Montparnasse cemetery, but cafés favoured by the likes of Picasso are still going strong on boulevard du Montparnasse, and there are plentiful artistic attractions: from the intimate museums dedicated to sculptors Zadkine and Bourdelle, to the contemporary exhibits at the Fondation Cartier and Fondation Cartier-Bresson. Further south, the riverside offers some intriguing attractions: to the east, the cutting-edge Paris Rive Gauche, and to the west, the futuristic Parc André-Citroën.

TOUR MONTPARNASSE

33 av du Maine Ⓜ Montparnasse-Bienvenüe
☎ 01.45.38.52.56, Ⓦ www.tourmontparnasse56
.com. April–Sept daily 9.30am–11.30pm; Oct–
March Sun–Thurs 9.30am–10.30pm, Fri & Sat
9.30am–11pm. €13. MAP P.134, POCKET MAP E11

THE TOUR MONTPARNASSE

At the station end of boulevard du Montparnasse, the 200-metre-high Tour Montparnasse skyscraper is one of the city's principal and most despised landmarks. That said, the 360° view from the top is better than the one from the Eiffel Tower, in that it includes the Eiffel Tower – and excludes the Tour Montparnasse. It also costs less to ascend, and queues are far shorter. The 56th-storey café-gallery offers a tremendous view westwards; sunset is the best time to visit.

JARDIN ATLANTIQUE

Access by lifts on rue Cdt. R. Mouchotte and bd Vaugirard, or by the stairs alongside platform #1 in Montparnasse station Ⓜ Montparnasse-Bienvenüe. Daily dawn–dusk. MAP P.134, POCKET MAP E11

Montparnasse station was once the great arrival and departure point for travellers heading across the Atlantic, a

FOUNTAIN AT THE JARDIN ATLANTIQUE

connection commemorated in the unexpected Jardin Atlantique, suspended above the train tracks behind the station. Hemmed in by cliff-like high-rise apartment blocks, the park is a fine example of Parisian flair, with fields of Atlantic-coast grasses, wave-like undulations in the lawns (to cover the irregularly placed concrete struts underneath) – and well-hidden ventilation holes that reveal sudden glimpses of TGV roofs and rail sleepers below.

MUSÉE BOURDELLE

16–18 rue A. Bourdelle ⓂMontparnasse-Bienvenüe/Falguière ☎01.49.54.73.73, Ⓦwww.bourdelle.paris.fr. Tues–Sun 10am–6pm. Free, €7 during temporary exhibitions. MAP P.134, POCKET MAP E10

One block northwest of the tower, the Musée Bourdelle has been built around the atmospheric atelier of the early twentieth-century sculptor. Rodin's pupil and Giacometti's teacher, Antoine Bourdelle created bronze and stone works that move from a naturalistic style – as in the series of Beethoven busts – towards a more geometric Modernism, seen in his better-known, monumental sculptures, some of which sit in the garden.

MUSÉE DU MONTPARNASSE

21 av du Maine ⓂMontparnasse-Bienvenüe ☎01.42.22.91.96, Ⓦwww.museedu montparnasse.net. Tues–Sun 12.30–7pm. €6. MAP P.134, POCKET MAP E10

A secretive, ivy-clad cobbled alley – a lovely remnant of the interwar years, lined today with bijou architects' studios – leads to what was once the Russian painter Marie Vassilieff's studio. Between 1912 and 1929, Vassilieff hosted fellow artists like Picasso, Léger, Modigliani, Chagall and Braque; the delightful space, now the Musée du Montparnasse, displays temporary cutting-edge exhibitions.

MUSÉE ZADKINE

100bis rue d'Assas ⓂVavin/RER Port-Royal ☎01.55.42.77.20, Ⓦwww.zadkine.paris.fr. Tues–Sun 10am–6pm. Free; €4 during exhibitions. MAP P.134, POCKET MAP F10–11

The cottage-like home and garden studios of Russian-born Cubist sculptor Ossip Zadkine, where he lived from 1928 to 1967, are occupied by the tiny Musée Zadkine. A mixture of elongated figures and blockier works are displayed in the intimate rooms, while Cubist bronzes are scattered about the minuscule garden, sheltering under trees or emerging from clumps of bamboo.

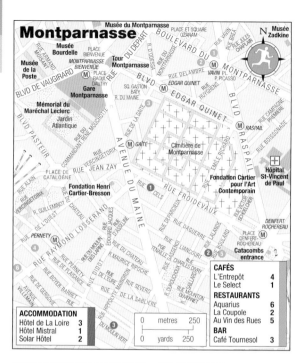

Montparnasse

FONDATION CARTIER POUR L'ART CONTEMPORAIN

261 bd Raspail Ⓜ Raspail ☎ 01.42.18.56.50, Ⓦ www.fondation.cartier.fr. Tues 11am–10pm, Wed–Sun 11am–8pm. €9.50. MAP P.134, POCKET MAP F11–12

Rue Schoelcher and boulevard Raspail, on the east side of Montparnasse cemetery, have some interesting examples of twentieth-century architecture, from Art Nouveau to the translucent glass-and-steel façade of the Fondation Cartier pour l'Art Contemporain. Designed in 1994 by Jean Nouvel, the venue presents contemporary installations, videos, graffiti and multimedia – often by foreign artists little known in France – in high-quality temporary exhibitions that use the light-filled spaces to maximum advantage.

THE CATACOMBS

Place Denfert-Rochereau Ⓜ Denfert-Rochereau ☎ 01.43.22.47.63, Ⓦ www .catacombes-de-paris.fr. Tues–Sun 10am–4pm. €8. MAP P.134, POCKET MAP F12

For a surreal, somewhat chilling experience, head down into the catacombs below place Denfert-Rochereau, formerly place d'Enfer (Hell Square). Abandoned quarries stacked with millions of bones, cleared from overstocked charnel houses and cemeteries between 1785 and 1871, the catacombs are said to hold the remains of around six million Parisians, more than double the population of the city, not counting the suburbs. Lining the gloomy passageways, long thigh bones are stacked end-on, forming a wall to keep in the smaller bones and shards, which can be seen in dusty heaps behind. These femoral walls are further inset with gaping, hollow-eyed skulls, forming elaborate geometric patterns, while plaques carrying macabre quotations loom out of the gloom. It's a fascinating place, but note that there are a good couple of kilometres to walk, and it can quickly become claustrophobic.

FONDATION HENRI CARTIER-BRESSON

2 Impasse Lebouis ⓜ Gaîté ☏ 01.56.80.27.00, ⓦ www.henricartierbresson .org. Tues, Thurs, Fri & Sun 1–6.30pm, Wed 1–8.30pm, Sat 11am–6.45pm; closed Aug. €6. MAP P.134. POCKET MAP E12

Old-fashioned networks of streets still exist in the Pernety and Plaisance *quartiers*, south of Montparnasse cemetery, where the slender steel-and-glass Fondation Henri Cartier-Bresson is hidden away. The foundation houses the archive of the great Parisian photojournalist, and showcases the work of his contemporaries and of younger photographers.

MONTPARNASSE CEMETERY

Bd Edgar Quinet ⓜ Raspail/Gaîté/Edgar Quinet. Mid-March to Nov 5 Mon–Fri 8am–6pm, Sat 8.30am–6pm, Sun 9am–6pm; Nov 6 to mid-March closes 5.30pm. Free. MAP P.134. POCKET MAP E11–F12

Second in size and celebrity to Père Lachaise, Montparnasse cemetery is an intriguing city of the dead, its ranks of miniature temples paying homage to illustrious names from Baudelaire to Beckett; pick up a free map at the entrance gate. The unembellished joint grave of Jean-Paul Sartre and Simone de Beauvoir lies right of the main entrance, while down avenue de l'Ouest, which follows the western wall, you'll find the tombs of Baudelaire, the painter Soutine, Dadaist Tristan Tzara and Ossip Zadkine. Across rue Emile-Richard, in the eastern section, lie car-maker André Citroën, Guy de Maupassant, César Franck, and the celebrated victim of French anti-Semitism at the end of the nineteenth century, Captain Dreyfus.

MONTPARNASSE CEMETERY FROM ABOVE

MONTPARNASSE AND SOUTHERN PARIS

ALLÉE DES CYGNES

Ⓜ Bir-Hakeim. MAP P.138–139, POCKET MAP A8–9

One of Paris's most charming walks leads down from the middle of the Pont de Bir-Hakeim along the tree-lined Allée des Cygnes, a narrow, mid-stream island built up on raised concrete embankments. Once you've taken in the views of the Eiffel Tower and both banks of the river, admired the passing coal barges and visited the curious small-scale version of the Statue of Liberty at the southern tip of the island, you might just share Samuel Beckett's opinion of the place – it was one of his favourite spots in Paris.

PARC ANDRÉ-CITROËN

Quai André-Citroën Ⓜ Balard. MAP P.138–139

The riverfront south of the Eiffel Tower is a dull swathe, bristling with office blocks and miniature skyscrapers; it's brightened up at the south-western extreme of the city limits by the Parc André-Citroën, the site of the old Citroën motor works. This is not a park for traditionalists: there is a central grassy

area, but elsewhere concrete terraces and walled gardens with abstract themes define the modernist space. Its best features are the huge glass-houses full of exotic-smelling shrubs, the capricious set of automated fountains – on hot days you'll see excitable teens dashing to and fro through its sudden spurts – and the tethered balloon (fine days only: 9am to roughly one hour before dusk; Mon–Fri €10, Sat and Sun €12), which rises and sinks regularly on calm days (call ☎01.44.26.20.00 to check conditions).

BUTTE-AUX-CAILLES

Ⓜ Corvisart/Place d'Italie. MAP P.137

Between boulevard Auguste-Blanqui and rue Bobillot, the lively hilltop quarter of Butte-aux-Cailles, with its little streets and cul-de-sacs of prewar houses and studios, is typical of pre-1960s Paris. The rue de la Butte-aux-Cailles itself is the animated heart of the area, lined with unpretentious, youthful and vaguely lefty bars and restaurants, most of which stay open late.

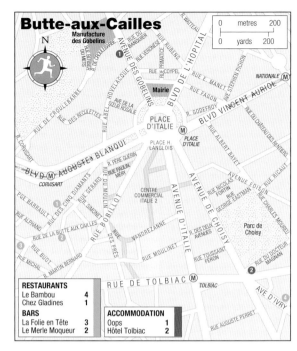

Butte-aux-Cailles

| 0 | metres | 200 |
| 0 | yards | 200 |

RESTAURANTS
Le Bambou — 4
Chez Gladines — 1

BARS
La Folie en Tête — 3
Le Merle Moqueur — 2

ACCOMMODATION
Oops — 1
Hôtel Tolbiac — 2

PARIS RIVE GAUCHE

Ⓜ Quai de la Gare/Bibliothèque François
Mitterrand. MAP P.138–139, POCKET MAP K11–L12

The easternmost edge of the 13ᵉ arrondissement, between the river and the Austerlitz train tracks, has been transformed as part of the Paris Rive Gauche development. The **Passerelle Simone de Beauvoir**, a €21-million footbridge crossing the Seine in a double-ribbon structure, sets the tone, while tethered barges have made the area a nightlife attraction. The floating swimming pool, **Piscine Josephine Baker**, is a wonderful place to do a few laps, while south of rue Tolbiac, **Les Frigos** warehouse, once used for cold-storage of produce destined for Les Halles, is now an anarchic studio space, with a bar-restaurant and occasional exhibitions.

Along Quai d'Austerlitz, warehouses are being transformed into **Docks en Seine**, an ultra-modern complex whose open spaces are set to hold a fashion museum, **La Cité de la Mode et du Design**.

CHINATOWN

Ⓜ Tolbiac. MAP P.138–139

Paris's best southeast Asian cuisine is to be found in Chinatown, home to several east Asian communities. Avenues de Choisy and d'Ivry are full of Vietnamese, Chinese, Thai, Cambodian and Laotian restaurants and food shops, as is **Les Olympiades**, a tattily futuristic pedestrian area seemingly suspended between tower blocks and accessed by escalators from rue Nationale, rue de Tolbiac and avenue d'Ivry.

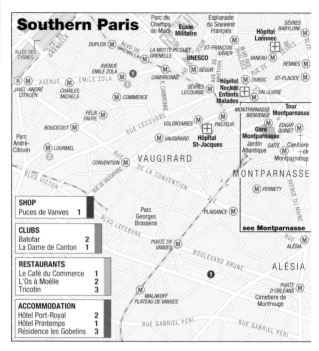

Southern Paris

Parc du	Esplanade
Champs	du Souvenir
de Mars	Français

Ecole
Militaire

SÈVRES
BABYLONE (M)

Hôpital
Laënnec (M)

ALLÉE DES
CYGNES

DUPLEIX (M)

BLVD DE
GRENELLE

BLVD DE
GRENELLE

LA MOTTE-PICQUET
GRENELLE

ST-FRANÇOIS
XAVIER

VANEAU (M)

SÈVRES (M)

RENNES (M)

BLVD
AVENUE
EMILE ZOLA (M)

AVENUE
EMILE ZOLA (M)

CAMBRONNE

(M) SÉGUR

UNESCO

BLVD DES
INVALIDES

AVE DE
BRETEUIL

ST-PLACIDE (M)

(R)(M) AVENUE
JAVEL-ANDRÉ
CITROËN

CHARLES
MICHELS

(M) COMMERCE

SÈVRES
LECOURBE

Hôpital (M)
Necker
Enfants
Malades (M)

DUROC (M)

FALGUIÈRE (M)

FÉLIX
FAURE (M)

RUE LECOURBE

MONTPARNASSE
BIENVENÜE (M)

Tour
Montparnasse

BOUCICOUT (M)

VOLONTAIRES (M)

Hôpital
PASTEUR (M)

Gare
Montparnasse

EDGAR
QUINET (M)

Parc
André-
Citroën

(M) LOURMEL

(M) VAUGIRARD

St-Jacques

Jardin
Atlantique

GAÎTÉ (M)

Cimitière
de
Montparnasse

BLVD VICTOR

RUE DE VAUGIRARD

CONVENTION (M)

VAUGIRARD

DE LA CONVENTION

MONTPARNASSE

(M) PERNETY

AVENUE DU MAINE

PLAISANCE (M)

see Montparnasse

CONVENTION (M)

Parc
Georges
Brassens

BLVD LEFEBVRE

RUE
ALÉSIA (M)

PORTE DE
VANVES (M)

BOULEVARD BRUNE

ALÉSIA

PORTE
D'ORLÉANS (M)

(M)
MALAKOFF
PLATEAU DE VANVES

Cimitiere de
Montrouge

RUE GABRIEL PÉRI

RUE GABRIEL PÉRI

SHOP	
Puces de Vanves	1

CLUBS	
Batofar	2
La Dame de Canton	1

RESTAURANTS	
Le Café du Commerce	1
L'Os à Moëlle	2
Tricotin	3

ACCOMMODATION	
Hôtel Port-Royal	2
Hôtel Printemps	1
Résidence les Gobelins	3

BIBLIOTHÈQUE NATIONALE DE FRANCE

Quai de la Gare (M) Quai de la Gare/
Bibliothèque François Mitterrand
🕿 01.53.79.40.43, 🕸 www.bnf.fr. Tues–Sat
9am–8pm, Sun 1–7pm. €3.50 for a reading
room pass. MAP P.138–139, POCKET MAP L12

Architect Dominique Perrault's
Bibliothèque Nationale
de France dominates this
modernized section of the
riverbank with four enormous
L-shaped towers – intended to
look like open books – framing
a sunken pine copse. Glass
walls alongside the trees allow
dappled light to filter through
to the underground library
spaces. It's worth wandering
around inside to experience
the structure at first hand, and
to see the pair of wonderful
globes that belonged to
Louis XIV; the garden level
is reserved for accredited
researchers only.

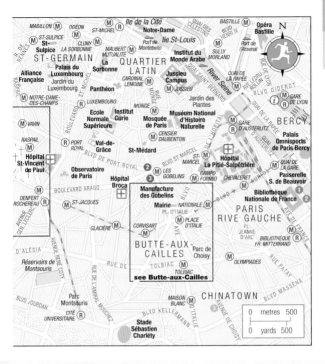

Shopping

PUCES DE VANVES

Av Georges-Lafenestre/av Marc-Sangnier
ⓜ Porte-de-Vanves. Sat & Sun 7am–1pm
(Marc-Sangnier), all day (Georges-Lafenestre).
MAP P.138–139

The city's best flea market for
original finds, bric-a-brac and
Parisian knick-knacks. It starts
at daybreak and spreads along
the pavements of avenues
Marc-Sangnier and Georges-
Lafenestre, petering out in
place de la Porte-de-Vanves.

Cafés

L'ENTREPÔT

7–9 rue Francis-de-Pressensé ⓜ Pernety.
Daily noon–2am; food served noon–3pm &
7.30–10.30pm. MAP P.134, POCKET MAP E12

This is a lively, innovative
arts cinema with a spacious,
relaxed café and outdoor
seating in the courtyard. Great
Sunday brunch for €26, *plats
du jour* for around €15–25,
and occasional concerts held
in the evening.

LE SELECT

99 bd du Montparnasse ⓜ Vavin.
Daily 7pm–2am, Fri & Sat till 4am.
MAP P.134, POCKET MAP F11

If you want to visit one of the
great Montparnasse cafés,
as frequented by Picasso,
Matisse, Henry Miller and
F. Scott Fitzgerald, make it this
one. It's the least spoilt and
most traditional of them all,
and has the lowest prices – it's
also conveniently located on
the sunny side of the street.
The food, however, can be
disappointing.

Restaurants

AQUARIUS

40 rue de Gergovie Ⓜ Pernety/Plaisance
☎ 01.45.41.36.88. Mon–Sat noon–2.30pm &
7–11pm. MAP P.134, POCKET MAP D12

The food is wholesome, if
unspectacular, at this homely,
welcoming and popular
vegetarian restaurant. Nut
roast, chilli and lasagne cost
around €12, and there's a *menu*
at €15 (€12 at lunch).

LE BAMBOU

70 rue Baudricourt Ⓜ Tolbiac
☎ 01.45.70.91.75. Tues–Sun 11.30am–3.30pm
& 6–10.30pm. MAP P.137

Tiny Asian-quarter restaurant
crammed with French and
Vietnamese punters tucking
into sublimely fresh-tasting
Vietnamese dishes, such as *pho*
soup (€8).

LE CAFÉ DU COMMERCE

51 rue du Commerce Ⓜ Emile-Zola
☎ 01.45.75.03.27. Daily noon–3pm &
7pm–midnight. MAP P.138–139.
POCKET MAP B10

L'OS À MOELLE

This huge, former workers'
brasserie is a buzzing, dramatic
place to eat, set on three lofty
levels around a patio. Honest,
high-quality meat is the
speciality; expect to pay €15–18
for a *plat*. The lunch *menu* is a
bargain at €15.

CHEZ GLADINES

30 rue des Cinq-Diamants Ⓜ Corvisart
☎ 01.45.80.70.10. Mon, Tues & Sun noon–3pm
& 7pm–midnight, Wed–Sat noon–3pm &
7pm–1am. MAP P.137

Cosy, welcoming and packed,
this rickety corner *bistrot*
serves hearty Basque and
southwestern dishes – try
mashed/fried potato with
magret de canard (€11.90), a
plat du jour for €10 or a giant
warm salad for under €10.

LA COUPOLE

102 bd du Montparnasse Ⓜ Vavin
☎ 01.43.20.14.20. Mon–Wed & Sun 8.30am–
midnight, Thurs–Sat 8.30–1am. MAP P.134,
POCKET MAP F11

The largest and loveliest of the
old Montparnasse brasseries.
Now part of the *Flo* chain, it
remains a genuine institution,
its Art Deco interior buzzing
with atmosphere. Tasty food
choices range from oysters to
Welsh rarebit, with plenty of
classics in between; *menus* at
€28 and €32.50.

L'OS À MOËLLE

3 rue Vasco da Gama Ⓜ Lourmel
☎ 01.45.57.27.27. Tues–Sat noon–2.30pm &
7.30–10.30pm; closed 3 weeks in Aug.
MAP P.138–139, POCKET MAP A11

The highlight of chef Thierry
Faucher's relaxed *bistrot* is
the €55 menu of four courses
of superb French cuisine.
La Cave de l'Os à Moelle
(☎01.45.57.28.88), across the
road, is a no-frills offshoot with
communal, help-yourself tables
laden with homely food. Book
in advance for either.

TRICOTIN

15 av de Choisy Ⓜ Porte-de-Choisy
☎ 01.45.85.51.52 & 01.45.84.74.44. Daily
9am–11pm. MAP P.138–139

Set back from the avenue at
the south end of Chinatown,
the ever-popular *Tricotin*
comprises two restaurants.
While broadly similar, no. 1
(closed Tues) specializes in
Thai and grilled dishes, and
the larger no. 2 has a longer
list of Vietnamese, Cambodian
and steamed foods. At both,
the *pho* and Thai soups,
starting at €5, are exceptional.
Plats from €8.

AU VIN DES RUES

21 rue Boulard Ⓜ Denfert-Rochereau
☎ 01.43.22.19.78. Mon–Sat noon–3pm &
7.30–11pm, Sun 7.30–11pm. MAP P.134,
POCKET MAP F12

This wonderfully unreconstructed *bistrot* offers French
classics (*andouillette*, *pavé* of
salmon and so on) and good
wines. The atmosphere is casual
and convivial. Main courses
around €20.

Bars

CAFÉ TOURNESOL

9 rue de la Gaîté Ⓜ Edgar Quinet. Daily
8am–2am. MAP P.134, POCKET MAP E11

This corner café-bar attracts
bohemian twenty-somethings
for its distressed chic, outside
tables and cool playlists.

LA FOLIE EN TÊTE

33 rue Butte-aux-Cailles
Ⓜ Place-d'Italie/Corvisart. Mon–Sat
5pm–2am, Sun 5pm–midnight. Happy hour
6–8pm. MAP P.137

The classic Butte-aux-Cailles
bar: friendly and alternative,
serving drinks and snacks in
the day and playing a wide-
ranging soundtrack, from world
music to *chanson*, at night.

LA FOLIE EN TÊTE

LE MERLE MOQUEUR

11 rue Butte-aux-Cailles
Ⓜ Place-d'Italie/Corvisart. Daily 5pm–2am.
MAP P.137

This narrow, distressed-chic
bar – which saw the Parisian
debut of Manu Chao – serves
up flavoured rums and an
alternative playlist to a young,
noisy crowd.

Clubs

BATOFAR

Quai François Mauriac Ⓜ Quai-de-la-Gare
☎ 01.53.60.17.30, ⓦ www.batofar.org.
MAP P.138–139, POCKET MAP L12

Atmospherically moored on
the river in front of the
Bibliothèque Nationale, this
lighthouse boat offers a quirky
space for electro, house, techno,
hip-hop, experimental funk
and all sorts. Entry €8–13.

LA DAME DE CANTON

Quai François Mauriac Ⓜ Quai-de-la-Gare
☎ 01.53.61.08.49, ⓦ www.damedecanton
.com. MAP P.138–139, POCKET MAP L12

Another kooky floating
venue, *Batofar*'s neighbour is
a beautiful Chinese junk that
hosts relaxed but upbeat world
music, *chanson* and DJ nights,
along with edgy music hall and
kids' shows.

Montmartre and northern Paris

One of Paris's most romantic quarters, Montmartre is famed for its association with artists like Renoir, Degas, Picasso and Toulouse-Lautrec. It long existed as a hilltop village outside the city walls, and today the steep streets around the Butte Montmartre, Paris's highest point, preserve an attractively village-like atmosphere – although the crown of the hill, around place du Tertre, is overrun with tourists. The Butte is topped by the church of Sacré-Coeur and its landmark bulbous white domes. While Montmartre continues to gentrify, brassy Pigalle still laps up against the foot of the Butte, its boulevards buzzing with fast-food outlets, cabarets, clubs and, of course, strip shows. South again is the genteel 9ᵉ arrondissement, while on the northern edge of the city, the mammoth St-Ouen market hawks everything from antiques to hand-me-downs.

METRO AT PLACE DES ABBESSES

BUTTE MONTMARTRE

Ⓜ Anvers/Abbesses. MAP P.144–145, POCKET MAP G3–H3

Despite being one of the city's chief tourist attractions, the slopes of the Butte Montmartre manage to retain the quiet, almost secretive, air of their rural origins, charming streets offering lovely views back over the city. The quickest way up is by the funicular, which is part of the city's métro system, but it's more fun to walk up through the winding streets from Abbesses métro.

PLACE DES ABBESSES

Ⓜ Anvers/Abbesses. MAP P.144–145, POCKET MAP G3

Shady place des Abbesses, featuring one of Paris's few complete surviving Guimard Art Nouveau métro entrances, is the hub of a lively neighbourhood. The streets immediately around the square are relatively

EXHIBIT AT THE MUSÉE DE L'EROTISME

chichi for Montmartre, filled with buzzing wine bars, laid-back restaurants and little boutiques – good to explore if you're after one-off outfits and accessories, and great to hang out in of an evening. From here you can head up rue de la Vieuville, from where the stairs in rue Drevet lead to the minuscule place du Calvaire, which has a lovely view back over the city.

PLACE EMILE-GOUDEAU

Ⓜ Abbesses/Anvers. MAP P.144–145, POCKET MAP G3

Halfway up steep, curving rue Ravignan is tiny place Emile-Goudeau, where Picasso, Braque and Juan Gris initiated the Cubist movement in an old piano factory known as the Bateau-Lavoir. The current building, a faithful recon-struction, is still occupied by studios. With its bench and little iron fountain, the *place* is a lovely spot to draw breath on your way up the Butte.

PLACE DU TERTRE

Ⓜ Abbesses. MAP P.144–145, POCKET MAP G3

The bogus heart of Montmartre, the place du Tertre is best avoided: clotted with tour groups, overpriced restaurants, tacky souvenir stalls and jaded street artists. At the east end of the *place*, however, stands the serene church of **St-Pierre-de-Montmartre**, the oldest in Paris, along with St-Germain-des-Prés. Although much altered since it was built as a Benedictine convent in the twelfth century, the church retains its Romanesque and early Gothic character, with four ancient columns, probably leftovers from the Roman shrine that stood on the hill (which they knew as *mons mercurii* – Mercury's Hill).

MUSÉE DE L'EROTISME

72 bd Clichy Ⓜ Blanche ☎ 01.42.58.28.73, Ⓦ www.musee-erotisme.com. Daily 10am–2am. €10. MAP P.144–145, POCKET MAP F3

Appropriately set amongst the sex shops and shows of Pigalle, the Musée de l'Erotisme explores different cultures' approaches to sex. Two floors brim with sacred and ethno-graphic art – displaying proud phalluses and well-practised positions from Asia, Africa and pre-Colombian Latin America, plus satirical European curio-sities – and feature a fascinating history of Parisian brothels; the remaining five floors are filled with temporary exhibits.

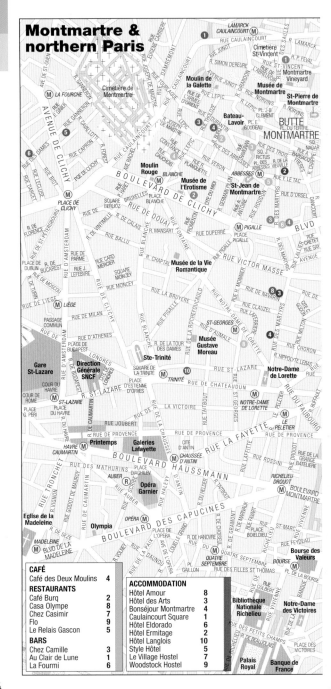

Montmartre & northern Paris

CAFÉ
Café des Deux Moulins — 4

RESTAURANTS
Café Burq — 2
Casa Olympe — 8
Chez Casimir — 7
Flo — 9
Le Relais Gascon — 5

BARS
Chez Camille — 3
Au Clair de Lune — 1
La Fourmi — 6

ACCOMMODATION
Hôtel Amour — 8
Hôtel des Arts — 3
Bonséjour Montmartre — 4
Caulaincourt Square — 1
Hôtel Eldorado — 6
Hôtel Ermitage — 2
Hôtel Langlois — 10
Style Hôtel — 5
Le Village Hostel — 7
Woodstock Hostel — 9

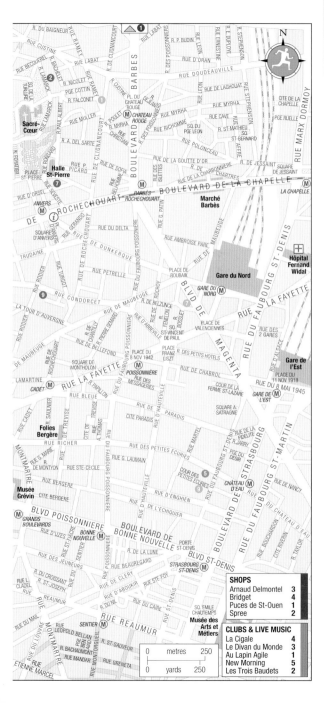

SHOPS	
Arnaud Delmontel	3
Bridget	4
Puces de St-Ouen	1
Spree	2

CLUBS & LIVE MUSIC	
La Cigale	4
Le Divan du Monde	3
Au Lapin Agile	1
New Morning	5
Les Trois Baudets	2

SACRÉ-COEUR

Ⓜ Anvers/Abbesses. Daily 6.45am–10.30pm. Free. Dome daily: April, May, Sept & Oct 9.30am–6.45pm; June-Aug 9.30am–8pm. €6.
MAP P.144–145, POCKET MAP G3

Crowning the Butte, Sacré-Coeur is a pastiche of Byzantine-style architecture, whose white tower and ice-cream-scoop dome has become an icon of the Paris skyline. Construction was started in the 1870s on the initiative of the Catholic Church to atone for the "crimes" of the revolutionary Commune, which first attempted to seize power from the heights of Montmartre. There's little to see in the soulless interior, but the view from the dome is fantastic – best enjoyed early in the morning or later in the afternoon if you don't want to look straight into the sun. **Square Willette**, at the foot of the monumental staircase, is named after the local artist who turned out on inauguration day to shout "Long live the devil!" Today the staircase acts as impromptu seating for visitors enjoying views, munching on picnics and tolerating the street entertainers; the crowds, and the guitar strumming, only increase as night falls.

MOULIN DE LA GALETTE

Rue Lepic Ⓜ Abbesses/Lamarck–Caulaincourt. MAP P.144–145, POCKET MAP G3

One atmospheric way to get to the top of the Butte is to head up rue Tholozé, turning right below the wooden Moulin de la Galette into rue des Norvins. The moulin is one of two survivors of Montmartre's forty-odd windmills (the other sits on an adjacent street corner, on top of a restaurant confusingly given the same name), and was once a *guinguette*, holding fashionable dances – as immortalized by Renoir in his *Bal du Moulin de la Galette*, which hangs in the Musée d'Orsay.

MUSÉE DE MONTMARTRE

12 rue Cortot Ⓜ Lamarck-Caulaincourt
☎ 01.49.25.89.37, Ⓦ www.museede
montmartre.fr. Daily 10am–6pm. €8.
MAP P.144–145, POCKET MAP G3

The intriguing little Musée de Montmartre, set in an old house on a quiet street, recaptures something of the feel of the quarter's bohemian days, lining its period rooms with old posters, paintings and personal photos. The house, rented variously by Renoir, Dufy, Suzanne Valadon and her alcoholic son Utrillo, also offers views over the neat terraces of the tiny **Montmartre vineyard**

THE SACRÉ CŒUR

MONTMARTRE CEMETERY

– which produces some 1500 bottles a year – on the north side of the Butte. You can walk round to the vineyard, where the steep rue de Saules falls away past the famous cabaret club **Au Lapin Agile** (see p.151); these are among the quietest and least touristy streets in Montmartre, and lovely for a romantic stroll.

MONTMARTRE CEMETERY

Entrance on av Rachel, underneath rue Caulaincourt Ⓜ Blanche/Place-de-Clichy. Mid-March to Nov 5 Mon–Fri 8am–6pm, Sat 8.30am–6pm, Sun 9am–6pm; Nov 6 to mid-March closes 5.30pm. Free. MAP P.144–145, POCKET MAP F2–3

West of the Butte, the Montmartre cemetery is an intimate, melancholy place: tucked down below street level in the hollow of an old quarry, its steep tomb-dotted hills create a sombre ravine of the dead. The graves of Nijinsky, Zola, Stendhal, Berlioz, Degas, Feydeau, Offenbach and Truffaut, among others, are marked on a free map available at the entrance.

PIGALLE

Ⓜ Pigalle. MAP P.144–145, POCKET MAP F3–H4

From place Clichy in the west to Barbès-Rochechouart in the east, the southern slopes of

Montmartre are bordered by the broad boulevards de Clichy and Rochechouart. At the Barbès end of bd Rochechouart crowds teem around the cheap Tati department stores, while African street vendors hawk textiles, watches and trinkets from the pavements. At the place de Clichy end, tour buses spill their contents into massive hotels. The area where the two roads meet, around **place Pigalle**, has long been associated with sleaze, with sex shows, sex shops and streetwalkers vying for custom. There are a few trendy bars, but it's still pretty tawdry.

THE MOULIN ROUGE

82 bd de Clichy Ⓜ Blanche ☎ 01.53.09.82.82. Ⓦ www.moulinrouge.fr. Shows at 9pm & 11pm. From €95. MAP P.144–145, POCKET MAP F3

Though its environs have lost the glamour they once had, you can't help but be drawn towards the tatty red windmill, its windows filled with photos of beaming showgirls. When Toulouse-Lautrec immortalized Moulin Rouge in his paintings, it was one of many such bawdy, populist cabarets in the area; nowadays, it survives on its reputation, offering expensive Vegas-style dinner-and-show deals to coachloads of package-tourists.

MUSÉE DE LA VIE ROMANTIQUE

16 rue Chaptal ⓂSt-Georges/Blanche/
Pigalle ☏01.55.31.95.67, ⓌWww.vie
-romantique.paris.fr. Tues–Sun 10am–6pm. €7
for (all) temporary exhibitions, otherwise free.
MAP P.144–145, POCKET MAP F4

The Musée de la Vie
Romantique evokes the era
when this quarter was the
home of Chopin, Delacroix,
Dumas and other prominent
figures in the Romantic
movement. The bourgeois
shuttered house, on a cobbled
courtyard, once belonged to
the painter Ary Scheffer; in
addition to his sentimental
portraits and the restored
period interiors, you can see
bits and pieces associated with
his friend George Sand.

INSIDE THE MUSÉE MOREAU

MUSÉE MOREAU

14 rue de La Rochefoucauld ⓂTrinité
☏01.48.74.38.50, ⓌWww.musee-moreau.fr.
Mon & Wed–Thurs 10am–12.45pm &
2–5.15pm, Fri–Sun 10am–5.15pm. €5. MAP
P.144–145, POCKET MAP F4

The little-visited museum
dedicated to the fantastical
Symbolist works of **Gustave
Moreau** was conceived by the
artist himself, to be carved out
of the house he shared with his
parents for many years – you
can visit their tiny apartments,
crammed with furniture and
trinkets. Connected by a
beautiful spiral staircase, the
two huge, studio-like spaces
are no less cluttered: Moreau's
decadent canvases hang
cheek by jowl, every surface
crawling with figures and
decorative swirls, or alive with
deep colours and provocative
symbolism, as in the museum's
pièce de résistance, *Jupiter and
Séméle*.

MARCHÉ BARBÈS

Boulevard de la Chapelle ⓂBarbès
Rochechouart. Wed 8am–1pm, Sat 7am–3pm.
MAP P.144–145, POCKET MAP H3

After World War I, when
large numbers of North
Africans were first imported
to replenish the ranks of
Frenchmen dying in the
trenches, the swathe of
Paris north of the Gare du
Nord gradually became an
immigrant ghetto. Today, while
the *quartier* remains poor, it is
a vibrant place, home to a host
of mini-communities, predominantly West African and
Congolese, but with pockets of
South Asian, Haitian, Turkish
and other ethnicities as well.
Countless shops sell ethnic
music and fabrics, but to get a
feel for the place, head to the
twice-weekly Marché Barbès,
heaving with African groceries,
exotic fish and and halal meat.

ITEMS FOR SALE AT THE PUCES DE ST-OUEN

St-Ouen claims to be the largest flea market in the world, though nowadays it's predominantly a proper – and pricey – antiques market. Mainly selling furniture, with all sorts of fashionable junk like old café-bar counters, telephones, traffic lights, jukeboxes and the like, it offers many quirky treasures. Of the twelve or so individual markets, you could concentrate on Marché **Dauphine**, good for movie posters, *chanson* and jazz records, comics and books, and Marché **Vernaison** for curios and bric-a-brac. Under the flyover of the *périphérique*, vendors hawk counterfeit clothing, sunglasses and pirated DVDs, while cup-and-ball scam merchants try their luck.

Shops

ARNAUD DELMONTEL

39 rue des Martyrs Ⓜ St-Georges. Mon & Wed–Sun 7am–8.30pm. MAP P.144–145, POCKET MAP G4

Exquisite Parisian patisserie with a funky twist, its *bavaroises*, *macarons* and tarts decorated in fresh candy colours. The award-winning bread is outstanding, too.

BRIDGET

17 rue des Martyrs Ⓜ Pigalle. Mon–Sat 11am–8pm, Sun 11am–4pm. MAP P.144–145, POCKET MAP G4

Long known for gourmet foods, rue des Martyrs is fast becoming the trendiest shopping street in Paris. This boutique stocks mostly fashionable and feminine womenswear (€60–150)..

PUCES DE ST-OUEN

Ⓜ Porte de Clignancourt. Officially (many stands closed Mon) Sat–Mon 9am–6.30pm – unofficially, from 5am. MAP P.144–145

Spreading beyond the *périphérique* at the northern edge of the city, between the Porte de St-Ouen and the Porte de Clignancourt, the **puces de**

SPREE

16 rue de la Vieuville Ⓜ Abbesses. Tues–Thurs 11am–7.30pm, Fri–Sat 10.30am–7.30pm, Sun 3–7pm. MAP P.144–145, POCKET MAP G3

This funky, feminine clothing store/gallery led by designers such as Vanessa Bruno, Isabel Marant and Christian Wijnants is typical of the trendy Abbesses scene. It also stocks vintage pieces, accessories, furniture and beauty products.

Café

CAFÉ DES DEUX MOULINS

15 rue Lepic Ⓜ Blanche. Daily 7.30–1am.. MAP P.144–145, POCKET MAP F3

Once a must-see for fans on the *Amélie* trail (she waited tables here in the film), this comfortably shabby retro diner/café is now a down-to-earth neighbourhood hangout once more – burly *ouvriers* in the morning, hipsters in the evening – serving breakfasts, brunches and standard *plats* at good prices.

Restaurants

CAFÉ BURQ

6 rue Burq Ⓜ Blanche/Abbesses
☎ 01.42.52.81.27. Mon–Sat 8pm–midnight.
MAP P.144–145, POCKET MAP G3

Trendy neighbourhood restaurant offering simple, delicious food – guacamole of peas and chorizo, dorade with asparagus pesto. The only decoration is provided by the unfailingly beautiful – not unfriendly – crowd, with whom you'll be pressed elbow to elbow. *Menus* €26/€30 at dinner.

CASA OLYMPE

48 rue St-Georges Ⓜ St-Georges
☎ 01.42.85.26.01. Mon–Wed noon–2pm & 7.30–10.30pm, Thurs–Fri noon–2pm & 7.30–11pm, Sat 7.30–11pm. MAP P.144–145, POCKET MAP G4

This classy but unstuffy little *bistrot* offers exceptional cooking featuring lots of offal and sauces with powerful, sunnily Corsican accents. Deeply satifsying set menu at €43.

CHEZ CASIMIR

6 rue de Belzunce Ⓜ Gare-du-Nord
☎ 01.48.78.28.80. Mon–Tues noon–2pm & 7.30–10.30pm, Wed–Fri noon–10.30pm, Sat & Sun 10am–7pm. MAP P.144–145, POCKET MAP H4

This no-frills corner *bistrot*, in a quiet spot a stone's throw from the Gare du Nord, is a gem: traditional but imaginative French cuisine at bargain prices (around €30), with a fine brunch at weekends.

FLO

7 cour des Petites-Ecuries Ⓜ Château-d'Eau
☎ 01.47.70.13.59. Daily noon–3pm & 7pm–12.30am. MAP P.144–145, POCKET MAP J5

This dark and splendid old-time Alsatian brasserie is so beautiful that even the stroppy service and insalubrious neighbourhood can't spoil the experience. Hearty brasserie fare, with lots of fish and seafood – and butter in everything. *Menus* €20–40.

LE RELAIS GASCON

6 rue des Abbesses & 13 rue de Joseph Maistre Ⓜ Abbesses ☎ 01.42.58.58.22.
Mon–Thurs 10.30am–midnight, Fri-Sun 10.30am–12.30am (food from noon). MAP P.144–145, POCKET MAP G3 & F3

Dishing up filling meals all day, these noisy restaurants provide a welcome blast of Gascon heartiness. Enormous hot salads start at €11.50, tasty *plats* around €12, and there's a good-value lunch *menu* at €15.50.

Bars

CHEZ CAMILLE

8 rue Ravignan Ⓜ Abbesses. Tues–Sat 6pm–1.30am, Sun 6pm–midnight MAP P.144–145, POCKET MAP G3

With an effortlessly stylish decor – creamy walls, ceiling fans, a few old mirrors, mismatched seating – this tiny bar pulls a local crowd of all ages who could just as easily be enjoying a quiet chat as dancing to Elvis or raï.

LA FOURMI

AU CLAIR DE LUNE

1 rue Ramey Ⓜ Chateau-Rouge. Daily 8am–2am. MAP P.144–145, POCKET MAP H3

Scruffily edgy bar – all neglected Art Deco fittings, 1970s shaggy pouffes and peeling 1950s movie posters – a million miles away, in spirit, from the touristy Montmartre hubbub. Drinks are cheap, and there's occasional live music.

LA FOURMI

74 rue des Martyrs Ⓜ Pigalle/Abbesses. Mon–Thurs 8am–2am, Fri & Sat 8am–3am, Sun 10am–1am. MAP P.144–145, POCKET MAP G4

Artfully distressed, high-ceilinged café-bar full of Parisian bohos sipping coffee and cocktails. Light meals available during the day.

Clubs and live music

LA CIGALE

120 bd de Rochechouart Ⓜ Pigalle ☎ 01.49.25.81.75, Ⓦ www.lacigale.fr. MAP P.144–145, POCKET MAP G4

This historic 1400-seater Pigalle theatre is a leading venue for rock and indie acts from France and continental Europe. For more rock and dance music, as well as club nights, head to *Elysée Montmartre* at no. 72 (☎ 01.44.92.45.47, Ⓦ www.elyseemontmartre.com).

LE DIVAN DU MONDE

75 rue des Martyrs Ⓜ Anvers ☎ 01.40.05.06.99, Ⓦ www.divandumonde.com. MAP P.144–145, POCKET MAP G4

A youthful venue in a former café whose regulars once included Toulouse-Lautrec, with an exciting programme ranging from poetry slams through swing nights to Congolese rumba.

PERFORMER AT NEW MORNING

AU LAPIN AGILE

22 rue des Saules Ⓜ Lamarck–Caulaincourt ☎ 01.46.06.85.87, Ⓦ www.au-lapin-agile.com. Tues–Sun 9pm–1am. MAP P.144–145, POCKET MAP G2

Painted and patronized by Picasso and other leading lights of the Montmartre scene, this legendary club – in a shuttered building hidden in a pretty garden – still hosts cabaret, poetry and *chanson* nights (€24). Touristy crowd, but authentic musicians.

NEW MORNING

7–9 rue des Petites-Ecuries Ⓜ Chateau d'Eau ☎ 01.45.23.51.41, Ⓦ www.newmorning.com. MAP P.144–145, POCKET MAP J5

One of the most exciting venues in Paris, mixed and buzzing, and *the* place to catch big international names in jazz and world music. It's usually standing room only.

LES TROIS BAUDETS

64 bd de Clichy Ⓜ Blanche/Pigalle ☎ 01.42.62.33.33, Ⓦ www.lestroisbaudets.com. MAP P.144–145, POCKET MAP F3

This historic pocket theatre was refitted in 2009, and has found a proud place on the *chanson* scene. Specializes in young, upcoming French performers. Tickets around €10–15.

The Bois de Boulogne and western Paris

The Bois de Boulogne, with its trees, lakes, cycling trails and beautiful floral displays, is a favourite Parisian retreat from the city. It runs all the way down the west side of the well-manicured 16e arrondissement. The area is mainly residential with few specific sights, the chief exception being the Musée Marmottan, with its dazzling collection of late Monets. The most rewarding areas for exploration are the old villages of Auteuil and Passy, which were incorporated into the city in the late nineteenth century. They soon became desirable districts, and well-to-do Parisians commissioned houses here. As a result, the area is rich in fine examples of architecture, notably by Hector Guimard and Le Corbusier. Further west, modern architecture brings the area bang up to date with the gleaming skyscrapers of the purpose-built commercial district of La Défense, dominated by the enormous Grande Arche.

BOIS DE BOULOGNE

Ⓜ Porte Maillot/Porte Dauphine. MAP P.155, POCKET MAP A5

The Bois de Boulogne was designed by Baron Haussmann and supposedly modelled on London's Hyde Park – though it's a very French interpretation. The "bois" of the name is somewhat deceptive, but the extensive parklands (just under 9 square kilometres) do contain

RIDE AT THE JARDIN D'ACCLIMATATION

some remnants of the once great Forêt de Rouvray. As its location would suggest, the Bois was once the playground of the wealthy. It also gained a reputation as the site of the sex trade and its associated crime; the same holds true today and you should avoid it at night. By day, however, the park is an extremely pleasant spot for a stroll. The best, and wildest, part for walking is towards the southwest corner. Bikes are available for rent at the entrance to the Jardin d'Acclimatation and you can go boating on the Lac Inférieur.

PARC DE BAGATELLE

Bois de Boulogne Ⓜ Porte Maillot. Daily 9.30am to dusk. €5. MAP P.155

The Parc de Bagatelle, within the Bois de Boulogne, comprises a range of garden styles from French and English to Japanese. Its most famous feature is the stunning rose garden, at its best in June, while in other parts of the garden

there are beautiful displays of tulips, hyacinths and daffodils in early April, irises in May, and waterlilies in early August. In June and July the park's orangery is the attractive setting for the prestigious Chopin Festival (Ⓦ www .frederic-chopin.com).

THE JARDIN D'ACCLIMATATION

Bois de Boulogne Ⓜ Porte Maillot
ⓣ 01.40.67.90.82, Ⓦ www.jardindacclimatation
.fr. Daily: April–Sept 10am–7pm; Oct–March
10am–6pm. €2.90 or €5.60 including return train
ride from métro; rides from €2.70. MAP P.155

The children's Jardin d'Acclimatation is an action-packed funfair, zoo and amusement park all rolled into one. The fun starts at the Porte-Maillot métro stop: a little train runs from here to the Jardin (every 15min 11am–6pm). The park's many attractions include bumper cars, donkey rides, sea lions, bears and monkeys, a huge trampoline and a magical mini-canal ride (*la rivière enchantée*).

FONDATION LOUIS VUITTON POUR LA CRÉATION

Av du Mahatma Gandhi Ⓜ Porte Maillot.
MAP P.155

Within the Jardin d'Acclimatation, construction of the Fondation Louis Vuitton pour la Création, a contemporary arts space, designed by Frank Gehry, should be complete by autumn 2013. Alongside galleries for permanent and temporary exhibitions, there will be activities aimed at children and a café. As with other Gehry designs, the building itself also promises to be worthy of a visit in its own right.

VILLA LA ROCHE

Square du Dr Blanche Ⓜ Jasmin
☎ 01.42.88.75.72, Ⓦ www.fondationlecorbusier
.asso.fr. Mon 1.30–6pm, Tues–Thurs 10am–6pm, Sat & Sun 10am–5pm; usually closed 1st week of Aug. €5. POCKET MAP A7

Le Corbusier's first private houses, dating to 1923, were the adjoining Villa Jeanneret and the Villa La Roche. The latter is in strictly cubist style, with windows in bands, the only extravagance being a curved frontage. It may look commonplace now from the outside, but at the time it was built it was in great contrast to anything that had gone before.

The interior is appropriately decorated with Cubist paintings.

PLACE DE PASSY

Ⓜ Passy. MAP P.155

The heart of the Passy *quartier* is pleasant place de Passy, with its crowded but leisurely *Le Paris Passy* café. Leading off from here is the old high street, rue de Passy, with its eye-catching parade of boutiques, and the cobbled, pedestrianized rue de l'Annonciation.

MAISON DE BALZAC

47 rue Raynouard Ⓜ Passy ☎ 01.55.74.41.80.
Tues–Sun 10am–6pm. Free. MAP P.155

The Maison de Balzac is a summery little house with pale green shutters, tucked away down some steps that lead through a shady, rose-filled garden – a delightful place to dally on wrought-iron seats, surrounded by busts of the writer. Balzac wrote some of his best-known works here, including *La Cousine Bette* and *Le Cousin Pons*. The museum preserves his study, while other exhibits include a complex family tree of around a thousand of the characters that feature in his *Comédie Humaine*.

EXHIBITS IN THE MAISON DE BALZAC

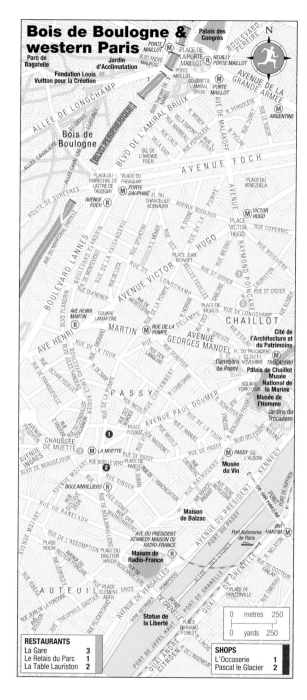

Bois de Boulogne & western Paris

RESTAURANTS	
La Gare	3
Le Relais du Parc	1
La Table Lauriston	2

SHOPS	
L'Occaserie	1
Pascal le Glacier	2

AUTEUIL

Ⓜ Michel-Ange-Auteuil. MAP P.155

The Auteuil district is now an integral part of the city, but there's still a village-like feel about its streets. It has some attractive *villas* (leafy lanes of old houses), fronted with English-style gardens, not to mention some fine Art Nouveau buildings by Hector Guimard – there's a concentration on rue de la Fontaine, such as Castel Béranger at no. 14, with exuberant decoration and shapes in the windows, roofline and chimney.

MUSÉE MARMOTTAN

2 rue Louis-Boilly Ⓜ Muette ☎ 01.44.96.50.33, Ⓦ www.marmottan.com. Tues–Sun 10am–6pm, Thurs till 8pm. €10. POCKET MAP A7

The Musée Marmottan is best known for its excellent collection of Monet paintings. One of the highlights is *Impression, soleil levant*, a canvas from 1872 of a misty Le Havre morning, and whose title the critics usurped to give the Impressionist movement its name. There's also a selection of works from Monet's last years at Giverny, including several *Nymphéas* (Waterlilies) and *Le Pont Japonais*. The collection also features some of his contemporaries – Manet, Renoir and Berthe Morisot – and a room full of beautiful medieval illuminated manuscripts.

LA DÉFENSE

Ⓜ /RER Grande-Arche-de-la-Defense/ Esplanade de la Défense. POCKET MAP A4

An impressive complex of gleaming skyscrapers, La Défense is Paris's prestige business district. Its most popular attraction is the huge Grande Arche. Apartment blocks and big businesses loom between the arch and

THE GRANDE ARCHE AT LA DÉFENSE

the river, while avant-garde sculptures by artists such as Joan Miró relieve the jungle of concrete and glass. A new wave of towers is currently under construction; most eagerly awaited is American architect Thom Mayne's **Tour Phare**, a skyscraper set to rival the Eiffel Tower in height, due to be completed in 2015.

GRANDE ARCHE DE LA DÉFENSE

Ⓜ /RER Grande-Arche-de-la-Defense ☎ 01.49.07.27.27, Ⓦ www.grandearche.com. POCKET MAP A4

The Grande Arche de la Défense, built in 1989 for the bicentenary of the Revolution, is an astounding 112-metre-high structure clad in white marble, standing 6km out and at a slight angle from the Arc de Triomphe, completing the western axis of this monumental east–west vista. Sadly, the thrillingly transparent lifts have been closed since an accident in 2010. The views from the steps that lead up to the base of the arch, however, are almost as good. For the most dramatic approach to the arch get off the métro a stop early at Esplanade-la-Défense, and walk along Esplanade de Général de Gaulle.

Shops

L'OCCASERIE

30 rue de la Pompe Ⓜ Muette/Passy.
Tues–Sat 11am–7pm. MAP P.155

Specialists in secondhand haute couture – Dior, Prada, Cartier and the like – and a great hunting ground for Chanel suits and Louis Vuitton handbags. While prices are much cheaper than new, you're still looking at around €720 for a designer suit and about €300 for a handbag. There are smaller branches nearby at 16 and 21 rue de l'Annonciation, 14 rue Jean-Bologne and 19 rue de la Pompe.

PASCAL LE GLACIER

17 rue Bois-le-Vent Ⓜ Muette.
Tues–Sat 10.30am–7pm; closed Aug.
MAP P.155

Exquisite home-made sorbets, made with Evian water and fresh fruits, in more than fifty seasonal flavours, such as sanguino orange, mango, white peach, raspberry, pear, and even rhubarb.

Restaurants

LA GARE

19 Chaussée de la Muette Ⓜ Muette
Ⓣ 01.42.15.15.31. Daily: restaurant noon–3pm & 7–10.30pm, bar noon–midnight.
MAP P.155

The focus is firmly on French classics at this renovated former train station turned elegant restaurant-bar, which boasts a huge, sunny dining room and serves, among other things, a popular €21–23 lunch *menu*. You can sit out on the attractive terrace on sunny days, and the bar upstairs (which often has samba, soul and house DJs in the evenings) is well worth a look.

LE RELAIS DU PARC

59 av Raymond Poincaré Ⓜ Victor Hugo
Ⓣ 01.44.05.66.10. Mon–Fri noon–2.30pm & 7.30–10.30pm, Sat 7.30–10.30pm; closed Aug.
MAP P.155, POCKET MAP A6

Celebrated chef Alain Ducasse's menu revolves around fish, beef, lamb, vegetables and fruit in imaginative permutations, such as milk-fed lamb with spring vegetables, or "American-style" angler fish with Madras rice. In the summer, meals are served outdoors in a lovely garden. Lunch *menu* from €29, dinner is à la carte (mains €20).

LA TABLE LAURISTON

129 rue Lauriston Ⓜ Trocadéro
Ⓣ 01.47.27.00.07. Mon–Fri noon–2.30pm & 7.30–10.30pm, Sat 7.30–10.30pm; closed Aug.
MAP P.155, POCKET MAP A7

A traditional *bistrot* run by chef-to-the-stars Serge Rabey. Game terrine with chanterelle mushrooms and *poularde fondante au vin jaune* (chicken croquettes with Arbois wine) are indicative of the upscale dishes here, and be sure to taste their famed *Baba au rhum*. The lunch menu is €26; dinner is à la carte (mains €25).

LA GARE

Excursions

Even if you're on a weekend break, a couple of major sights may tempt you beyond the city limits. It's worth making an effort to get out to the château de Versailles, the ultimate French royal palace, awesome in its size and magnificence, and boasting exquisite gardens that are free to visit. At the other end of the spectrum, there's Disneyland Paris. Love it or loathe it, the French version of the theme park offers a good variety of fear-and-thrill rides, and it's easy to visit as a day-trip.

VERSAILLES

Twenty kilometres southwest of Paris, the royal town of **VERSAILLES** is renowned for Louis XIV's extraordinary **Château de Versailles**. With 700 rooms, 67 staircases and 352 fireplaces alone, Versailles is, without doubt, the apotheosis of French regal indulgence. It's not advisable, or indeed possible, to see the whole behemoth in one day – if you can, avoid the unbearable morning crowds by heading for the grounds and Marie Antoinette's estate first, moving on to the palace proper in the relative peace of late afternoon.

THE PETIT TRIANON GARDENS AT VERSAILLES

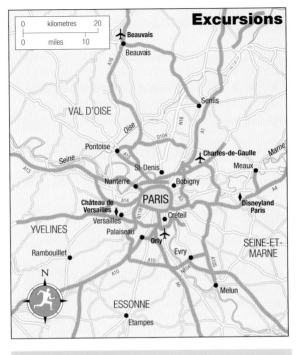

Excursions

Versailles practicalities

To **get to Versailles**, take the RER line C5 from Champs de Mars or another Left Bank station to Versailles-Rive Gauche; it's a 25-minute journey, and the palace is less than ten minutes' walk from the station.

Tickets for the **château** cost €15 (€13 after 3pm), including audioguide, while admission to Marie-Antoinette's estate is €10. Queues can be nightmarish, so by far the best option is to buy the one-day **Passeport Versailles** at ⓦ www.chateauversailles.fr (€18, or €25 during the Grandes Eaux Musicales fountain show, ie April–Oct Sat and Sun) in advance. It's available online (print at home) from branches of Fnac (see p.107), in the tourist office at Versailles (on the way to the palace), and, in Paris, on the Carrousel du Louvre (see p.187). You can also buy the Passeport at the château itself up until 3pm on the day, though this of course means queuing with everyone else. Ticket-holders walk straight in through the gate marked "A".

Guided tours (Tues–Sun 9am–5pm; €16), many of which are expertly conducted in English, take you into some of the wings and private apartments that you don't otherwise get to see. You can book online or just turn up on the day, but arrive early to guarantee a place; they're well worth it. The more specialized 90min "themed tours" have to be booked by phone (ⓣ 01.30.83.78.00); they focus on subjects such as music and women, and are usually in French.

BRONZE STATUE OUTSIDE THE CHÂTEAU DE VERSAILLES

CHÂTEAU DE VERSAILLES

☎ 01.30.83.78.00, ⊕ www.chateauversailles
.fr. April–Sept Tues–Sun 9am–6.30pm;
Oct–March Tues–Sun 9am–5.30pm.

Driven by envy of his finance minister's château at Vaux-le-Vicomte, the young Louis XIV recruited the same design team – architect Le Vau, painter Le Brun and gardener Le Nôtre – to create a **palace** a hundred times bigger. Construction began in 1664 and lasted virtually until Louis XIV's death in 1715. Second only to God, and the head of an immensely powerful state, Louis was an institution rather than a private individual. His risings and sittings, comings and goings, were minutely regulated and rigidly encased in ceremony, attendance at which was an honour much sought after by courtiers. Versailles was the headquarters of every arm of the state, and the entire court of around 3500 nobles lived in the palace (in a state of squalor, according to contemporary accounts).

Following the king's death, the château was abandoned for a few years before being reoccupied by Louis XV in 1722. It remained a residence of the royal family until the Revolution of 1789, when the furniture was sold and the pictures dispatched to the Louvre. Thereafter, Versailles fell into ruin until Louis-Philippe established his giant museum of French Glory here – it still exists, though most is mothballed. In 1871, during the Paris Commune, the château became the seat of the nationalist government, and the French parliament continued to meet in Louis XV's opera building until 1879.

Without a guide you can visit the **State Apartments**, used for the king's official business. A procession of gilded drawing rooms leads to the dazzling **Galerie des Glaces** (Hall of Mirrors), where the Treaty of Versailles was signed after World War I. More fabulously rich rooms, this time belonging to the **queen's apartments**, line the northern wing, beginning with the queen's bedchamber, which has been restored exactly as it was in its last refit of 1787, with hardly a surface unadorned with gold leaf or pretty floral decoration.

THE DOMAINE DE MARIE-ANTOINETTE

Daily: April–Oct Tues–Sun noon–6.30pm; Nov–March noon–5.30pm.

Hidden away in the northern reaches of the park is the Domaine de Marie-Antoinette, the young queen's country retreat, where she found relief from the stifling etiquette of the court. Here she commissioned some dozen or so buildings, sparing no expense and imposing her own style and tastes throughout (and gaining herself a reputation for extravagance that did her no favours).

The centrepiece is the elegant Neoclassical **Petit Trianon** palace, built by Gabriel in the 1760s for Louis XV's mistress, Mme de Pompadour, and given to Marie-Antoinette by her husband Louis XVI as a wedding gift. The airy, sunlit interior provides a lovely contrast to the stuffy pomp of the Versailles palace proper, and boasts an intriguing *cabinet des glaces montantes*, a pale-blue salon fitted with sliding mirrors that could be moved to conceal the windows, creating a more intimate space. West of the palace, in the formal Jardin français, is the Queen's Theatre where Marie-Antoinette would regularly perform, often as a maid or shepherdess, before the king and members of her inner circle.

On the other side of the palace lies the bucolic **Jardin anglais**, with its little winding stream, grassy banks and artificial grotto, and the enchanting, if bizarre, **Hameau de la Reine**, an olde-worlde play village and farm (now re-stocked with real animals) where the queen indulged her fashionable Rousseau-inspired fantasy of returning to the "natural" life.

The Italianate **Grand Trianon** palace, designed by Hardouin-Mansart in 1687 as a country retreat for Louis XIV, was refurbished in Empire style by Napoleon, who stayed here intermittently between 1805 and 1813.

VERSAILLES PARK & GARDEN

April–Oct 7am–8.30pm, Nov–March 8am–6pm.

You could spend a whole day exploring the lovely **park** (free, except when *spectacles* are on), with its symmetrical gardens, grand vistas, statuary, fountains and pools; trails of varying length are detailed on notice boards. Take a picnic, or stop at one of the tearooms, cafés or more formal restaurants dotted around the grounds. Baroque music is played in the garden (Tues spring & summer; €7.50), and on weekends the fountains dance to the music (€8.50; Ⓦwww.chateauversaillesspectacles.fr).

Distances in the park are considerable. A *petit train* shuttles between the terrace in front of the château and the Trianons (€3.50; every 15min–1hr). You could also rent a buggy (driving licence needed), a bike or a rowing boat.

THE MARBLE COURT AT THE CHÂTEAU DE VERSAILLES

161

DISNEYLAND PARIS

There are no two ways about it – children will love Disneyland Paris (ⓦ www.disneylandparis .co.uk), and the young at heart will find much to enjoy. Quite why American parents might bring their charges here is hard to fathom, though; even British parents might deem it better to buy a family package to Florida, where sunshine is assured, the rides are bigger and better, and where the conflict between enchanted kingdom and enchanting city does not arise.

Carping aside, at a distance of just 25km east of Paris, it's easy to visit as a day-trip from the capital, and there's a far wider choice of things to do than at a funfair or ordinary theme park. The complex is divided into three areas: Disneyland Park,

with most of the big rides; Walt Disney Studios Park, a more technology-based attempt to recreate the world of cartoon film-making, with a few thrill rides; and Disney Village, with its expensive hotels.

DISNEYLAND PARK

Disneyland Park has a variety of serious thrill rides, though the majority of attractions remain relatively sedate. The Magic Kingdom is divided into four "lands" radiating out from **Main Street USA**. **Fantasyland** appeals to the tinies, with "It's a Small World", Sleeping Beauty's Castle, Peter Pan's Flight and Dumbo the Flying Elephant among its attractions. **Adventureland** has the most outlandish sets and two of the best rides – Pirates of the Caribbean and Indiana

Disneyland practicalities

To **reach Disneyland** from Paris, take RER line A from Châtelet-Les Halles, Gare de Lyon or Nation to Marne-la-Vallée/Chessy station, which is opposite the main park gates. The journey takes around 35 minutes. If you're coming straight **from the airport**, there are shuttle buses from Charles de Gaulle, Beauvais and Orly, taking 45 minutes from each (every 30min–1hr from 8.30am; check ⓦ www.vea.fr/uk for timetables and pick-up points). Tickets cost €17 one-way, but children under 12 pay €13, and under-3s go free. Marne-la-Vallée/Chessy also has its own TGV train station, linked to Lille, Lyon – and London via special Eurostar trains. By car, the park is a 32-kilometre drive east of Paris along the A4: take the "Porte de Bercy" exit off the ring road (périphérique), then follow "direction Metz/Nancy", leaving at exit 14. From Calais, follow the A26, changing to the A1, the A104 and finally the A4.

Most people buy their Disney passes online, taking advantage of seasonal online offers, but you can also get them at tourist offices. Prices vary throughout the year and there is a dizzying array of options available, among them a "1-day/1-Park" ticket (from €53 adult), which allows entry to either the Disneyland Park or Walt Disney Studios Park. One-day tickets allowing access to both parks cost €64; two-and three-day tickets are also available. Tickets for children between 3–11 years tend to be €10 less than the price of adults. **Opening hours** vary, and should be checked when you buy your ticket, but are usually 9/10am–6/8/10pm, or until 11pm in high summer.

THE TEACUP RIDE AT DISNEYLAND PARIS

Jones and the Temple of Peril. **Frontierland**, loosely set in the Wild West, features the hair-raising roller coaster Big Thunder Mountain, modelled on a runaway mine train, and the gothic Phantom Manor. In **Discoveryland** there's a 3D experience called "Honey, I Shrunk The Audience", an interactive Buzz Lightyear laser battle, and the terrifyingly fast Space Mountain roller coaster. The grand **parade** of floats representing all your favourite characters sallies down Main Street USA at about 7pm every day, with smaller events, special shows and firework displays occurring regularly.

WALT DISNEY STUDIOS PARK

Though it has its share of big rides, the Walt Disney Studios Park focuses largely on what Disney was and is still renowned for – animation. You can try your hand at drawing, be part of the audience in a mocked-up film or TV set, and enjoy special effects and stunt shows. The virtual-reality Armageddon ride is genuinely thrilling – your space-station is bombarded by meteors – the tram tour through the collapsing Catastrophe Canyon is good fun, and smaller children will be bowled over by their live interactions with that crazed blue alien, Stitch.

Hotels

Paris is extremely well supplied with hotels. The ones reviewed here are all classics, places that offer something special – a great location, unusually elegant decor or a warm welcome. The grandest establishments are mostly found in the Champs-Elysées area, while the trendy Marais quarter is a good bet for something elegant but relatively relaxed. You'll find more homely, old-fashioned hotels around the Quartier Latin, St-Germain and the Eiffel Tower quarter.

Most hotels offer two categories of rooms: at the bottom end of the scale this means choosing between an en-suite bathroom or shared facilities, while more expensive places may charge a premium rate for larger or more luxurious rooms. Prices aren't exorbitant, by European standards, but then rooms can be surprisingly small for the money. Many hotels offer lower rates than those publicly advertised; the reviews below show the lowest rate you're likely to get for a double room. Continental breakfast is normally an extra €6 to €12 per person.

The Islands

HÔTEL HENRI IV > 25 place Dauphine ⓜ Pont Neuf/Cité ☎ 01.43.54.44.53, ⓦ www.henri4hotel.fr. MAP P.38–39, POCKET MAP C16. An ancient, slightly ramshackle budget hotel on a beautiful square. A narrow staircase leads to fifteen rooms spread over five storeys (no lift). Rooms are basic, but most have been renovated to an acceptable standard. Book in advance and ring to confirm nearer the time. **Doubles €78**

HÔTEL DE LUTÈCE > 65 rue St-Louis-en-l'Ile ⓜ Pont-Mairie ☎ 01.43.26.23.52, ⓦ www.paris -hotel-lutece.com. MAP P.38–39, POCKET MAP E17. This slender seventeenth-century townhouse, located on the most desirable island in France, has a cosy old-world charm and is run by helpful and friendly staff. The rooms are small, but comfy and characterful, with wood beams and fresh contemporary decor in shades of terracotta and cream. **Doubles €210**

Booking accommodation

It's wise to reserve your accommodation as early as possible. All receptionists speak some English – but it's worth bearing in mind that more and more places offer online booking as well. If you book by phone you may be asked for just a credit card number, or sometimes for written or faxed confirmation. The tourist office can make bookings for you for free – either in person at one of their offices (see p.187 for addresses) or online at ⓦ www.parisinfo; many hotels on the site offer discounted rates.

The Champs-Elysées and Tuileries

BEST WESTERN PREMIER L'HOTEL PERGOLÈSE > 3 rue Pergolèse ⓜ Argentine ☏ 01.53.64.04.04, ⓦ www.hotelpergolese.com. MAP P.48–49, POCKET MAP A5. This classy boutique hotel occupies a tall building on a quiet side street near the Arc de Triomphe. The decor is contemporary – wood floors, cool colours, chic styling – but sofas and friendly service add a cosy touch. Rooms face the street or the internal courtyard; some are a little poky but most are comfortable and well appointed, with great designer bathrooms. Doubles from €132

HÔTEL BRIGHTON > 218 rue de Rivoli ⓜ Tuileries ☏ 01.47.03.61.61, ⓦ www.brightonhotelparis.com. MAP P.48–49, POCKET MAP A14. An elegant hotel dating back to the late nineteenth century. The "classic" rooms with internal views are fine, but the "superior" rooms are much better, particularly those with magnificent views of the Tuileries gardens. Classic €180, superior €240

HÔTEL LE BRISTOL > 112 rue du Faubourg St-Honoré ⓜ Miromesnil ☏ 01.53.43.43.00, ⓦ www.lebristol paris.com. MAP P.48–49, POCKET MAP D5. The city's most luxurious hotel manages to remain discreet and warm. Gobelins tapestries adorn the walls and some rooms have private roof gardens. There's also a garden, swimming pool, health club and gourmet restaurant. Doubles from €800

HOSPES LANCASTER > 7 rue de Berri ⓜ George V ☏ 01.40.76.40.76, ⓦ www.hotel-lancaster.fr. MAP P.48–49, POCKET MAP C5. Once the *pied-à-terre* for the likes of Garbo and Dietrich, this elegantly restored nineteenth-century townhouse is still a favourite hideout for those fleeing the paparazzi. Rooms retain original features and are full of Louis XVI and rococo antiques, but with a touch of contemporary chic. There's also a superlative restaurant and zen-style interior garden. Doubles from €410

HÔTEL DE LA TRÉMOILLE > 14 rue de la Trémoille ⓜ Alma-Marceau ☏ 01.56.52.14.00, ⓦ www.hotel -tremoille.com. MAP P.48–49, POCKET MAP C6. A swanky four-star boasting understated rooms with harmonious decor and shimmering black-and-white bathrooms; room service is delivered through a specially designed hatch to avoid disturbing guests. There's also a revamped spa and gym. Doubles from €345

Eiffel Tower Area

HÔTEL DU CHAMPS-DE-MARS > 7 rue du Champs-de-Mars ⓜ École-Militaire ☏ 01.45.51.52.30, ⓦ www.hotelduchampdemars.com. MAP P.56–57, POCKET MAP C8. Cosy, colourful, excellent-value rooms in a well-run hotel. The location is great, too, in a nice neighbourhood just off the lively rue Cler market. Doubles €115

HÔTEL DU PALAIS BOURBON > 49 rue de Bourgogne ⓜ Varenne ☏ 01.44.11.30.70, ⓦ www .hotel-palais-bourbon.com. MAP P.56–57, POCKET MAP E8. This substantial, handsome old building on a quiet street in the hushed, posh district near the Musée Rodin offers spacious, prettily furnished rooms, with parquet floors and plenty of period detail. Homely family rooms (€250) are also available. Breakfast is included in the price. Doubles from €190

HÔTEL SAINT DOMINIQUE > 62 rue Saint-Dominique ⓜ Invalides/La Tour-Maubourg ☏ 01.47.05.51.44, ⓦ www .hotelstdominique.com. MAP P.56–57, POCKET MAP D8. Welcoming hotel in the heart of this upmarket, villagey neighbourhood near the Eiffel Tower. Smallish but tastefully decorated rooms are arranged around a bright little courtyard where you can sit outside among the greenery. Singles and triples available. Doubles €100–160

The Grands Boulevards and *passages*

HÔTEL CHOPIN > 46 passage Jouffroy, entrance on bd Montmartre, near rue du Faubourg-Montmartre Ⓜ Grands-Boulevards ☎ 01.47.70.58.10, Ⓦ www.hotelchopin.fr. MAP P.68–69, POCKET MAP G5. A charming, quiet hotel set in an atmospheric period building hidden away at the end of a picturesque 1850s *passage*. Rooms are pleasantly furnished, though the cheaper ones are on the small side and a little dark. **Doubles €98–114**

HÔTEL MANSART > 5 rue des Capucines Ⓜ Opéra/Madeleine ☎ 01.42.61.50.28, Ⓦ www.paris -hotel-mansart.com. MAP P.68–69, POCKET MAP A13.This gracious hotel is just a stone's throw from the Ritz, but with rooms at a fraction of the price, and while they're not quite in the luxury bracket they're very agreeably decorated in Louis XIV style. It's worth asking to see a few rooms, as three in the standard class have balconies (€225) and some have huge bathrooms. The more expensive rooms look out onto place Vendôme. **Doubles €150–350**

RELAIS ST HONORÉ > 308 rue St Honoré Ⓜ Tuileries ☎ 01.42.96.06.06, Ⓦ http://relaissainthonore.com. MAP P.68–69, POCKET MAP B14. A snug little hotel run by friendly and obliging staff, and set in a stylishly renovated seventeenth-century townhouse. The pretty wood-beamed rooms are done out in warm colours and rich fabrics. Facilities include free broadband internet access and flat-screen TVs. **Doubles €229**

HÔTEL THÉRÈSE > 5–7 rue Thérèse Ⓜ Palais Royal-Musée du Louvre ☎ 01.42.96.10.01, Ⓦ www.hotel therese.com. MAP P.68–69, POCKET MAP B14. A very attractive boutique hotel, on a quiet street within easy walking distance of the Louvre, offering more expensive "traditional" rooms, pared-down and stylish with dark wood fittings, and "classic" rooms, smaller but good value. Book in advance as it's very popular. **Doubles from €165**

HÔTEL VIVIENNE > 40 rue Vivienne Ⓜ Grands-Boulevards/Bourse ☎ 01.42.33.13.26, Ⓦ www .hotel-vivienne.com. MAP P.68–69, POCKET MAP G6. Ideally located for the Opéra Garnier and the Grands Boulevards, this is a friendly place, with good-sized rooms done up in nice woods and prints. Doubles with shower only and shared toilet €83; doubles with full bathroom €86.

Beaubourg and Les Halles

RELAIS DU LOUVRE > 19 rue des Prêtres St-Germain l'Auxerrois Ⓜ Palais Royal-Musée du Louvre ☎ 01.40.41.96.42, Ⓦ www.relaisdu louvre.com. MAP P.80, POCKET MAP C15. A discreet hotel with eighteen rooms set on a quiet back street opposite the church of St-Germain l'Auxerrois. Decor is traditional, with rich fabrics, Turkish rugs and solid furniture. The relaxed atmosphere and charming service attract a faithful clientele. **Doubles €141**

HÔTEL SAINT-MERRY > 78 rue de la Verrerie Ⓜ Rambuteau ☎ 01.42.78.14.15, Ⓦ www.hotel -saintmerry.com. MAP P.80, POCKET MAP E15. This is a unique, quirky little hotel, where you can indulge your Gothic medieval fantasies in a former presbytery attached to the Eglise Saint-Merry. There are ten wonderfully atmospheric rooms and two suites, all with dark wood furniture, exposed stone walls and wrought iron; room 9, incorporating a flying buttress, is the most popular (and possibly the most unusual hotel room in Paris). **Doubles €160, suite €335**

The Marais

HÔTEL DU BOURG TIBOURG > 19 rue du Bourg-Tibourg Ⓜ Hôtel-de-Ville ☎ 01.42.78.47.39, Ⓦ www.hotelbourgtibourg.com. MAP P.86–87, POCKET MAP F16. Oriental meets medieval, with a dash of Second

Empire, at this sumptuously designed, and perennially fashionable, boutique hotel. Tiny rooms are packed with rich velvets, silks and drapes. The hotel would make a perfect romantic hideaway. Doubles €250–270

HÔTEL DE LA BRETONNERIE >
22 rue Ste Croix de la Bretonnerie Ⓜ Hôtel-de-Ville ☎ 01.48.87.77.63, Ⓦ www.bretonnerie.com. MAP P.86–87, POCKET MAP F16. A charming place on one of the Marais' liveliest streets; the rooms are decorated with quality fabrics, oak furniture, and, in some cases, four-poster beds. The beamed attic rooms on the fourth floor are particularly appealing. Front-facing rooms may suffer from street noise at night. Doubles €145–175, suites from €200

HÔTEL CARON DE BEAUMARCHAIS
> 12 rue Vieille-du-Temple Ⓜ Hôtel-de-Ville ☎ 01.42.72.34.12, Ⓦ www.carondebeaumarchais.com. MAP P.86–87, POCKET MAP F16. Named after the eighteenth-century French playwright Beaumarchais, this gem of a hotel has only nineteen rooms. Everything – down to the original engravings and Louis XVI-style furniture, not to mention the pianoforte in the foyer – evokes the refined tastes of high-society pre-Revolutionary Paris. Rooms overlooking the courtyard are small but cosy while those on the street (€195) are more spacious, some with balconies, others with chandeliers. Doubles €145–195

HÔTEL DUO > 11 rue du Temple
Ⓜ Hôtel-de-Ville ☎ 01.42.72.72.22, Ⓦ duo-paris.com. MAP P.86–87, POCKET MAP E16. Two adjoining elegant town houses harbour this contemporary boutique hotel, with small, but stylish rooms, decorated in soothing colours. Doubles €210

GRAND HÔTEL JEANNE D'ARC >
3 rue de Jarente Ⓜ St-Paul ☎ 01.48.87.62.11, Ⓦ www.hoteljeanne darc.com. MAP P.86–87, POCKET MAP G16. A recent makeover has brightened up this budget hotel set in an old Marais townhouse, just off lovely place du Marché-Ste-Catherine. The en-suite rooms are very small, have brightly coloured walls and often clashing carpets and duvets, but it all seems to work. Doubles €96–119

HÔTEL DE NICE > 42 bis rue de Rivoli
Ⓜ Hôtel-de-Ville ☎ 01.42.78.55.29, Ⓦ www.hoteldenice.com. MAP P.86–87, POCKET MAP F16. A delightful old-world charm pervades this six-storey establishment, its pretty rooms hung with old prints and furnished with deep-coloured fabrics. Double-glazing helps to block out the traffic on rue de Rivoli. Doubles €110

HÔTEL PAVILLON DE LA REINE >
28 pl des Vosges Ⓜ Bastille ☎ 01.40.29.19.19, Ⓦ www .pavillon-de-la-reine.com. MAP P.86–87, POCKET MAP G16. A perfect honeymoon hideaway in a beautiful ivy-covered mansion off the adorable place des Vosges, it preserves an intimate ambience, with friendly, personable staff. Doubles from €330

HÔTEL DU PETIT MOULIN >
29–31 rue du Poitou Ⓜ Saint Sébastien Froissart/Filles du Calvaire ☎ 01.42.74.10.10, Ⓦ www.paris-hotel -petitmoulin.com. MAP P.86–87, POCKET MAP G15. A glamorous boutique hotel, set in an old bakery and designed top to bottom by Christian Lacroix. The designer's *joie de vivre* reigns in the seventeen rooms, with a fusion of styles from elegant Baroque to Sixties kitsch: pinks and lime greens vie with *toile de Jouy* prints, and pod chairs sit by antique dressing tables. Doubles €190–350

HÔTEL ST-LOUIS MARAIS >
1 rue Charles-V Ⓜ Sully-Morland ☎ 01.48.87.87.04, Ⓦ www.saintlouis marais.com. MAP P.86–87, POCKET MAP G17. Formerly part of the seventeenth-century Célestins Convent, this characterful, quiet place retains its period feel, with stone walls, exposed beams and tiled floors. Standard rooms have private showers, while superior ones have bathtubs; all have flat-screen TVs. The cheaper doubles are very small. Doubles €115 and €140

Bastille and eastern Paris

LE CITIZEN HÔTEL > 96 quai de Jemmapes Ⓜ Jacques Bonsergent ☎ 01.83.62.55.50, Ⓦ www .lecitizenhotel.com. MAP P.104, POCKET MAP K5. *The Citizen* is a new eco-friendly design hotel with only twelve rooms. The Zen-style decor of light wood and pale tones makes for nice, airy rooms, all of which have windows overlooking the Canal St Martin. The cheaper rooms are compact, the more expensive are twice as big. **Doubles €175**

LE GÉNÉRAL HÔTEL > 5–7 rue Rampon Ⓜ République ☎ 01.47.00.41.57, Ⓦ www.legeneral hotel.com. MAP P.104, POCKET MAP G14. This cool boutique hotel, run by helpful staff, is a lesson in restrained modern design. The bright rooms have spotless bathrooms and rosewood furnishings. Facilities include a sauna and fitness centre, and the breakfast area turns into a bar in the evenings. **Doubles €200–260**

MAMA SHELTER > 109 rue de Bagnolet Ⓜ Alexandre-Dumas ☎ 01.43.48.48.48, Ⓦ www.mama shelter.com. POCKET MAP C21. One of the most talked-about hotels in Paris, *Mama Shelter*, owned by Club Med founders the Trigano family, justifies the hype. Philippe Starck-designed, with an industrial-chic theme, it's also extremely good value. The sharp en suites come with an arty graffiti motif on the carpets and ceilings, swanky bathrooms, iMacs and decorative superhero masks. An excellent bar-restaurant, sun terrace and top-notch service complete the package. **Doubles €119**

HÔTEL MARAIS BASTILLE > 36 bd Richard-Lenoir Ⓜ Bréguet-Sabin/ Bastille ☎ 01.48.05.75.00, Ⓦ www .maraisbastille.com. MAP P.100, POCKET MAP H16. Part of the Best Western chain, this 37-room hotel has recently undergone a stylish refurbishment by interior designer Michel Jouannet. The rooms are small but bright, done out in beige, taupe and moss green, with splashes of orange. **Doubles €125**

HÔTEL DU NORD > 47 rue Albert Thomas Ⓜ Jacques Bonsergent/ Republique ☎ 01.42.01.92.10, Ⓦ www .hoteldunord-leparivelo.com. POCKET MAP K6. A pretty ivy-strewn entrance leads into a cosy reception and 23 simple en-suite rooms. The cheaper ones look onto the courtyard and are smaller and darker. Ten bicycles are available for guests to use for free. **Doubles €71–84.50**

NOUVEL HÔTEL > 24 av du Bel Air Ⓜ Nation ☎ 01.43.43.01.81, Ⓦ www .nouvel-hotel-paris.com. MAP P.100, POCKET MAP M10. A quiet, family-run hotel, with a faintly provincial air and small but neat rooms, each with private shower or bath, TV and phone. Some overlook the lovely garden (no. 9 opens directly onto it). It's a bit out of the way, but the nearby RER gets you into the centre in no time. **Doubles €95 (shower), €109 (bath)**

HÔTEL DE LA PORTE DORÉE > 273 av Daumesnil Ⓜ Porte-Dorée ☎ 01.43.07.56.97, Ⓦ www.hotel delaportedoree.com. MAP P.100, POCKET MAP M11. A welcoming hotel tastefully refurbished by an American-French family. Preserves period features such as ceiling mouldings and fireplaces, and many of the furnishings are antique, but all rooms have private shower or bath, cable TV and comfy beds. **Doubles from €60**

LE QUARTIER BERCY SQUARE > 33 boulevard de Reuilly Ⓜ Daumesnil/ Dugommier ☎ 01.44.87.09.09, Ⓦ www.lequartierhotelbs.com. MAP P.100, POCKET MAP M11. A worthy addition to Paris's stable of design hotels, *Le Quartier* is located in a cool, untouristy neighbourhood. The sleek en suites are small but perfectly formed: think smooth curves and subdued lighting, as well as thoughtful features like tea/coffee makers. Staff can be a little haughty, but are generally fine. **Doubles from €107**

HÔTEL SAINT LOUIS BASTILLE > 114 bd Richard Lenoir Ⓜ Oberkampf ☎ 01.43.38.29.29, Ⓦ www.saintlouis bastille.com. MAP P.104, POCKET MAP H14. A comfy and pleasant hotel, whose rooms are attractively decorated in soothing tones of dove grey, cream and beige, with rococo-style furnishings and Boucher prints on the walls, and sleek white bathrooms. The front-facing rooms get some traffic noise. **Doubles from €135**

The Quartier Latin

HÔTEL DU COMMERCE >
14 rue de la Montagne-Ste-Geneviève Ⓜ Maubert-Mutualité ☏ 01.43.54.89.69, Ⓦ www.commerce-paris-hotel.com. MAP P.114–115, POCKET MAP D18. Business-like budget hotel with a range of rooms from washbasin-only cheapies (€54, €44 for one person) up to modern en suites (€74) and family rooms (€144). The communal kitchen and dining area are handy, there's free internet access, and the location is excellent. **Doubles €64–74**

LES DEGRÉS DE NOTRE DAME >
10 rue des Grands Degrés Ⓜ St-Michel/Maubert-Mutualité ☏ 01.55.42.88.88, Ⓦ www.lesdegreshotel.com. MAP P.114–115, POCKET MAP E17. This charming, superbly idiosyncratic hotel has just ten rooms, so book in advance. The building is ancient and the rooms all very different, with prices corresponding to size. Unique, personal touches are everywhere: hand-painted murals, antique mirrors and curious nooks. Perhaps the loveliest room of all is under the roof, with its own stairs. Breakfast included. **Doubles €115–170**

ESMERALDA > 4 rue St-Julien-le-Pauvre Ⓜ St-Michel/Maubert-Mutualité ☏ 01.43.54.19.20, Ⓔ hotel.esmeralda ⓐorange.fr. MAP P.114–115, POCKET MAP D17. Dozing in an ancient house on square Viviani, this rickety old hotel offers a deeply old-fashioned feel, with cosily unmodernized en-suite rooms done up in worn red velvet or faded florals. A few rooms have superb views of Notre-Dame (€100–110). **Doubles €100–115**

FAMILIA HÔTEL > 11 rue des Ecoles Ⓜ Cardinal-Lemoine/Maubert-Mutualité/Jussieu ☏ 01.43.54.55.27, Ⓦ www.familiahotel.com. MAP P.114–115, POCKET MAP E18. Friendly, family-run hotel in the heart of the *quartier*. Rooms are small but attractive, with beams and *toile de Jouy* wallpaper; some have views of Notre-Dame, others have balconies. Breakfast €6. **Doubles €102–132**

HÔTEL DES GRANDES ECOLES >
75 rue du Cardinal-Lemoine Ⓜ Cardinal-Lemoine ☏ 01.43.26.79.23, Ⓦ www.hotel-grandes-ecoles.com. MAP P.114–115, POCKET MAP E19. Follow the cobbled alleyway to a large, peaceful garden and this tranquil hotel, with its pretty, old-fashioned rooms. Reservations are taken three months in advance, on the 15th of the month; don't be even a day late. **Doubles €120–145**

HÔTEL MARIGNAN > 13 rue du Sommerard Ⓜ Maubert-Mutualité ☏ 01.43.54.63.81, Ⓦ www.hotel-marignan.com. MAP P.114–115, POCKET MAP D18. Great value place, totally sympathetic to the needs of rucksack-toting foreigners, with free wi-fi, laundry, ironing and kitchen facilities, a library of guidebooks – and rooms for up to five people. The cheapest share bathrooms with one other room. No credit cards (except for over €400). **Doubles €66–103**

HÔTEL RÉSIDENCE HENRI IV >
50 rue des Bernardins Ⓜ Maubert-Mutualité ☏ 01.44.41.31.81, Ⓦ www.residencehenri4.com. MAP P.114–115, POCKET MAP E18. Set back from busy rue des Ecoles on a cul-de-sac, this hotel is discreet and elegant, with classically styled rooms. Some have period features like fireplaces, and all have miniature kitchenettes. **Doubles from €120**

SELECT HÔTEL > 51 place de la Sorbonne Ⓜ Cluny-Sorbonne ☏ 01.46.34.14.80, Ⓦ www.selecthotel.fr. MAP P.114–115, POCKET MAP C18. Situated right on the *place*, this hotel has had the full designer makeover, with exposed stone walls, leather and recessed wood trim much in evidence. **Doubles from €218**

St-Germain

HÔTEL DU GLOBE > 15 rue des Quatre-Vents Ⓜ Odéon
☎ 01.43.26.35.50, Ⓦ www.hotel-du -globe.fr. MAP P.124–125, POCKET MAP C17. Welcoming hotel in a tall, narrow, seventeenth-century building decked out with four-posters, stone walls, roof beams and the like. Rooms can be small, but aren't expensive for the location. **Doubles €99–170**

GRAND HÔTEL DES BALCONS > 3 rue Casimir-Delavigne Ⓜ Odéon
☎ 01.46.34.78.50, Ⓦ www.balcons .com. MAP P.124–125, POCKET MAP C18. Appealing, comfortable hotel with a few Art Deco motifs remaining in the modernized rooms. It's fair value, and in a lovely location near the Odéon and Luxembourg gardens. Other than those on the fifth floor, the balconies in question are small, decorative affairs. **Doubles €119–222**

HÔTEL DES MARRONNIERS > 21 rue Jacob Ⓜ St-Germain-des-Prés
☎ 01.43.25.30.60, Ⓦ www.hotel -marronniers.com. MAP P.124–125, POCKET MAP B16. A romantic hotel, with small rooms swathed in deep velvet curtains and expensive fabric wall-coverings. The breakfast room gives onto a pleasant pebbled courtyard garden. **Doubles from €205**

HÔTEL MICHELET-ODÉON > 6 place de l'Odéon Ⓜ Odéon ☎ 01.53.10.05.60, Ⓦ www.hotelmicheletodeon.com. MAP P.124–125, POCKET MAP C18. A serious bargain for a hotel so close to the Jardin du Luxembourg. Rooms are unusually attractive (especially those facing onto the *place*) and larger than most at this price. **Doubles from €120**

HÔTEL DE NESLE > 7 rue de Nesle Ⓜ St-Michel ☎ 01.43.54.62.41, Ⓦ www.hoteldenesleparis.com. MAP P.124–125, POCKET MAP C16. Eccentric and sometimes chaotic hotel whose rooms are decorated with cartoon historical murals that you'll either love or hate. Rooms are tiny, but inexpensive for the amazingly central location. **Doubles from €75**

RELAIS CHRISTINE > 3 rue Christine Ⓜ Odéon/St Michel ☎ 01.40.51.60.80, Ⓦ www.relais-christine.com. MAP P.124–125, POCKET MAP C17. Deeply elegant, romantic four-star in a sixteenth-century former convent set around a deliciously hidden courtyard. It's well worth paying the 20 percent premium for one of the *supérieure* rooms. **Doubles from €320**

RELAIS SAINT-SULPICE > 3 rue Garancière Ⓜ St-Sulpice/ St-Germain-des-Prés ☎ 01.46.33.99.00, Ⓦ www.relais-saint-sulpice.com. MAP P.124–125, POCKET MAP B18. Set in an aristocratic townhouse immediately behind St-Sulpice's apse, this is a discreetly classy small hotel with well-furnished rooms painted in cheerful Provencal colours. The sauna is a nice touch. **Doubles from €222**

HÔTEL DE L'UNIVERSITÉ > 22 rue de l'Université Ⓜ Rue du Bac ☎ 01.42.61.09.39, Ⓦ www. hoteluniversite.com. MAP P.124–125, POCKET MAP A16. Cosy, quiet boutique three-star with antique details, including beamed ceilings and fireplaces in the larger, slightly pricier rooms. **Doubles €190–250**

Montparnasse and southern Paris

HÔTEL DE LA LOIRE > 39bis rue du Moulin Vert Ⓜ Pernety/Alésia
☎ 01.45.40.66.88, Ⓦ www.hoteldela loire-paris.com. MAP P.134. On a pedestrianized street lies this delightful family hotel. En-suite doubles, with spotless, if tiny, bathrooms, are a bargain. There are cheaper options (with shared WC) in the slightly darker rooms in the annexe, which runs the length of the peaceful garden. Each room is different, and all have charming personal touches. Free wi-fi. **Doubles around €75**

HÔTEL MISTRAL > 24 rue de Cels Ⓜ Pernety/Alésia ☎ 01.43.20.25.43, Ⓦ www.hotel-mistral-paris.com. MAP P.134, POCKET MAP E12. Welcoming, cosy and pleasantly refurbished hotel on a very quiet street, with a little courtyard garden and a shared dining room/kitchen. Some rooms come with showers and shared WC facilities only (€70). **Doubles €90**

HÔTEL PORT-ROYAL > 8 bd Port-Royal Ⓜ Gobelins ☎ 01.43.31.70.06, Ⓦ www.hotelportroyal.fr. MAP P.138–139, POCKET MAP H12. A friendly, good-value one-star that has been in the same family since the 1930s. Doubles, though small, are attractive and very clean; those with shared bath are considerably cheaper (€58, showers €2.50). It's in a quiet, residential area at the rue Mouffetard end of the boulevard, near the métro and the Quartier Latin. No credit cards. **Doubles €58–89**

HÔTEL PRINTEMPS > 31 rue du Commerce Ⓜ La Motte-Picquet-Grenelle/Émile-Zola ☎ 01.45.79.83.36. MAP P.138–139, POCKET MAP B10. The cheap furnishings, thin walls and ageing decor don't prevent this being a good backpacker choice: benefits include its lively and safe neighbourhood location, cheery welcome and low prices. The nicer rooms have small balconies. **Doubles €50**

RÉSIDENCE LES GOBELINS > 9 rue des Gobelins Ⓜ Gobelins ☎ 01.47.07.26.90, Ⓦ www.hotelgobelins.com. MAP P.138–139, POCKET MAP H12. Nicely old-fashioned and quiet place, with a flower-filled garden, on a narrow street an easy walk away from the Quartier Latin's rue Mouffetard. Its large, simple, comfortable rooms are a well-known bargain, so book in advance. **Doubles €98**

HÔTEL TOLBIAC > 122 rue de Tolbiac Ⓜ Tolbiac/Place d'Italie ☎ 01.44.24.25.54, Ⓦ www.hotel-tolbiac.com. MAP P.137. Situated on a noisy junction, this big, friendly budget hotel has a bright colour scheme, free internet and wi-fi, and good prices (doubles with shared facilities for €50). **Doubles €67**

SOLAR HÔTEL > 22 rue Boulard Ⓜ Denfert-Rochereau ☎ 01.43.21.08.20, Ⓦ www.solarhotel.fr. MAP P.134,

POCKET MAP F12. Set on an old-fashioned Montparnasse street, this budget hotel has an original and friendly spirit – there are paintings by local artists on the walls, cultural events in the back garden and the hotel strives to be ecological, with low-energy fittings, organic breakfasts and free bike rental. Don't be put off by the exterior: rooms are basic, but comfortable and bright, with a/c, TV and free wi-fi. **Doubles €69**

Montmartre and northern Paris

HÔTEL AMOUR > 8 rue Navarin Ⓜ Pigalle ☎ 01.48.78.31.80, Ⓦ www.hotelamourparis.fr. MAP P.144–145, POCKET MAP G4. Designer hotel for an achingly cool clientele, with old parquet, new paintwork and a deliberately boho Pigalle porn theme. Every room is decorated differently – one is all black with disco balls above the bed – but none has phone or TV, and all have iPod speakers. There's also a spacious dining area and a vodka bar. **Doubles from €155**

HÔTEL DES ARTS > 5 rue Tholozé Ⓜ Abbesses/Blanche ☎ 01.46.06.30.52, Ⓦ www.montmartrehotel.com. MAP P.144–145, POCKET MAP G3. The decor is a little bland but the welcome excellent (not least from the family dog) and the location – on a romantically sloping, cobbled street in the heart of the Abbesses quarter, opposite a classic arts cinema –fantastic. The "superior" rooms have fine views. **Doubles from €95–140**

HÔTEL BONSÉJOUR MONTMARTRE > 11 rue Burq Ⓜ Abbesses ☎ 01.42.54.22.53, Ⓦ www.hotel-bonsejour-montmartre.fr. MAP P.144–145, POCKET MAP G3. The location is a dream – on a quiet, untouristy street on the slopes of Montmartre, footsteps away from great neighbourhood bars and restaurants – and the simple, old-fashioned, clean rooms (with shower, WC down the hall) are a serious bargain. Ask for the corner rooms 23, 33, 43 or 53, which have balconies. **Doubles from €68**

CAULAINCOURT SQUARE > 2 sq Caulaincourt, by 63 rue Caulaincourt Ⓜ Lamarck-Caulaincourt ☎ 01.46.06.46.06, Ⓦ www.caulaincourt .com. MAP P.144–145, POCKET MAP G2. You can choose shared facilities (€59) or en suites at this lively budget hotel/ hostel on the heights of Montmartre. Dorm beds are €29–31 a night. Rooms are small and faintly shabby but decent enough, and breakfast is free. Free wi-fi; bike rental available. **Doubles €70–80**

HÔTEL ELDORADO > 18 rue des Dames Ⓜ Place-de-Clichy ☎ 01.45.22.35.21, Ⓦ www.eldoradohotel.fr. MAP P.144–145, POCKET MAP E3. Idiosyncratic hotel in the bohemian Batignolles village. Characterful rooms with some vintage fittings are brightened up with vivid colour schemes and furnishings, and there's a secluded annexe at the back of the courtyard garden. Rooms with shared bath available for €58. Good onsite *bistrot*. **Doubles €58–85**

HÔTEL ERMITAGE > 24 rue Lamarck Ⓜ Anvers ☎ 01.42.64.79.22, Ⓦ www.ermitagesacrecoeur.fr. MAP P.144–145, POCKET MAP H3. Hushed, family-run hotel set on the lofty heights behind Sacré-Coeur. Rooms are old-fashioned and chintzy; those at the back have views across northern Paris. Complimentary breakfast served in rooms. Approach via the funicular to avoid a steep climb. No credit cards. **Doubles €96**

HÔTEL LANGLOIS > 63 rue St-Lazare Ⓜ Trinité ☎ 01.48.74.78.24, Ⓦ www .hotel-langlois.com. MAP P.144–145, POCKET MAP F5. Despite having all the facilities of a two-star, this genteel hotel has barely changed in the last century, with antique furnishings and some handsome rooms. **Doubles €140**

STYLE HÔTEL > 8 rue Ganneron (av Clichy end) Ⓜ Place-de-Clichy ☎ 01.45.22.37.59. MAP P.144–145, POCKET MAP F3. An unpromising exterior in Batignolles hides a really lovely budget place, with wooden floors, marble fireplaces and a secluded courtyard. Great value, especially the rooms with shared bathrooms (€40). **Doubles €60**

Hostels

Hostels are an obvious choice for a tight budget, but won't necessarily be cheaper than sharing a room in a budget hotel. Many take advance bookings, including all three main hostel groups: FUAJ (Ⓦ www.fuaj.fr), which is part of Hostelling International; UCRIF (Ⓦ www.ucrif.asso.fr), which caters largely to groups; and MIJE (Ⓦ www.mije.com), which runs three excellent hostels in historic buildings in the Marais. Independent hostels tend to be noisier places, often with bars attached.

D'ARTAGNAN > 80 rue Vitruve Ⓜ Porte-de-Bagnolet ☎ 01.40.32.34.56, Ⓦ www.fuaj.org. POCKET MAP C21. This colourful, modern HI hostel is the largest in France with 440 beds and facilities including a small cinema, restaurant and bar, internet access and a swimming pool nearby. Guests have to vacate the rooms between 11am and 3pm for cleaning. It's very popular, so get here early or book online or by phone on the central reservations number: ☎ 01.44.89.87.27. Doubles and rooms for three to five are a few euros more per head than the dorm price. **Dorm beds from €27.80**

BVJ LOUVRE > 20 rue Jean-Jacques-Rousseau Ⓜ Louvre/Châtelet-Les-Halles ☎ 01.53.00.90.90, Ⓦ www.bvjhotel .com. MAP P.68–69, POCKET MAP C14.

With 200 beds, the *BVJ Louvre* attracts an international studenty crowd, though dorms (sleeping eight) have a slightly institutional feel. Single rooms are available. **Dorm beds €30, twins €70**

BVJ PARIS QUARTIER LATIN > 44 rue des Bernardins Ⓜ Maubert-Mutualité ☎ 01.43.29.34.80, Ⓦ www.bvjhotel.com. MAP P.114–115, POCKET MAP E18. Spick and span hostel in a good location. Single rooms (€45) and dorm beds are good value; for double rooms (€66) you can do better elsewhere. **Dorm beds €29**

LE FAUCONNIER > 11 rue du Fauconnier Ⓜ St-Paul/Pont Marie ☎ 01.42.74.23.45, Ⓦ www.mije.com. MAP P.86–87, POCKET MAP F17. MIJE hostel in a superbly renovated seventeenth-century building. Dorms sleep three to eight, and there are some single (€51) and double rooms too (€76), with en-suite showers. **Dorm beds €31**

LE FOURCY > 6 rue de Fourcy Ⓜ St Paul ☎ 01.42.74.23.45. MAP P.86–87, POCKET MAP F17. Another excellent MIJE hostel (same prices and deal as *Le Fauconnier*, see above). Housed in a beautiful mansion, this place has a small garden and an inexpensive restaurant. Doubles and triples also available.

JULES FERRY > 8 bd Jules-Ferry Ⓜ République ☎ 01.43.57.55.60, Ⓦ www.fuaj.fr. MAP P.104, POCKET MAP H13. Fairly central HI hostel, in a lively area at the foot of the Belleville hill. Difficult to get a place, but they can help find a bed elsewhere. Two to four people in each room. **Dorm beds from €25.80**

MAUBUISSON > 12 rue des Barres Ⓜ Pont Marie/Hôtel de Ville ☎ 01.42.74.23.45. MAP P.86–87, POCKET MAP F16. A MIJE hostel in a magnificent medieval building on a quiet street. Shared use of the restaurant at *Le Fourcy* (see above). Dorms only, sleeping four. **Dorm beds €31**

OOPS > 50 ave des Gobelins Ⓜ Gobelins ☎ 01.47.07.47.00, Ⓦ www.oops-paris.com. MAP P.137, POCKET MAP J12. This "design hostel", opened in 2007, is brightly decorated with funky patterns. All dorms are en suite, there's free wi-fi, a/c and a basic breakfast, and it's open 24 hours. Private doubles from €80–100. Unexceptional location, but it's just a couple of métro stops south of the Quartier Latin. **Dorm beds €28–32**

ST CHRISTOPHER'S PARIS > 68–74 Quai de la Seine Ⓜ Crimée/Laumière ☎ 01.40.34.34.40, Ⓦ www.st-christophers.co.uk/paris-hostels. MAP P.104, POCKET MAP L3. Massive hostel overlooking the waters of the Bassin de la Villette – some way from the centre. Rooms sleep six to eight and are pleasant in a functional, cabin-like way, but there's a great bar, inexpensive restaurant, and free internet access. As well as dorms there are also twins and doubles available. **Dorm beds €27–37**

LE VILLAGE HOSTEL > 20 rue d'Orsel Ⓜ Anvers ☎ 01.42.64.22.02, Ⓦ www.villagehostel.fr. MAP P.144–145, POCKET MAP H3. Attractive independent hostel in a handsome building, with good facilities and a view of Sacré-Coeur from the terrace. Breakfast included. Small discounts in winter. **Dorm beds €28–48**

WOODSTOCK HOSTEL > 48 rue Rodier Ⓜ Anvers/St-Georges ☎ 01.48.78.87.76, Ⓦ www.woodstock.fr. MAP P.144–145, POCKET MAP H4. A reliable hostel with its own bar, set in a great location on a pretty street near Montmartre. Breakfast included. **Dorm beds €25–27**

YOUNG AND HAPPY HOSTEL > 80 rue Mouffetard Ⓜ Monge/Censier-Daubenton ☎ 01.47.07.47.07, Ⓦ www.youngandhappy.fr. MAP P.114–115, POCKET MAP H11. Noisy, basic and studenty independent hostel in a lively, touristy location. Dorms, with shower, sleep four, and there are a few doubles (€26 per person). Lockout 11am–4pm. **Dorm beds from €19–30**

Arrival

It's easy to get from both of Paris's main airports to the city centre using the efficient public transport links. The budget airline airport, Beauvais, is served by buses. If you're arriving by train, of course, it's easier still: just get on the métro.

By air

The two main Paris **airports** that deal with international flights are Roissy-Charles de Gaulle and Orly, both well connected to the centre. Information on them can be found on ⓦ www.aeroportsdeparis.fr. A third airport, Beauvais, is used by Ryanair. Bear in mind that you can buy a Paris Visite card at the airports which will cover multiple journeys to and within the city (see p.181).

ROISSY-CHARLES DE GAULLE AIRPORT

Roissy-Charles de Gaulle Airport (24hr information in English ⓣ 01.70.36.39.50), usually referred to as Charles de Gaulle and abbreviated to CDG, is 23km northeast of the city. The airport has two main terminals linked by a shuttle bus.

The simplest way to reach the city centre is by the **Roissyrail** train link, on RER line B, which takes thirty minutes (every 15min 5am–midnight; €9.25 one way). You can pick it up direct at CDG 2, but from CDG 1 you have to get a shuttle bus (*navette*) to the RER station first. The train is fast to Gare du Nord, then stops at Châtelet-Les Halles, St-Michel and Denfert-Rochereau, all of which have métro stations for onward travel. Ordinary commuter trains also run on this line, but make more stops and have fewer facilities for luggage storage.

Various **bus companies** provide services from the airport direct to a number of city-centre locations, though may take longer than Roissy-rail. The **Roissybus**, for instance, connects CDG 1 and CDG 2 with the Opéra-Garnier (corner of rues Auber and Scribe; ⓜ Opéra/RER Auber); it runs every fifteen to thirty minutes from 5.45am to 11pm, costs €10 one-way and takes around an hour. There are also two Air France buses (ⓦ http://videocdn.airfrance.com/cars-airfrance): one stops outside Charles-de-Gaulle-Etoile RER/métro and the other at the Gare de Lyon before terminating near the Gare Montparnasse. Timings are similar to the Roissybus, but tickets are more expensive at €24–27 return.

A more useful alternative is the **minibus door-to-door service**, Paris Blue, which costs from €32 for two people, with no extra charge for luggage. It operates round-the-clock but bookings must be made at least 24 hours in advance on ⓣ 01.30.11.13.00 or via ⓦ www.paris-blue-airport-shuttle.fr.

Taxis into central Paris from CDG cost around €50 on the meter and should take between fifty minutes and an hour. Note that if your flight gets in after midnight your only means of transport is a taxi or the minibus service.

ORLY AIRPORT

Orly Airport (ⓣ 01.70.36.39.50), 14km south of Paris, has two terminals, Orly Sud (south; for international flights) and Orly Ouest (west; for domestic flights), linked by shuttle bus but easily walkable.

The easiest way into the centre is the **Orlyval**, a fast train shuttle link to RER station Antony, from where you can pick up RER line B trains to the central RER/métro stations

Denfert-Rochereau, St-Michel and Châtelet-Les Halles; it runs every four to seven minutes from 6am to 11pm (€10.90 one way including shuttle; 35min to Châtelet). Another service connecting with the RER is the "**Paris par le train" shuttle bus** (*navette*): this takes you to RER line C station Pont de Rungis, from where trains leave every twenty minutes from 5am to 11.30pm for the Gare d'Austerlitz and other métro connection stops (€6.45 one way; train 35min, total journey around 50min). Leaving Paris, the train runs from Gare d'Austerlitz from 5.40am to 10.40pm.

Taxis take about 35 minutes to the city centre and cost around €35.

BEAUVAIS AIRPORT

Beauvais Airport (☎ 08.92.68.20.66, ⓦ www.aeroportbeauvais.com) is a fair distance from Paris – some 65km northwest – and is used by Ryanair. Coaches (€15 one-way) shuttle between the airport and Porte Maillot, at the northwestern edge of Paris, where you can pick up métro line 1 to the centre. Coaches take about an hour, and leave between fifteen and thirty minutes after the flight has arrived and about three hours before the flight departs on the way back. Tickets can be bought via the airport's website, at Arrivals or from the Beauvais shop at 1 boulevard Pershing, near the Porte Maillot terminal.

By rail

Eurostar (☎ 08.92.35.35.39, ⓦ www.eurostar.com) trains terminate at the **Gare du Nord** in the northeast of the city – a bustling convergence of international, long-distance and suburban trains, the métro and several bus routes. Coming off the train, turn left for the métro and the

RER, immediately right and through the side door for taxis (roughly €10 to the centre). The Eurostar offices and check-in point for departures are both located on the mezzanine level, above the main station entrance.

Gare du Nord is also the arrival point for trains from Calais and northern European countries, such as Belgium. Paris has five other mainline train stations, part of the national SNCF network: the **Gare de l'Est** serves eastern France and central and eastern Europe; the **Gare St-Lazare** serves the Normandy coast and Dieppe; the **Gare de Lyon** serves Italy, Switzerland and TGV trains to southeast France. South of the river, the **Gare Montparnasse** is the terminus for Chartres, Brittany, the Atlantic coast and TGV lines to southwest France and the Loire Valley; the **Gare d'Austerlitz** runs ordinary trains to the Loire Valley and the Dordogne. The motorail station, **Gare de Paris-Bercy**, is down the tracks from the Gare de Lyon on boulevard de Bercy.

For **information** on national train services and reservations phone ☎ 36.35 (within France only), or consult: ⓦ www.sncf.com. For information on suburban lines call ☎ 36.58 or look up ⓦ www.transilien.com. You can buy **tickets** at any train station, at travel agents and online at the SNCF website.

By road

If arriving by bus – international or domestic – you'll almost certainly arrive at the main **Gare Routière**, at the eastern edge of the city; métro Gallieni (line 3) links it to the centre. If you're driving in yourself, don't travel straight across the city. Use the ring road – the **boulevard périphérique** – to get around to the nearest *porte*: it's quicker, except at rush hour, and easier to navigate.

Getting around

While walking is undoubtedly the best way to discover Paris, the city's integrated **public transport system** of bus, métro, tram and trains – the RATP (Régie Autonome des Transports Parisiens; ⓦ www .ratp.fr) – is reasonably priced, fast and meticulously signposted. You'll find a métro map at the front of this book; alternatively, free métro and bus maps of varying sizes and detail are available at most stations, bus terminals and tourist offices: the largest and most useful is the *Grand Plan de Paris numéro 2*, which overlays the métro, RER and bus routes on a map of the city so you can see exactly how transport lines and streets match up. If you just want a handy pocket-sized métro/ bus map ask for the *Petit Plan de Paris* or the smaller *Paris Plan de Poche*. You can download a useful searchable interactive online version at ⓦ www.ratp.fr.

Tickets and passes

For a short stay, it's worth buying a **carnet** of ten tickets, available from any station or *tabac* (€12.70, as opposed to €1.70 for an individual ticket, or €1.90 when bought on buses). The RATP is divided into **five zones**, and the métro system itself more or less fits into zones 1 and 2. The same tickets are valid for the buses (including the night bus), métro and, within the city limits and immediate suburbs (zones 1 and 2), the RER express rail lines, which also extend far out into the Ile de France. Only one ticket is ever needed on the métro system, and within zones 1 and 2 for any RER or bus journey, but you can't switch between buses or between bus and métro/RER on the same ticket. Children under 4 travel free and from ages 4 to 10 at half-price. Don't buy from the touts who hang round the main stations – you may pay well over the odds, quite often for a used ticket – and be sure to keep your ticket until the end of

Touring Paris by public transport

A good way to take in the sights is to hop on a **bus**. Bus #20 (wheelchair accessible) from the Gare de Lyon follows the Grands Boulevards and does a loop through the 1er and 2e arrondissements. Bus #24 (also wheelchair accessible) between Porte de Bercy and Gare St-Lazare follows the left bank of the Seine. Bus #29 is one of the best routes for taking in the city: it ventures from the Gare St-Lazare past the Opéra Garnier, the Bourse and the Centre Pompidou, through the Marais and past Bastille to the Gare de Lyon. For La Voie Triomphale, take a trip on bus #73 between La Défense and the Musée d'Orsay, while bus #63 drives a scenic route along the Seine on the Rive Gauche, then crosses the river and heads up to Trocadéro, where there are wonderful views of the Eiffel Tower. Many more bus journeys – outside rush hours – are worthwhile trips in themselves: get hold of the *Grand Plan de Paris* from a métro station and check out the routes of buses #38, #48, #64, #67, #68, #69, #82, #87 and #95.

The **métro**, surprisingly, can also provide some scenery: the overground line on the southern route between Charles-de-Gaulle-Etoile and Nation (line 6) gives you views of the Eiffel Tower, the Ile des Cygnes, the Invalides, the new Bibliothèque Nationale and the Finance Ministry.

Fly Less – Stay Longer!

Rough Guides believes in the good that travel does, but we are deeply aware of the impact of fuel emissions on climate change. We recommend taking fewer trips and staying for longer. If you can avoid travelling by air, please use an alternative, especially for journeys of under 1000km/600miles. And always offset your travel at ⓦ www.roughguides.com/climatechange.

the journey as you'll be fined on the spot if you can't produce one.

If you're doing a fair number of journeys for just one day, it might be worth getting a **Mobilis day pass** (€6.40 for zones 1 and 2; €8.55 zones 1–3), which offers unlimited access to the métro, buses, trams and, depending on which zones you choose, the RER – note that the Mobilis pass is not valid to or from the airports.

Other possibilities are the **Paris Visite** passes (ⓦ www.ratp.info/touristes), one-, two-, three- and five-day visitors' passes at €9.75, €15.85, €21.60 and €31.15 for Paris and close suburbs, or €20.50, €31.15, €44.65 and €53.40 to include the airports, Versailles and Disneyland Paris (make sure you buy this one when you arrive at Roissy-Charles de Gaulle or Orly to get maximum value). A half-price child's version is also available. You can buy them from métro and RER stations, tourist offices and online from ⓦ www.helloparis.co.uk or ⓦ www.parismetro.com. Paris Visite passes become valid on the first day you use them and entitle you to unlimited travel (in the zones you have chosen) on bus, métro, trams, RER, SNCF, the Montmartrobus around Montmartre and the Montmartre funicular between the hours of 5.30am and 1.30am; they also allow you discounts at certain monuments, museums and tours, including day tickets to Disneyland Paris. If you're going to Paris by Eurostar, you could

save time by buying passes from the info point at the St Pancras International Eurostar terminal.

The métro and RER

The **métro**, combined with the **RER** (Réseau Express Régional) suburban express lines, is the simplest way of moving around the city. The métro runs from 5.20am to 1.20am, RER trains from 4.45am to 1.30am. Stations (abbreviated: ⓂConcorde, RER Luxembourg, etc) are evenly spaced and you'll rarely find yourself more than 500m from one in the centre, though the interchanges can involve a lot of legwork, including many stairs. Every station has a big plan of the network outside the entrance and several inside, as well as a map of the local area. The métro lines are colour-coded and designated by numbers for the métro and by letters for the RER, although they are signposted within the system with the names of the terminus stations: for example, travelling from Montparnasse to Châtelet, you follow the sign "Direction Porte-de-Clignancourt"; from Gare d'Austerlitz to Grenelle on line 10 you follow "Direction Boulogne–Pont-de-St-Cloud". The numerous interchanges (*correspondances*) make it possible to travel all over the city in a more or less straight line. For RER journeys beyond the city, make sure that the station you want is illuminated on the platform display board.

Buses and trams

The city's **buses** (5.30am–8.30pm, with some continuing to 1.30am) are easy to use, and allow you to see much more than on the métro. However, many lines don't operate on Sundays and holidays – log onto ⓦ www.ratp.fr for a map of the most useful tourist routes.

Bus stops display the name of the stop, the numbers of the buses that stop there, a map showing all the stops on the route, and the times of the first and last services. As with all forms of transport you can buy a single ticket (€1.70, or €1.90 from the driver), or a pre-purchased carnet ticket or pass (see p.180); insert it into one of the machines on board to validate. Press the red button to request a stop.

On Sunday afternoons and holidays from mid-April to mid-September, a special **Balabus service** (not to be confused with Batobus, see opposite) passes all the major tourist sights between the Grande Arche de la Défense and Gare de Lyon (every 15–20min noon–9pm). Bus stops are marked "Balabus", and you'll need one to three bus tickets, depending on the length of your journey. Paris Visite and Mobilis passes are also valid.

Night buses (Noctilien; ⓦ www .noctilien.fr) ply 47 routes at least every hour from 12.30am to 5.30am between place du Châtelet and the suburbs. Details of routes are available online.

There are currently four **tram lines** in and around Paris, with more planned; currently the most useful is line T3, which runs along the southern edge of the city from the Pont du Garigliano on the Seine in the 15e arrondissement to Pont d'Ivry métro. Trams every five or ten minutes or so between 4.50am and 11.40pm; stops are marked by a large "T".

Taxis

Taxi charges are fairly reasonable, though considerably more if you call one out; there's a pick-up charge of €2.30. The minimum charge for a journey is €6.20, and you'll pay €1 for each piece of luggage. Waiting time costs from €29.95 an hour. Drivers don't have to take more than three passengers (they don't like people sitting in the front); if a fourth passenger is accepted, €3 will be added to the fare. A **tip** of ten percent is expected.

Waiting at a **taxi rank** (arrêt taxi) is usually more effective than hailing one from the street. If the large green light on top of the vehicle is lit up, the taxi is free. Taxis can be rather thin on the ground at lunchtime and after 7pm, when you might prefer to call one out – the main firms are all on one number (ⓣ 01.45.30.30.30).

Cycling

Parisians have taken enthusiastically to Velib' (ⓦ www.velib.paris.fr), the self-service bike scheme set up in 2007. Thousands of sleek, modern – and heavy – bicycles are stationed at around 1500 locations around the city; you simply pick one up at one rack, or borne, ride to your destination, and drop it off again. The scheme hasn't been without its problems, mainly owing to vandalism and theft, but it's certainly popular and widely admired.

Passes – one-day €1.70, weekly €8 – are sold online and from meters at each borne; plug in your credit card details (which will also secure a €150 deposit, not cashed unless you damage the bike). The first thirty minutes on top of the cost of the pass are free, but after that costs mount; €1 for the next half-hour, €2 for the next, and €4 for every further half hour. Helmets are not provided. There are between twelve and twenty bike stands at each *borne*, which are around 300m apart. Maps of the network are displayed at the *bornes*, and available to print in advance from their website. Incidentally, if you're caught running a red light while cycling in Paris, you'll be fined €100 on the spot.

Boats

One of the most enjoyable ways to get around Paris is on the **Batobus** (☎ 08.25.05.01.01, ⓦ www.batobus .com), which operates all year round, apart from January, stopping at eight points along the Seine, including the Eiffel Tower and the Jardin des Plantes. Boats run every fifteen to thirty minutes (Feb, March, Nov and Dec 10.30am–4.30pm; March to May, Sept and Oct 10am–7pm; June–Aug 10am–9.30pm). The total journey time for a round-trip is around ninety minutes and you can hop on and off as many times as you like – a day pass costs €15, two consecutive days €18 and five consecutive days €21 (kids half price).

Driving

Travelling **by car** – in the daytime at least – is hardly worth it because of the difficulty of finding parking spaces. You're better off locating a motel-style place on the edge of the city and using public transport. If you're determined to use the pay-and-display parking system you must buy a **Paris Carte** (like a phonecard) worth €15–40 from a *tabac*, then look for the blue "P" signs alongside grey parking meters. Put the card in the meter and it automatically deducts from the value on the card – it costs €1.20–3.60 an hour depending on location, for a maximum of two hours. Alternatively, make for an underground **car park**; these cost up to €2.50 per hour, or around €25 for 24 hours.

If you want to rent a car in Paris your cheapest option is the city's pioneering electric car rental scheme, **Autolib'** (ⓦ autholib.eu), operating on the same model as Velib' (see opposite). Some 3000 cars are available to rent from numerous stands all over the city. Cars can be picked up at one station and deposited at another. As with Velib', you need to buy a subscription card first, either online or from one of the 75 Espaces Autolib' in the city. Cards are valid for a day (€10) or a week (€15). The first 30min costs €7, the second €6 and subsequent ones €8. The scheme is open to anyone with a driving licence over the age of 18, and you don't have to have been driving for 2 years to be eligible.

Boat trips

Most tourists are keen to take a **boat trip** on the Seine. The faithful old Bateaux-Mouches (ⓦ www.bateaux-mouches.fr) is the best-known operator. Leaving from the Embarcadère du Pont de l'Alma on the Right Bank in the 8ᵉ (Ⓜ Alma-Marceau), the rides last 1hr 10min, cost €11 (€5.50 for children and over-65s) and take you past the major Seine-side sights, such as Notre-Dame and the Louvre. From April to September boats leave every 30–45 minutes from 10.15am to 7pm, then every 20 minutes from 7 to 11pm; winter departures are less frequent, and a minimum of fifty passengers is needed.

Directory A–Z

Addresses

Paris is divided into twenty districts, or arrondissements. The first arrondissement, or "1er" is centred on the Louvre, in the heart of the city. The rest wind outward in a clockwise direction like a snail's shell: the 2e, 3e and 4e are central; the 5e, 6e and 7e lie on the inner part of the left (south) bank; while the 8e–20e make up the outer districts. Parisian addresses often quote the arrondissement, along with the nearest métro station or stations, too.

Banks and exchange

All **ATM**s – *distributeurs* or *points argent*, found everywhere – give instructions in French or English. You can also use credit cards for (interest-paying) cash advances at banks and ATMs.

On the whole, the best **exchange rates** are offered by banks, though there's always a commission charge on top. Be very wary of bureaux de change, which cluster round arrival points and tourist spots, as they can really rip you off. Standard banking hours are Monday to Friday from 9am to 4 or 5pm. A few banks close for lunch; some are open on Saturday 9am to noon; all are closed on Sunday and public holidays. Money-exchange bureaux stay open until 6 or 7pm, tend not to close for lunch and may even open on Sundays in the more touristy areas.

Cinemas

Paris has a world-renowned concentration of cinemas, and moviegoers can choose from around three hundred films showing in any one week. Tickets rarely need to be purchased in advance and are good value at around €9. Among the more interesting cinemas in the city are: **Le Grand Rex**, 1 bd Poissonnière (Ⓜ Bonne Nouvelle), a famously kitsch Art Deco cinema showing blockbusters (usually dubbed); **Max Linder Panorama**, 24 bd Poissonnière (Ⓜ Bonne Nouvelle), a 1930s cinema showing films in the original format, with state-of-the-art sound; **La Pagode**, 57bis rue de Babylone (Ⓜ François-Xavier), a reproduction Japanese pagoda and the most beautiful of the city's cinemas; and the cluster of inventive cinemas at the junction of rue Champollion and rue des Ecoles, **Reflet Medicis**, **La Filmothèque** and **Le Champo** (Ⓜ Cluny-La Sorbonne), which offer up rare screenings and classics. **The Cinémathèque Française**, 51 rue de Bercy (Ⓦ www.cinematheque .fr; Ⓜ Bercy) shows dozens of films every week, including lots of art-house fare, and costs just €6.50.

Crime

Petty theft sometimes occurs on the métro, at train stations and at tourist hotspots such as Les Halles and around rue de la Huchette, in the Quartier Latin. Serious crime against tourists is rare. To report thefts, you have to make your way to the *commissariat de police* in the arrondissement where the theft took place. The Préfecture de Police de Paris is at 7 boulevard du Palais (☎ 01.53.73.53.73). For rape crisis (SOS Viol) call ☎ 08.00.05.95.95.

Embassies and consulates

Australia, 4 rue Jean-Rey, 15e (Ⓜ Bir-Hakeim) ☎ 01.40.59.33.00, Ⓦ www.france.embassy.gov.au; **Canada**, 35 av Montaigne, 8e (Ⓜ Franklin-D-Roosevelt) ☎ 01.44.43.29.00, Ⓦ www.amb -canada.fr; **Ireland**, 4 rue Rude, 16e (Ⓜ Charles-de-Gaulle-Etoile)

☎ 01.44.17.67.00, ⓦ embassyofire-land.fr; **New Zealand**, 7 rue Léonard-de-Vinci, 16ᵉ (Ⓜ Victor-Hugo) ☎ 01.45.01.43.43; **South Africa**, 59 quai d'Orsay, 7ᵉ; (Ⓜ Invalides) ☎ 01.53.59.23.23, ⓦ www.afriquesud.net; **UK**, 35 rue du Faubourg St-Honoré, 8ᵉ (Ⓜ Concorde) ☎ 01.44.51.31.00, ⓦ ukinfrance.fco.gov.uk; **US**, 2 rue St-Florentin, 1ᵉʳ (Ⓜ Concorde) ☎ 01.43.12.22.22, ⓦ http://france.usembassy.gov.

Gay and lesbian travellers

Paris has a vibrant, upfront gay community, and full-on prejudice or hostility is rare. Legally, France is liberal as regards homosexuality, with legal consent starting at 16 and laws protecting gay couples' rights. The Centre Gai Lesbien Bi et Trans, 63 rue Beaubourg, 3ᵉ, ☎ 01.43.57.21.47, ⓦ www.centrelgbtparis.org (Tues–Sat 3.30–8pm; Ⓜ Arts et Métiers), is a useful port of call for information and advice. Useful contacts and listings can be found in the excellent glossy monthly magazine, *Têtu* (ⓦ www.tetu.com).

Health

Pharmacies can give good advice on minor complaints, offer appropriate medicines and recommend a doctor. Most are open roughly 8am–8pm; details of the nearest one open at night are posted in all pharmacies. You can find a good English-speaking chemist at Swann, 6 rue Castiglione, 1ᵉʳ (☎ 01.42.60.72.96). Pharmacies open at night include Dérhy/Pharmacie des Champs-Elysées, 84 avenue des Champs-Elysées, 8ᵉ (☎ 01.45.62.02.41;

Emergency numbers

Ambulance ☎ 15; police ☎ 17; fire ☎ 18.

24hr; Ⓜ George-V); Pharmacie des Halles, 10 bd Sébastopol, 4ᵉ (☎ 01.42.72.03.23; Mon–Sat 9am–midnight, Sun 9am–10pm; Ⓜ Châtelet). British citizens with a European Health Insurance Card (available from post offices) can take advantage of French health services. Non-EU citizens are strongly advised to take out travel insurance.

Internet

Internet access is everywhere in Paris – if it's not in your hotel there'll be a café close by, and there are lots of *points internet* around the city centre. Most are open long hours but rates vary: expect to pay anything between €2.50 and €8 per hour. Most post offices, too, have a computer geared up for public internet access. Free wi-fi access is widespread and offered by many hotels, cafés, bars, train stations, sites like the Pompidou Centre and 200 public gardens.

Lost property

The **lost property office** (Bureau des Objets Trouvés) is at the Préfecture de Police, 36 rue des Morillons, 15ᵉ; ☎ 08.21.00.25.25 (Mon–Thurs 8.30am–5pm, Fri 8.30am–4.30pm; Ⓜ Convention). For property lost on public transport, phone the RATP on ☎ 01.40.30.52.00. If you lose your passport, report it at a police station, then your embassy (see opposite).

Museum/monument passes

The cost of entrance tickets to **museums and monuments** can add up, but with a little pre-planning you can sightsee relatively cheaply. The permanent collections at all municipal museums are free all year round, while all national museums (including the Louvre and Musée d'Orsay) are free on the first Sunday of the month – see ⓦ www.rmn.fr for a full list – and to under-18s.

Elsewhere, the cut-off age for free admission varies between 18, 12 and 4. Reduced admission is often available for 18 to 26-year-olds and for those over 60 or 65 (regardless of whether you are still working or not); you'll need to carry your passport or ID card with you as proof of age. Some discounts (often around one-third off) are available for students with an ISIC Card (International Student Identity Card; ⓦ www.isiccard.com); this is usually the only card accepted for student admissions.

If you're planning to visit a great many museums in a short time it might be worth buying the **Paris Museum Pass** (€39 for 2 consecutive days, €54 for 4 consecutive days, €69 for 6 consecutive days; ⓦ www.parismuseumpass.fr). Available online and from tourist offices and participating museums, it's valid for 35 or so of the most important museums and monuments including the Pompidou Centre, the Louvre and the Château de Versailles, and allows you to bypass ticket queues (though not the security checkpoints); it often doesn't cover the cost of special exhibitions. The Paris Visite multi-day transport pass (see p.181) also offers discounts on a number of museum admissions.

Opening hours

Most shops, businesses, information services, museums and banks in Paris stay open all day. The exceptions are the smaller shops and enterprises, which may close for lunch some time between 12.30pm and 2pm. Basic **hours of business** are from 8 or 9am to 6.30 or 7.30pm Monday to Saturday for the big shops, and Tuesday to Saturday for smaller shops (some of the smaller shops may open on Monday afternoon). You can always find boulangeries and food shops that stay open on days when others close – on Sunday normally until noon. Shops are also open on Sunday afternoons in the Marais and on the Champs Elysées.

Restaurants, **bars** and **cafés** often close on Sunday or Monday, and quite a few restaurants also close on Saturdays, especially at midday. It's common for bars and cafés to stay open to 2am, and even extend hours on a Friday and Saturday night, closing earlier on Sunday. Restaurants won't usually serve after 10pm, though some brasseries cater for night owls and serve meals till the early hours. Many restaurants and shops take a holiday between the middle of July and the end of August, and over Easter and Christmas.

Post

French post offices (la Poste) – look for bright yellow-and-blue signs – are generally open Mon–Fri 8am–7pm, Sat 8am–noon. However, Paris's main office, at 52 rue du Louvre, 1ᵉʳ (Ⓜ Etienne-Marcel), is open 24 hours for all postal services (but not banking). The easiest place to buy ordinary stamps (*timbres*) is at a tobacconist (*tabac*). Postcards (*cartes postales*) and letters (*lettres*) up to 20g cost €0.77 for the UK and EU, and €0.89 for North America, Asia and Oceania. For anything heavier, most post offices now have yellow *guichets automatiques* which weigh your letter or package and give you the correct stamps.

Racism

Paris has an unfortunate reputation for racism, but harassment of tourists is unlikely to be a problem. That said, there are reports of unpleasant incidents such as restaurants claiming to be fully booked, or shopkeepers with a suspicious eye, and travellers of north African or Arab appearance may be unlucky enough to encounter outright hostility or excessive police interest.

Telephones

Almost all public phones take phonecards (*télécartes*), sold at railway stations and *tabacs*. Many call boxes also accept credit cards, but coin-operated phones are rare. For calling within Paris, you'll always need to dial the regional code first – ☎01. Local calls are inexpensive, especially off-peak, though hotel phones usually carry a significant mark-up. Domestic and international off-peak rates run at weekends and weekdays from 7pm to 8am. At peak rates, €1 gets you about five minutes to the US or Britain. The number for French directory enquiries and operator assistance is ☎12.

France operates on the European GSM mobile phone standard, so travellers from Britain can bring theirs from home; US cellphones, however, won't work in Paris unless they're tri-band.

Time

Paris, and all of France, is in the Central European Time Zone (GMT+1): one hour ahead of the UK, six hours ahead of Eastern Standard Time and nine hours ahead of Pacific Standard Time. In France, and all of the EU, Daylight Saving Time (+1hr) lasts from the last Sunday of March through to the last Sunday of October, so for one week in late March and/or early April North American clocks lag an extra hour behind.

Tipping

Service is almost always included in restaurant bills, so you don't need to leave more than small change. Taxi drivers and hairdressers expect around ten percent. You should tip only at the most expensive hotels; in other cases you're probably tipping the proprietor.

Tourist information

At Paris's **tourist offices** (Ⓦwww .parisinfo.com) you can pick up maps and information, book accommodation and buy travel passes and the Paris Museum Pass (see opposite). The main **office** is at 25 rue des Pyramides (daily 10am–7pm; ⓂPyramides). Other useful locations include Carrousel du Louvre, accessed from 99 rue de Rivoli (daily 10am–6pm; ⓂPalais Royal-Musée du Louvre), which also has information on the Ile de France. Montmartre has its own office on place du Tertre (daily 10am–7pm; ⓂAnvers) and there are booths at the Gare du Nord (daily 8am–6pm) and Gare de Lyon (Mon–Sat 8am–6pm).

Of Paris's inexpensive weekly **listings magazines**, sold at newsagents and kiosks, *Pariscope* has the edge, with a comprehensive section on films. On Wednesdays, *Le Monde* and *Le Figaro* also bring out free listings supplements, while for more detail, the webzines *Paris Voice* (Ⓦwww.parisvoice.com) and *GoGo Paris* (Ⓦwww.gogoparis.com) cover the latest events.

Travellers with disabilities

While the situation is certainly improving, Paris has never had any special reputation for access facilities. The narrow pavements make wheelchair travel stressful, and the métro system has endless flights of steps. Museums, however, are getting much better. Up-to-date information is best obtained from organizations at home before you leave.

Festivals and events

Paris hosts an impressive roster of festivals and events. In addition to the festivals listed below, France celebrates thirteen **national holidays**: January 1; Easter Sunday; Easter Monday; Ascension Day; Whitsun; Whit Monday; May 1; May 8; July 14; August 15; November 1; November 11; December 25.

FÊTE DE LA MUSIQUE

June 21 Ⓦwww.fetedelamusique.culture.fr
During the annual Fête de la Musique, buskers take to the streets and free concerts are held across the whole city in a fun day of music-making.

PRIDE MARCH

Last Saturday of June
Ⓦhttp://marche.inter-lgbt.org
The Marche des Fiertés LGBT, or gay pride march, is a flamboyant parade of floats and costumes making its way from Montparnasse to Bastille, followed by partying and club events.

FÊTE DU CINÉMA

End June Ⓦwww.feteducinema.com
A superb opportunity to view a wide range of films, from classics to the cutting-edge in French and foreign cinema. Buy one full-price ticket and you can see any number of films during the weekend-long festival for €3.

BASTILLE DAY

July 14
The Big One: on Bastille Day the city celebrates the 1789 storming of the Bastille. The party starts the evening before, with dancing around place de la Bastille; in the morning there's a military march down the Champs-Elysées followed by fireworks.

TOUR DE FRANCE

3rd or 4th Sunday in July Ⓦwww.letour.fr
Paris stages the final romp home of the Tour de France, and thousands line the route to cheer cyclists to the finish line on the Champs-Elysées.

PARIS PLAGE

Mid-July to mid-August
Three sections of the Seine – from the Louvre to the Pont de Sully, at the foot of the Mitterand National Library near the Josephine Baker swimming pool, and at Bassin de la Villette – are transformed into "beaches", complete with real sand, deckchairs and palm trees. Various extras, from tai chi classes to lending libraries and cafés are available.

JOURNÉES DU PATRIMOINE

3rd weekend in September
Ⓦwww.journeesdupatrimoine.culture.fr
Off-limits and private buildings throw open their doors to a curious public for the "heritage days".

FESTIVAL D'AUTOMNE

Last week of September up to Christmas
Ⓦwww.festival-automne.com
The Festival d'Automne is an international festival of theatre and music, much of it avant-garde and exciting.

NUIT BLANCHE

Early October Ⓦwww.paris.fr
Nuit Blanche is a night-long festival of poetry readings, concerts and performance art, held in galleries, bars, restaurants and public buildings across the city.

Chronology

Third-century BC > A tribe known as the Parisii begins to settle on the Ile de la Cité.

52 AD > When Julius Caesar's conquering armies arrive they find a thriving settlement of some 8000 people.

Around 275 > St Denis brings Christianity to Paris. He is martyred for his beliefs at Montmartre.

451 > The marauding bands of Attila the Hun are repulsed supposedly thanks to the prayerful intervention of Geneviève, a peasant girl from Nanterre who becomes the city's patron saint.

486 > The city falls to Clovis the Frank. His dynasty, the feuding Merovingians, governs Paris for the next two hundred years or so.

768 > Charlemagne is proclaimed king at St-Denis. Over the next forty years he conquers half of Europe – but spends little time in Paris.

845–85 > Vikings repeatedly sack Paris.

987 > Hugues Capet, one of the counts of Paris, is elected king of Francia and makes Paris his capital.

1200s > Paris experiences an economic boom, its university becomes the centre of European learning and King Philippe-Auguste constructs a vast city wall.

1330s to 1430s > The French and English nobility struggle for power in the Hundred Years' War.

1348 > The Black Death kills some 800 Parisians a day, and over the next 140 years one year in four is a plague year, and Paris's population falls by half.

1429 > Joan of Arc attempts to drive the English out of Paris, but it is not until 1437 that Charles VII regains control of his capital.

1528 > François I finally brings the royal court back from the Loire to his new palace at the Louvre. He sets about building the Tuileries palace.

1572 > On St Bartholomew's Day, August 25, some 3000 Protestants gathered in Paris are massacred at the instigation of the ultra-Catholic Guise family.

1607 > The triumphant monarch Henri IV builds the Pont Neuf and sets about creating a worthy capital.

1661–1715 > Louis XIV transfers the court to Versailles, but this doesn't stop the city growing in size, wealth and prestige.

1786 > The wall of the Fermiers Généraux is erected around Paris. The wall has 57 toll gates (one of which survives at place Stalingrad), which levy a tax on all goods entering Paris, a source of irritation in the lead-up to revolution.

1789 > Long-standing tensions explode into revolution. Ordinary Parisians, the "sans-culottes", storm the Bastille prison on July 14.

1793 > The revolutionaries banish the monarchy and execute Louis XVI. A dictatorship is set up, headed by the ruthless Robespierre.

1799 > Army general Napoleon Bonaparte seizes control in a coup and, in 1804, crowns himself emperor in Notre-Dame.

1820s > Paris acquires gas lighting and its first omnibus.

1830 > After three days of fighting, known as *les trois glorieuses*, Louis-Philippe is elected constitutional monarch.

1848 > In June, revolution erupts once again. Louis Napoleon Bonaparte, Napoleon's nephew, is elected president. In 1851 he declares himself Emperor Napoleon III.

1850s and 1860s > Baron Haussmann literally bulldozes the city into the modern age, creating long, straight boulevards and squares.

1863 > At the Salon des Refusés, Manet's proto-impressionist painting *Déjeuner sur l'Herbe* scandalizes all of Paris.

1870 > Hundreds die of starvation as the city is besieged by the Prussians.

1871 > Paris surrenders in March, but the Prussians withdraw after just three days. In the aftermath, workers rise up and proclaim the Paris Commune. It is speedily and bloodily suppressed by French troops.

1874 > The first Impressionist exhibition is held in photographer Nadar's studio to mixed critical response.

1889 > The all-new Eiffel Tower steals the show at the Exposition Universelle, or "great exhibition".

1894 > Captain Alfred Dreyfus, a Jew, is convicted on the flimsiest of evidence of spying for the Germans. The Dreyfus Affair divides Parisian society into two camps: the Dreyfusards (including republicans and left-wing intellectuals Jean Jaurès, Anatole France and Léon Blum), suspecting a cover-up by the army, and anti-Dreyfusards, including clerics, monarchists and conservatives, who suspect a Jewish conspiracy.

1895 > Parisians are the first people anywhere in the world to see the jerky cinematic documentaries of the Lumière brothers.

1900 > The Métropolitain underground railway, or "métro", is unveiled.

1910 > The Great Flood of Paris: the River Seine bursts its banks, rendering thousands homeless and paralysing the city. Parisians get around by boat and hastily constructed wooden walkways. Damage is estimated at 400 million francs.

1914 > War with Germany calls time on the "belle époque". In September, the Kaiser's armies are just barely held off by French troops shuttled from Paris to the front line, just fifteen miles away.

1920s > In the aftermath of war, the decadent *années folles* (or "mad years") of the 1920s rescue Paris's international reputation for hedonism.

1940 > In May and June, the government flees Paris, and Nazi soldiers are soon marching down the Champs-Elysées. Four years of largely collaborative fascist rule ensue.

1942 > Parisian Jews are rounded up – by other Frenchmen – and shipped off to Auschwitz.

1944 > Liberation arrives on August 25, with General de Gaulle motoring up the Champs-Elysées to the roar of a vast crowd.

1961 > As France's brutal repression of its Algerian colony reaches its peak, at least two hundred Algerians are murdered by police during a civil rights demonstration.

1968 > In May, left-wing students occupying university buildings are supported by millions of striking and marching workers.

1969 > President de Gaulle loses a referendum, and retires to his country house.

1973 > Paris's first skyscraper, the Tour Montparnasse, tops out at 56 hideous storeys. The *périphérique* ring road is completed in April.

1981 > Socialist François Mitterand becomes president but Paris remains firmly right wing, under Mayor Jacques Chirac.

1998 > In July, a multiracial French team wins the World Cup at the new Stade de France, in the suburb of St-Denis.

2001 > Unassuming Socialist candidate, Bertrand Delanoë, is elected Mayor of Paris in March.

2002 > Parisians find themselves paying a little extra for their coffees and baguettes with the introduction of the euro, on January 1.

2002 > Far Right candidate Jean-Marie Le Pen makes it through the first round of the presidential elections, sending shock waves through the city. Consequently, some 800,000 people pack the boulevards in the biggest demonstration since 1968. In the second round run-off Chirac is elected, winning 90 percent of the vote in Paris.

2002 > Mayor Bertrand Delanoë launches Paris's new image by turning three kilometres of riverbank expressway into a summer beach: "Paris Plage" is an immense success.

2003 > Following Chirac's spat with George W. Bush over Iraq, US tourists temporarily vanish from the capital. In the summer, temperatures soar above an unprecedented 40 degrees C (104 degrees F).

2005 > In late October, disaffected youths riot in the impoverished Paris suburb of Clichy-sous-Bois. Right-wing interior minister, Nicolas Sarkozy, declares a state of emergency.

2007 > As Nicolas Sarkozy becomes President, Mayor Delanoë continues his greening of Paris: bus and cycle lanes appear everywhere, as do the Vélib' rental bikes.

2009 > Paris contemplates its future with an exhibition of architectural visions for the green mega-city of the future. It will incorporate its often-neglected suburbs, and is dubbed "Le Grand Paris".

2011 > Building on the success of the city's bike rental scheme, Autolib' is launched: around 3000 electric cars are made available to rent from 1000 locations in Paris.

French

Paris isn't the easiest place to learn French: many Parisians speak a hurried slang and will often reply to your carefully enunciated question in English. Despite this, it's worth making the effort, and knowing a few essentials can make all the difference. Even just saying "Bonjour monsieur/madame" will usually secure you a smile and helpful service.

What follows is a rundown of essential words and phrases. For more detail, get *French: A Rough Guide Dictionary Phrasebook*, which has an extensive vocabulary, a detailed menu reader and useful dialogues.

Pronunciation

Vowels are the hardest sounds to get right. Roughly:

a as in hat
e as in get
é between get and gate
è between get and gut
eu like the u in hurt
i as in machine
o as in hot
o/au as in over
ou as in food
u as in a pursed-lip, clipped version of toot

More awkward are the combinations in/im, en/em, on/om, un/um at the end of words, or followed by consonants other than n or m. Again, roughly:

in/im like the "an" in anxious
an/am, en/em like "on" said with a nasal accent
on/om like "on" said by someone with a heavy cold
un/um like the "u" in understand

Consonants are much as in English, except that ch is always sh, h is silent, th is the same as t, in some instances ll is like the y in "yes" when preceded by the letter "i", w is v, and r is growled (or rolled).

Words and phrases
BASICS

Yes	Oui
No	Non
Please	S'il vous plaît
Thank you	Merci
Excuse me	Pardon/excusez-moi
Sorry	Pardon/Je m'excuse
Hello	Bonjour
Hello (phone)	Allô
Goodbye	Au revoir
Good morning/ afternoon	Bonjour
Good evening	Bonsoir
Good night	Bonne nuit
How are you?	Comment allez-vous?/Ça va?
Fine, thanks	Très bien, merci
I don't know	Je ne sais pas
Do you speak English?	Vous parlez anglais?
How do you say ...in French?	Comment ça se dit...en français?
What's your name?	Comment vous appelez-vous?
My name is...	Je m'appelle...
I'm English/ Irish/ Scottish/ Welsh/ American/	Je suis anglais(e)/ irlandais(e)/ écossais(e)/ gallois(e)/ américain(e)/
OK/agreed	D'accord
I understand	Je comprends
I don't understand	Je ne comprends pas
Can you speak more slowly?	S'il vous plaît, parlez moins vite
Today	Aujourd'hui
Yesterday	Hier
Tomorrow	Demain
In the morning	Le matin
In the afternoon	L'après-midi
In the evening	Le soir
Now	Maintenant
Later	Plus tard

Here	Ici
There	Là
This one	Ceci
That one	Cela
Open	Ouvert
Closed	Fermé
Big	Grand
Small	Petit
More	Plus
Less	Moins
A little	Un peu
A lot	Beaucoup
Half	La moitié
Inexpensive	Bon marché/ Pas cher
Expensive	Cher
Good	Bon
Bad	Mauvais
Hot	Chaud
Cold	Froid
With	Avec
Without	Sans

QUESTIONS

Where?	Où?
How?	Comment?
How many	Combien?
How much is it?	C'est combien?
When?	Quand?
Why?	Pourquoi?
At what time?	À quelle heure?
What is/Which is?	Quel est?

GETTING AROUND

Which way is it to the Eiffel Tower?	S'il vous plaît, pour aller à la Tour Eiffel?
Where is the nearest métro?	Où est le métro le plus proche?
Bus	Bus
Bus stop	Arrêt
Train	Train
Boat	Bâteau
Plane	Avion
Railway station	Gare
Platform	Quai
What time does it leave?	Il part à quelle heure?
What time does it arrive?	Il arrive à quelle heure?

A ticket to...	Un billet pour...
Single ticket	Aller simple
Return ticket	Aller retour
Where are you going?	Vous allez où?
I'm going to...	Je vais à...
I want to get off at...	Je voudrais descendre à...
Near	Près/pas loin
Far	Loin
Left	À gauche
Right	À droite

ACCOMMODATION

A room for one/ two people	Une chambre pour une/deux personnes
With a double bed	Avec un grand lit
A room with a shower	Une chambre avec douche
A room with a bath	Une chambre avec salle de bains
For one/two/ three nights	Pour une/deux/trois nuit(s)
With a view	Avec vue
Key	Clef
To iron	Repasser
Do laundry	Faire la lessive
Sheets	Draps
Blankets	Couvertures
Quiet	Calme
Noisy	Bruyant
Hot water	Eau chaude
Cold water	Eau froide
Is breakfast included?	Est-ce que le petit déjeuner est compris?
I would like breakfast	Je voudrais prendre le petit déjeuner
I don't want breakfast	Je ne veux pas le petit déjeuner
Youth hostel	Auberge de jeunesse

EATING OUT

I'd like to reserve	Je voudrais réserver
...a table	...une table
...for two people	...pour deux personnes
at eight thirty	à vingt heures et demie

I'm having the €30 menu	Je prendrai le menu à trente euros
Waiter!	Monsieur/madame! (never "garçon")
The bill, please	L'addition, s'il vous plaît

DAYS

Monday	Lundi
Tuesday	Mardi
Wednesday	Mercredi
Thursday	Jeudi
Friday	Vendredi
Saturday	Samedi
Sunday	Dimanche

NUMBERS

1	un
2	deux
3	trois
4	quatre
5	cinq
6	six
7	sept
8	huit
9	neuf
10	dix
11	onze
12	douze
13	treize
14	quatorze
15	quinze
16	seize
17	dix-sept
18	dix-huit
19	dix-neuf
20	vingt
21	vingt-et-un
22	vingt-deux
30	trente
40	quarante
50	cinquante
60	soixante
70	soixante-dix
75	soixante-quinze
80	quatre-vingts
90	quatre-vingt-dix
95	quatre-vingt-quinze
100	cent
101	cent un
200	deux cents
1000	mille
2000	deux mille
1,000,000	un million

Menu reader
ESSENTIALS

déjeuner	lunch
dîner	dinner
menu	set menu
carte	menu
à la carte	individually priced dishes
entrées	starters
les plats	main courses
pain	bread
beurre	butter
fromage	cheese
oeufs	eggs
lait	milk
poivre	pepper
sel	salt
sucre	sugar
fourchette	fork
couteau	knife
cuillère	spoon
bio	organic
à la vapeur	steamed
au four	baked
cru	raw
frit	fried
fumé	smoked
grillé	grilled
rôti	roast
salé	salted/savoury
sucré	sweet
à emporter	takeaway

DRINKS

eau minérale	mineral water
eau gazeuse	fizzy water
eau plate	still water
carte des vins	wine list
une pression	a glass of beer
un café	coffee (espresso)
un crème	white coffee
bouteille	bottle

verre	glass
un quart/demi de rouge/blanc	a quarter/half-litre of red/white house wine
un (verre de) rouge/blanc	a glass of red/white wine

SNACKS

crêpe	pancake (sweet)
un sandwich/ une baguette	sandwich
croque -monsieur	grilled cheese and ham sandwich
omelette	omelette
nature	plain
aux fines herbes	with herbs
au fromage	with cheese
assiette anglaise	plate of cold meats
crudités	raw vegetables with dressings

FISH (POISSON) AND SEAFOOD (FRUITS DE MER)

anchois	anchovies
brème	bream
brochet	pike
cabillaud	cod
carrelet	plaice
colin	hake
coquilles st-jacques	scallops
crabe	crab
crevettes	shrimps/prawns
daurade	sea bream
flétan	halibut
friture	whitebait
hareng	herring
homard	lobster
huîtres	oysters
langoustines	crayfish (scampi)
limande	lemon sole
lotte de mer	monkfish
loup de mer	sea bass
maquereau	mackerel
merlan	whiting
morue	dried, salted cod
moules (marinière)	mussels (with shallots in white wine sauce)
raie	skate

rouget	red mullet
saumon	salmon
sole	sole
thon	tuna
truite	trout
turbot	turbot

FISH: DISHES AND RELATED TERMS

aïoli	garlic mayonnaise served with salt cod and other fish
béarnaise	sauce made with egg yolks, white wine, shallots and vinegar
beignets	fritters
la douzaine	a dozen
frit	fried
fumé	smoked
fumet	fish stock
gigot de mer	large fish baked whole
grillé	grilled
hollandaise	egg yolk and butter sauce
à la meunière	in a butter, lemon and parsley sauce
mousse/mousseline	mousse
quenelles	light dumplings

MEAT (VIANDE) AND POULTRY (VOLAILLE)

agneau	lamb
andouillette	tripe sausage
bavette	beef flank steak
bœuf	beef
bifteck	steak
boudin noir	black pudding
caille	quail
canard	duck
contrefilet	sirloin roast
dinde	turkey
entrecôte	ribsteak
faux filet	sirloin steak
foie	liver
foie gras	fattened (duck/goose) liver

gigot (d'agneau)	leg (of lamb)
grillade	grilled meat
hachis	chopped meat or mince hamburger
jambon	ham
lapin, lapereau	rabbit, young rabbit
lard, lardons	bacon, diced bacon
merguez	spicy red sausage
oie	goose
onglet	cut of beef
porc	pork
poulet	chicken
poussin	baby chicken
rognons	kidneys
tête de veau	calf's head (in jelly)
veau	veal
venaison	venison

STEAKS

bleu	almost raw
saignant	rare
à point	medium
bien cuit	well done

GARNISHES AND SAUCES

beurre blanc	sauce of white wine and shallots, with butter
chasseur	white wine, mushrooms and shallots
forestière	with bacon and mushroom
fricassée	rich, creamy sauce
mornay	cheese sauce
pays d'auge	cream and cider
piquante	gherkins or capers, vinegar and shallots
provençale	tomatoes, garlic, olive oil and herbs

MEAT AND POULTRY: DISHES AND RELATED TERMS

aile	wing
blanquette de veau	veal in cream and mushroom sauce
bœuf bourguignon	beef stew with red wine, onions and mushrooms
canard à l'orange	roast duck with an orange-and-wine sauce
carré	best end of neck, chop or cutlet
cassoulet	a casserole of beans and meat
choucroute garnie	sauerkraut served with sausages or cured ham
civet	game stew
confit	meat preserve
coq au vin	chicken with wine, onions and mushrooms, cooked till it falls off the bone
côte	chop, cutlet or rib
cou	neck
cuisse	thigh or leg
en croûte	in pastry
epaule	shoulder
daube estouffade, hochepot, navarin and ragoût	all are types of stew
farci	stuffed
au feu de bois	cooked over wood fire
au four	baked
garni	with vegetables
gésier	gizzard
grillé	grilled
magret de canard	duck breast
marmite	casserole
médaillon	round piece
mijoté	stewed
pavé	thick slice
rôti	roast
sauté	lightly cooked in butter
steak au poivre (vert/rouge)	steak in a black (green/red) peppercorn sauce
steak tartare	raw chopped beef, topped with a raw egg yolk

VEGETABLES (LÉGUMES), HERBS (HERBES) AND SPICES (ÉPICES)

ail	garlic
artichaut	artichoke
asperges	asparagus
basilic	basil
betterave	beetroot
carotte	carrot
céleri	celery
champignons	mushrooms
chou (rouge)	(red) cabbage
chou-fleur	cauliflower
concombre	cucumber
cornichon	gherkin
échalotes	shallots
endive	chicory
épinards	spinach
estragon	tarragon
fenouil	fennel
flageolets	white beans
gingembre	ginger
haricots	beans
verts	string (french)
rouges	kidney
beurres	butter
lentilles	lentils
maïs	corn (maize)
moutarde	mustard
oignon	onion
pâtes	pasta
persil	parsley
petits pois	peas
pois chiche	chickpeas
poireau	leek
poivron (vert, rouge)	sweet pepper (green, red)
pommes de terre	potatoes
primeurs	spring vegetables
riz	rice
safran	saffron
salade verte	green salad
tomate	tomato
truffes	truffles

FRUITS (FRUITS) AND NUTS (NOIX)

abricot	apricot
amandes	almonds
ananas	pineapple
banane	banana
brugnon, nectarine	nectarine
cacahouète	peanut
cassis	blackcurrants
cerises	cherries
citron	lemon
citron vert	lime
figues	figs
fraises	strawberries
framboises	raspberries
groseilles	redcurrants and gooseberries
mangue	mango
marrons	chestnuts
melon	melon
noisette	hazelnut
noix	nuts
orange	orange
pamplemousse	grapefruit
pêche	peach
pistache	pistachio
poire	pear
pomme	apple
prune	plum
pruneau	prune
raisins	grapes

DESSERTS (DESSERTS OR ENTREMETS) AND PASTRIES (PÂTISSERIE)

bavarois	refers to the mould, could be mousse or custard
brioche	sweet, high-yeast breakfast roll
coupe	a serving of ice cream
crème chantilly	vanilla-flavoured and sweetened whipped cream
crème pâtissière	thick eggy pastry-filling
fromage blanc	cream cheese
glace	ice cream
parfait	frozen mousse, sometimes ice cream
petits fours	bite-sized cakes/pastries
tarte	tart

PUBLISHING INFORMATION

This second edition published February 2013 by **Rough Guides Ltd**

80 Strand, London WC2R 0RL

11, Community Centre, Panchsheel Park, New Delhi 110017, India

Distributed by the Penguin Group

Penguin Books Ltd, 80 Strand, London WC2R 0RL

Penguin Group (USA) 375 Hudson Street, NY 10014, USA

Penguin Group (Australia) 250 Camberwell Road, Camberwell, Victoria 3124, Australia

Penguin Group (NZ) 67 Apollo Drive, Mairangi Bay, Auckland 1310, New Zealand

Rough Guides is represented in Canada by

Tourmaline Editions Inc., 662 King Street West, Suite 304, Toronto, Ontario, M5V 1M7

Typeset in Minion and Din to an original design by Henry Iles and Dan May.

Printed and bound in China

© Rough Guides 2013

Maps © Rough Guides

No part of this book may be reproduced in any form without permission from the publisher except for the quotation of brief passages in reviews.

208pp includes index

A catalogue record for this book is available from the British Library

ISBN 978-1-40936-021-6

The publishers and authors have done their best to ensure the accuracy and currency of all the information in **Pocket Rough Guide Paris**, however, they can accept no responsibility for any loss, injury, or inconvenience sustained by any traveller as a result of information or advice contained in the guide.

1 3 5 7 9 8 6 4 2

ROUGH GUIDES CREDITS

Text editors: Lucy Kane and Lara Kavanagh

Layout: Jessica Subramanian and Nikhil Agarwal

Cartography: Ed Wright, Simonetta Giori and Katie Bennett

Picture editor: Nicole Newman

Photographers: James McConnachie and Lydia Evans

Production: Rebecca Short

Proofreader: Susanne Hillen

Cover design: Nicole Newman, Daniel May and Mark Thomas

THE AUTHORS

James McConnachie is also author of the *Rough Guide to The Loire*, and he has travelled all over Europe and beyond for Rough Guides. His non-travel books include *Conspiracy Theories* (Rough Guides), *Sex* (Rough Guides) and *The Book of Love: A Biography of the Kamasutra* (Atlantic Books).

Ruth Blackmore is co-author of the *Rough Guide to Paris* and a contributor to the *Rough Guide to France* and the *Rough Guide to Classical Music*.

HELP US UPDATE

We've gone to a lot of effort to ensure that the first edition of **Pocket Rough Guide Paris** is accurate and up-to-date. However, things change – places get "discovered", opening hours are notoriously fickle, restaurants and rooms raise prices or lower standards. If you feel we've got it wrong or left something out, we'd like to know, and if you can remember the address, the price, the hours, the phone number, so much the better.

Please send your comments with the subject line "**Pocket Rough Guide Paris Update**" to ✉ mail@roughguides.com. We'll credit all contributions and send a copy of the next edition (or any other Rough Guide if you prefer) for the very best emails.

Find more travel information, connect with fellow travellers and book your trip on ⓦ www .roughguides.com

PHOTO CREDITS

All images © Rough Guides except the following:

Front cover Eiffel Tower © Marvin Newman/Axiom

Back cover Pont des Arts © Bruno De Hogues/Getty Images

p.2 Louvre Museum at night © Photolibrary

p.5 Jardin du Luxembourg © Sonnet Sylvain/Photolibrary

p.6 Seine and Eiffel Tower © J Pratt/Photolibrary

p.9 Fountain and obelisk in place de la Concorde © Factoria Singular/iStock

p.12 Sidewalk café in Jardin du Luxembourg © Bertrand Rieger/Corbis

p.15 Pont Neuf © Eleanor Farmer

p.15 Panthéon © Neilerua/iStock

p.19 Le Gallopin © Le Desk, Alamy

p.19 Le Gaigne © Claire Williams

p.19 Salle Arpège © Aurore Deligny/Courtesy of L'Arpège

p.25 Point Ephémère © Courtesy of Point Ephémère

p.26 Notre-Dame with cherry blossoms © Bertrand Gardel/Corbis

p.27 The Eiffel Tower on Bastille Day © Arnaud Chicurel/Corbis

p.27 Paris Plage © John Kellerman/Alamy

p.27 Nuit Blanche © Directphoto.org/Alamy

p.27 Ice skating at the Hôtel de Ville © Robert Armstrong/Photolibrary

p.28 Disneyland Paris © Michel Viard/Photolibrary

p.33 Place de l'Hôtel de Ville and Vélib bikes © Sonnet Sylvain/Photolibrary

p.33 Les Trois Baudets © Courtesy of Les Trois Baudets

p.36 Pont Neuf at night © Chad Ehlers/Photolibrary

p.39 Notre-Dame cathedral © Lillis photography/iStock

p.47 The Grand Palais © Matthew Dixon/iStock

p.64 Salle Arpège © Aurore Deligny/Courtesy of L'Arpège

p.73 Repetto © Paris Marais, Alamy

p.75 Drouant © Eleanor Farmer

p.79 Pompidou Centre © Ian Cumming/Axiom

p.85 Musée Picasso © Sonnet Sylvain/Photolibrary

p.90 Maison de Victor Hugo © Eleanor Farmer

p.94 Ambassade d'Auvergne © Eleanor Farmer

p.95 Le Potager du Marais © Paris Marais, Alamy

p.131 WAGG © Courtesy of WAGG

p.152 Bois de Boulogne © Isatis/iStock

p.158 Garden at Versailles © Isatis/iStock

p.160 Sunset at Versailles and Neptune fountain © Anton-Marlot/iStock

p.161 The Marble Court at Palace of Versailles © Terraxplorer/iStock

p.163 Teacup ride at Disneyland Paris © Mohammed Ansar/Photolibrary

Index

Maps are marked in **bold**.

SO NOW WE'VE TOLD YOU
ABOUT THE THINGS NOT TO
MISS, THE BEST PLACES TO
STAY, THE TOP RESTAURANTS,
THE LIVELIEST BARS AND THE
MOST SPECTACULAR SIGHTS,
IT ONLY SEEMS FAIR TO
TELL YOU ABOUT THE BEST
TRAVEL INSURANCE AROUND

 WorldNomads.com
keep travelling safely

RECOMMENDED BY ROUGH GUIDES

www.roughguides.com
MAKE THE MOST OF YOUR TIME ON EARTH™

 ROUGH GUIDES

MAKE THE MOST OF YOUR GADGETS

roughguides.com/downloads

FROM **ANDROID** TO **iPADS** TO **SOCIAL MEDIA**

BOOKS | EBOOKS | APPS

www.roughguides.com

MAKE THE MOST OF YOUR TIME ON EARTH

ROUGH GUIDES

AFFECT, ANIMATE, AROUSE, CARRY, CAUSE, COMMOVE, ELATE, EMBOLDEN, ENDUE, ENKINDLE, ENLIVEN, EXALT, EXCITE, EXHILARATE, FIRE UP, GALVANIZE, GIVE IMPETUS, GIVE RISE TO, HEARTEN, IMBUE, IMPRESS, INFECT, INFLAME, INFLUENCE, INFORM, INFUSE, INSPIRE, INSPIRIT, INSTILL, INVIGORATE, MOTIVATE, OCCASION, PRODUCE, PROVOKE, QUICKEN, REASSURE, SPARK, SPUR, START OFF, STIR, STRIKE, SWAY, TOUCH, TRIGGER, URGE, WORK UP

Whatever you call it, Rough Guides does it

www.roughguides.com
MAKE THE MOST OF YOUR TIME ON EARTH

ROUGH GUIDES

WE GET AROUND

ONLINE sign up to receive news & offers at www.roughguides.com

EBOOKS electronic books, cool eh?

IBOOKSTORE guidebooks on cool gadgets

MOBILE APPS travelling wherever you go

GUIDEBOOKS need we say more

PHRASEBOOKS learn the lingo

MAPS don't get lost

GIFTBOOKS inspiration is our middle name

LIFESTYLE from ipads to climate change

...so you can too

OVER 700 BOOKS, EBOOKS, MAPS & APPS

FOLLOW US ON  facebook & twitter

www.roughguides.com
MAKE THE MOST OF YOUR TIME ON EARTH™

ROUGH GUIDES